Urban Humanities

Los Angeles

Mexico City

Tokyo

Shanghai

Urban and Industrial Environments

Series editor: Robert Gottlieb, Henry R. Luce Professor of Urban and Environmental Policy, Occidental College

For a complete list of books published in this series, please see the back of the book.

Urban Humanities

New Practices for Reimagining the City

Dana Cuff, Anastasia Loukaitou-Sideris, Todd Presner,
Maite Zubiaurre, and Jonathan Jae-an Crisman

The MIT Press   Cambridge, Massachusetts   London, England

This book was set in Sabon and Helvetica by the MIT Press. Printed and bound in the United States of America.

Library of Congress Cataloging-in-Publication Data

Names: Cuff, Dana, 1953- author. | Loukaitou-Sideris, Anastasia, 1958- author. | Presner, Todd Samuel, author. | Zubiaurre, Maria Teresa, author. | Crisman, Jonathan, Jae-an, author.
Title: Urban humanities : new practices for reimagining the city / Dana Cuff, Anastasia Loukaitou-Sideris, Todd Presner, Maite Zubiaurre, and Jonathan Jae-an Crisman.
Description: Cambridge, MA : The MIT Press, 2020. | Series: Urban and industrial environments | Includes bibliographical references and index.
Identifiers: LCCN 2019017368 | ISBN 9780262538220 (pbk. : alk. paper)
Subjects: LCSH: Cities and towns. | Architecture and society. | Architecture--Study and teaching--Case studies.
Classification: LCC HT153 .C84 2020 | DDC 306.76--dc23 LC record available at https://lccn.loc.gov/2019017368

10 9 8 7 6 5 4 3 2 1

To Our Students

Contents

Series Foreword

2019 marked the twenty-fifth year of the Urban and Industrial Environments (UIE) series. When I first proposed the idea to then MIT Press editor Madeline Sunley, I envisioned the series attracting manuscripts that stretched disciplinary boundaries, appealed to both academic and general-interest audiences, focused on local and global questions, and expanded the definitions of "environment" to encompass the issues of everyday life. I wanted the series to have a strong social and environmental justice orientation, where its authors would see themselves as participants and not just observers.

With more than seventy-five books now in the series (see the list of titles at the back of this book), the books published have accomplished much of what I had originally proposed. The success of the series is also due to the role of the two subsequent MIT Press editors, Clay Morgan and currently Beth Clevenger, who helped support and nurture it, solicit new as well as recognized contributors, and advocate within the MIT Press for the kinds of books that often do not fit neatly into traditional disciplinary silos.

It is fitting then, as we continue to expand its reach, for the UIE series to be able to include *Urban Humanities: New Practices for Reimagining the City.* A collaborative work of people from different disciplines, the five authors see their collaboration as a means to establish what they call a "new ecology of teaching and learning." The term "urban humanities" (first originating at UCLA where these authors formed their collaboration) emphasized the "urban" in a global context. These would be places, as Richard Sennett has argued, where "people can turn outward, not inward . . . and give them the experience of otherness" to be, as Sennett puts it, "in the presence of difference." This concept of the urban contrasts with the "neoliberal city," a place of what Saskia Sassen called "expulsions," where lack of affordable housing, gentrification, financialization, displacement, and the privatization of public space all meet.

Research, in this context, is a practice rather than a set of methods; a "fusion of research, representation and action," write the *Urban Humanities* collaborators. This type of action-oriented research agenda situates many of the books in the UIE series as well as my own work and *practice* as well. It is a form of *engagement* with communities and with universities. It starts with the classroom, breaking down barriers, creating new ways of thinking. It could be "toxicology for poets" or "poetry for toxicologists"—as one of our students characterized a multilayered collaborative course of four faculty that I participated in at UCLA twenty-five years ago; two of the first titles in the UIE series were written by former students who had been in that class. It leads to the community, or rather communities needing or seeking transformation. The action research agenda challenges the very divide between university and researcher and community and community actor. Instead of seeing and accepting universities as places of power and privilege, the urban humanities approach challenges universities to be *of* the community, and in that way challenges the unequal power relations and the walls that traditionally divide town and gown.

Moreover, *Urban Humanities*, similarly to many of the books in the UIE series, provides research and engagement at local, national, and global levels. Spaces, particularly urban spaces, are at once local, particular, *and* transnational, especially in an era when the itineraries of the refugees and immigrants are changing the very character of those places. Urban places can be desolate places—spaces of camps and walls, as described by the *Urban Humanities* authors, but also places where crossing borders elevates the importance of spatial justice and the necessity of turning global cities into places of resistance.

This book is timely and well situated historically. While the walls have not entirely come down, universities (and, I would argue, the university presses and journals that had previously sustained the divide) are seeking, albeit still tentatively, to break out of their isolation. *Urban Humanities* includes the search for interdisciplinarity, although the university reward system still discourages it. It includes the need to develop greater transparency and openness to the immediate and broader worlds around universities, although they all too often remain closed and self-contained places. It seeks to engage with communities, although communities require not just engagement but also action. And it searches for diversity when what is also required is social justice and transformation.

Welcome then, reader, to these contested spaces and to the emerging world of *Urban Humanities*.

Preface

This book embodies the core principles of the Urban Humanities Initiative. This is a cross-disciplinary, project-oriented, and experimental curricular initiative at UCLA that draws from humanist practices to interpret and intervene in the city and is driven by a concern for social justice. We treat the format of this book as a generative framework for succinctly demonstrating the open-ended, transformative possibilities of urban humanities, and one possible and compelling way to present knowledge to a broader public audience. The creation of this book, like the urban humanities curricular and research initiative, was a deeply collaborative, design-oriented, experimental process involving all five authors at every step of the way. As we thought about how to articulate years of experiences in the classroom and research practices in multiple cities in a book format, we settled on several organizing ideas: first, a situated history of "urban humanities" as a developing concept and an intellectual framework; second, a set of emerging practices, with a wide range of research applications; third, a pedagogical component that examined how our teaching and curricula changed, especially through modes of public engagement and an emphasis on spatial justice; and, finally, a set of concrete projects about urban humanities practices in the field, composed and written by a range of collaborators.

We divided the book into five core chapters, and each of us served as the primary author for one chapter and the secondary author for another. Initial drafts of each chapter thus emerged from a collaboration of two authors, and then, the other three authors reviewed, edited, and even rewrote them in "round robin" style. Sometimes parts of one chapter moved to another; some chapters were expanded while others were condensed; debates flourished and were settled in the interlinear commentaries that emerged in the writing process. In the book's final form, it is virtually impossible to separate out each of the individual voices and contributions; instead, the book is a synergistic summation of the urban humanities experiment. We see this process, reflective as it is of collaborative work, not as one where each coauthor undertook some imaginary fraction of the necessary labor to produce a monograph but, rather, one where each author brought the intellectual and productive work necessary for the entirety of a book project to bear on each other's contributions, so that the whole is far greater than the sum of its parts.

The decision to list the authors in the order we did may thus need some clarification. Early on in the process, we all agreed to list Dana Cuff as first author in order to recognize her leadership efforts in moving the urban humanities program forward at UCLA and bringing the rest of the faculty and students together as part of the broader initiative. Her leadership as principal investigator is what allowed the program to flourish in the ways that it has. Next, we decided to list the core faculty and co-principal investigators at UCLA in alphabetical order, recognizing that they have each played important roles in developing the methods, practices, research, and teaching of urban humanities. While Jonathan Crisman is listed as the fifth author, we want to emphasize that this is not an indication of lesser importance or contribution to the book, but rather of his teaching and development of the urban humanities program. In the formative years when the Urban

Humanities Initiative was just getting off the ground at UCLA, he was part of the day-to-day creative leadership as associate director and teaching colleague. After three years, he began a new era by undertaking a doctoral degree at the University of Southern California, while the core faculty continued its regular, energetic engagement with the evolving program. The author list reflects the dual production of this volume's underlying theories and practices, that is, the coequal authorship of the book as well as our differential participation in the initiative at UCLA over nearly seven years.

Just as the authorial project of this book is shared, so is the substantial contribution made by our students, colleagues, collaborators, community partners, and advisors. The entire undertaking we call "urban humanities" would not have been born or nurtured to good health without the generous and intelligent support of the Andrew W. Mellon Foundation. Mariët Westermann and the late Hilary Ballon ventured that architecture and urban studies had an important role to play in the humanities, and moreover, that these fields needed to rebuild their humanist perspectives. Later, Dianne Harris joined Mariët to shepherd our energetic enthusiasms toward institutionally viable undertakings. The Mellon Foundation's Architecture, Urbanism, and the Humanities Initiative sponsored urban humanities not only at UCLA but also at more than a dozen other institutions, where our peers have served as collaborators and critics and deserve our thanks: Eve Blau, Alison Eisenberg, Kent Kleinman, Laura Kurgan, Bruce Lindsey, Vanessa Sellers, and Thaisa Way. We had an especially close relationship with our fellow University of California colleagues at UC Berkeley, who were led by Jennifer Wolch and Anthony Cascardi, and where we worked especially closely with Jennifer Wolch, Michael Dear, Greig Crysler, and Susan Moffat. Finally, our friend and colleague Diane Favro at UCLA was an original co-PI and leader for the initiative, and her insights were critical during the early years of its formation.

We have been fortunate to undertake this experiment at the University of California, Los Angeles where we have the support of our administrators and colleagues. Former provost and executive vice chancellor Scott Waugh's humanist and institutional wisdom has been invaluable, and we have relied on him deeply since the project's earliest days. The Urban Humanities Initiative operates within the domains of three different deans who have helped us navigate this uncharted, interdisciplinary terrain: Dean David Schaberg of the Humanities Division; Dean Gary Segura of the Luskin School of Public Affairs and his predecessors Interim Dean Lois Takahashi and Dean Frank Gilliam; and Dean Brett Steele, who took over from Interim Dean David Rousseve in the School of the Arts and Architecture. At UCLA, we have among our colleagues a luxury of riches when it comes to intelligence, expertise, compassion, and commitment. Each year we have brought together a monthly workshop with faculty who share an interest in urban humanities, and these conversations have pushed our thinking substantially. Among approximately fifty colleagues who have joined us over the years, we particularly wish to thank the following individuals who have consistently raised the level of discourse: Jon Christensen, Greg Cohen, Alicia Gaspar de Alba, Kian Goh, Ursula Heise, Tamara Levitz, Paavo Monkkonen, Michael Osman, Ananya Roy, and Jasmine Trice. Another group of faculty has joined us in the classroom, fieldwork abroad, or research undertakings to practice the very cross-disciplinary methods that we elaborate in this book: Eric Avila, Marisa Belausteguigoitia, Greg Cohen, Gabriel Fries-Briggs, Rubén Gallo, Wonne Ickx, Kelly Lytle Hernandez, William Marotti, Ignacio Padilla, Gaspar Rivera Salgado, and Sharon Traweek.

Benjamin Leclair-Paquet served as associate director of the Urban Humanities Initiative for two years, developing and teaching courses, and generally advancing our entire undertaking. Similarly, Jonathan Banfill has had an ongoing and deep participation in the initiative that belies his status as a PhD student: he is very much a colleague, friend, and teacher. cityLAB's assistant director, Gus Wendel, has been central to the substance and administration of the initiative. A number of people have lent their technical expertise and intelligence during our intensive summer institutes, including Albert Kochaphum, Miriam Posner, and Yoh Kawano. A number of graduate student alumni of the urban humanities program played a special role as colleagues, researchers, city guides, and co-teachers: Jacqueline Barrios, Maricela Becerra, Humberto Castro, Aaron Cayer, Brady Collins, Will Davis, Max Greenberg, Jia Gu, Joshua Nelson, Cameron Phillips, Maria Francesca Piazzoni, Carla Salehian, Gus Wendel, Kenny Wong, and Yang Yang.

Our initiative is really a collaboration with partners in our home city of Los Angeles, as well as in our sister cities of Tokyo, Shanghai, and Mexico City. Several groups stand out among the dozens that have worked with us: the Echo Park Film Center, the UCLA Labor Center, Waseda and Kogakuin Universities, Laboratorio para la Ciudad, Casa Gallina, PRODUCTORA and the LIGA Space for Architecture, the HKU-Shanghai Center, Tongji University, and Universidad Autónoma Metropolitana Unidad Cuajimalpa. We particularly thank our colleagues abroad, who have shared their knowledge and brought their own students to join us in some of our most meaningful interchanges: Yung Ho Chang, Christian Dimmer, Arata Endo, Keigo Kobayashi, Xiangning Li, Gabriela Gómez-Mont, Maria Moreno-Carranco, and Zheng Tang. Other individuals who have met or worked with us across this international geography and whose creative minds have been instrumental in the unfolding of urban humanities include Eric Cazdyn, Neil Goldberg, and Annette Kim.

The book could not have taken shape as beautifully, articulately, and swiftly without help in its production. We are fortunate to have partnered with a talented graphic designer, Will Davis, who is also an urban humanities alumnus. His artful visual interpretation of the text and all its components created a coherence from word, to image, to idea. From Will's capable art direction, Yasuyo Iguchi at the MIT Press produced the book's elegant end state. Gratitude is also in abundance for the MIT team: Beth Clevenger, Virginia Crossman, Robert Gottlieb, and Anthony Zannino.

This book is dedicated to all our students from whom we have learned much and received the greatest inspiration. We have high hopes that their varied, illustrious careers will demonstrate the true value of the field of urban humanities, extending its reach, commitments, and capacities.

1
Introducing Urban Humanities

The city is the social, physical, and political terrain of our collective lives, where we live in geographic proximity to people unlike ourselves, negotiating the varied understandings that comprise our coexistence. This definition of the city pertains as readily to historical as well as contemporary examples. However, the intensifying transnational urbanization, globalization, and immigration flows of the last decades have accentuated interactions, contestations, and negotiations of diverse bodies in urban settings.[1] Commuters, tourists, public housing tenants, civic leaders, parking attendants, business owners, migrant street vendors, Skid Row residents, school teachers, downtown cops, and corner drug dealers often rub shoulders in cities, articulating daily life in relation to physical spaces. This cosmopolitan congestion produces the friction to spark debates about various social, economic, and cultural issues, and these spatial politics most often play out in the city's common grounds. How space is understood, articulated, and regulated has a lot to do with how we interact in it.

Consider urban streets. In ancient Pompeii, cart traffic into the forum was blocked by large stones to afford both commerce and political discourse among citizens. Nineteenth-century arcades were fundamental to the creation of a vibrant Parisian street life, where strangers encountered one another in public, and consumer life blossomed. Built in 2017, Grand Park in downtown Los Angeles offers Angelenos from different walks of life a common ground for coming together to celebrate or protest. In each instance, a loose or coordinated consortium includes residents, visitors, writers, planners, and politicians who together braid stories about how to imagine, interpret, claim, and act within the city they share. Contested urban space and spaces of resistance also define a portion of this spectrum, as when the French Revolution flourished behind street barricades, the Occupy Movement presented itself to the world in Manhattan's Zuccotti Park, or Tahrir Square became the epicenter of Cairo's Arab Spring. In each instance, the public sphere of street and square situates collective life, inscribing potential for political interchange that in turn recomposes the metropolis.

The city has always been a social, spatial, and political terrain, where we coexist in continuously negotiated spaces, often (though certainly not always) marked by shared histories, narratives, and meanings. However, in the last decades, new urgencies demand our attention, as cities have become the transnational home to the majority of the world's population. These urgencies include vast disparities of wealth that create social tensions in urban settings, migrations of economic and political refugees, and affordable housing shortages globally.[2] At the same time, the world's cities produce and experience environmental crises that range from climate change and sea level rise to industrial pollution and toxic air quality.

Rather than rehearse alarmist refrains, these conditions serve as the groundwork for *urban humanities*, an emerging field and a new approach for not only understanding cities in a global context but also intervening in them, interpreting their histories, analyzing and engaging current circumstances, and speculating about their futures.[3] Urban humanities deploy urban studies, design, and the humanities to interpret and intervene in the city through engaged scholarship attentive to the settings of everyday life. The perspectives, interpretive practices, and content of the humanities are enriched by their interaction with those of urban planning and architecture, while the practices of architecture and planning are enhanced by their interaction with humanistic approaches that ground design, speculation, modeling, and intervention in the complex cultural-socio-historical networks that compose the urban.

Defining Urban Humanities

If we have hinted at our understanding of the urban, what then are the *urban humanities*? We begin this chapter by dwelling a bit longer on the constitutive concepts of this combined term. As a modifier, the "urban" in the "urban humanities" connotes a humanistic inquiry that is specifically centered on the city. This includes the cultural expressions created in cities, their social forms and structures, ethnic and racial composition, and varied and multilayered histories, the languages spoken and linguistic expressions of inhabitants, as well as the built and lived spaces. This inquiry is pursued through the many media forms (including literature, photography, film) that help to make sense of the city and its people, but also through direct interaction with them. By and large, this is a pedagogy of the city attuned to both the empirical and the interactive but also the representational forms that tend to be the way the humanities have conventionally approached the city—that is, by focusing on the reading and interpretation of its representations (i.e., "the city as text").

However, "urban" need not just modify "humanities." Rather, the term also connotes a new collective singular, a linkage defined by the productive and sometimes precarious tensions between the two constitutive terms. As a productive tension, neither term is overcome by the other. Instead, they exist in a push-and-pull relationship, in which new possibilities and potentialities are opened up for both the urban and the humanities by virtue of their coming together. In this respect, neither term is static or impermeable. The "urban humanities" emerges as a sublated, third term without, however, losing the elemental components of the urban and the humanities in the dialectical process. In many ways, this is the same logic that provides the dynamic intellectual and pedagogical framework for other new critical, experimental, and praxis-oriented interventions, such as "digital humanities," "environmental humanities," and "medical humanities."[4]

In each case, disciplinary formations that had been outside the conventional purview of the humanities (perhaps because of their methodological approach, content, professional ambitions, or pedagogies) are now defined by their intersection with the humanities. Far from "correcting" or merely augmenting the humanities, urban humanities (like digital, environmental, and medical humanities) bring the critical lineages, interpretive paradigms, historical depths, comparative cultural analyses, and ethical orientations of the humanities to bear upon the city (just as digital humanities, for example, do this for computation and digital technologies). What this means is that each of these "hyperobjects"—the city, the digital, the environment, medicine—to use Timothy Morton's coinage to refer to objects of study characterized by vast temporal and spatial dimensionality and complexity[5]—are conjoined with and interpreted, however provisionally and partially, by the critical practices of the humanities.

At the core of the humanities are, of course, human beings— with all their diverse and embodied cultural expressions, perspectives, languages, and histories. This is what the humanities study, interpret, and value. They do so through methods of interpretation and critical inquiry, which provide historical context, situated perspectives, and comparative frameworks for understanding and also exposing various epistemologies, ideologies, value systems, structuring principles, and world views. At the same time, the humanities are attentive to media form and media specificity, as form cannot be dissociated from content. In this sense, humanistic inquiry is also design-oriented because it opens up spaces for the imaginative, the speculative, and the future-oriented. The humanities are not just a retrospective analysis of the remains of the cultural record (the archive, the wisdom of the past, the archaeological artifacts of the past), but can be—and we argue, *should be*—attuned to futurity, the possibility of justice, reparation, and perhaps even redemption. As the German-Jewish philosopher Walter Benjamin famously said in a context of great historical urgency, as he fled the advances of the Nazi army: "We [human beings] have been endowed with a *weak* messianic power" by which the past makes a claim on both the present and the possibilities of the future.[6] For urban humanists, we see this transformative potential—grounded in and emerging from the injustices of the past—to be oriented toward the possibility of spatial justice. At the core of urban humanities pedagogy, then, is the ideal of spatial justice—a concept we will return to later. But to orient our pedagogy toward this ideal, we must first recognize and break from certain entrenched traditions that have tended to isolate the university and cut off the humanities from other disciplines (especially those in the social and applied sciences, as well as in schools of planning or architecture).

While there have been many calls for reform in the humanities (especially in graduate education), very few programs have made substantive changes beyond shortening the time to degree and supporting "alternative" professionalization opportunities outside the academy.[7] Perhaps this is because the humanities tend to be isolated from other disciplines and programs at the university. If we look beyond the humanities to the medical sciences, engineering, the applied social sciences, and other professional schools such as architecture, it is not uncommon to think in terms of "grand challenges" or "big problems": a cure for a disease, energy independence, global health, clean water, just cities, and so forth. These are not only big problems but ones that require years and years of effort to solve; they require many people from various disciplines to work collaboratively, including generations of scholars, often in labs and studios, and collaborators from public policy, the nonprofit and for-profit worlds, government, philanthropy, the arts, and more. The work takes years, perhaps even decades, to carry out. The research proceeds incrementally and may, in fact, fail. Nonetheless, it is cumulative, with students coming in, working in labs and studios for short periods of time, receiving their degrees focused on elemental aspects of the research process, and moving on.[8]

In the humanities, scholars tend to approach things exactly the opposite way: with ever smaller, ever more specialized problems, addressed by single individuals almost always working in isolation, with the highest achievement being a dissertation monograph. In fact, almost everything in the humanities is set up to support scholarship in isolation: individual achievement is valorized; single-authored texts are the norm; and even office space is organized by separating scholars from one another. While these practices may come from a tradition of fostering thoughtful (even monastic) contemplation and individualized writing, it means that collaborative, experimental, and speculative research is the exception in the humanities, and students are hardly ever brought into the experimental research process as partners and co-contributors.

What if we turn this approach on its head and ask, instead: "How can a hyperobject like the city be studied and taught? What would it mean to address this challenge with generations of students, who would work with faculty as well as outside collaborators—across multiple disciplines and institutions—to come up with ways to understand, address, contextualize, and respond to the challenge of spatial justice?" The idea is to think at many different scales at once—from the biggest to the smallest, in as many different directions as possible, with as many different methods and people as possible. To give a more concrete example: How might we compose a comprehensive history of immigration to a city as complex as Los Angeles? It would need to treat the topic historically, geographically, socially, culturally, economically, and architecturally; it would focus on issues of race, global histories of nation-states, technologies of mobility, assimilation, identity, public policy, gender, policing, and representations of difference and otherness; it would be multilingual, transnational, and multimedia; it would involve a multitude of voices, perspectives, languages, narratives, and neighborhoods. It would have primary materials, translations, annotations, commentaries, interactive media, historical analyses, datasets, interpretations, and maps; it would be a forum for debate and the development of public policy, a resource for courses, and a collaborative site for reviewing scholarly research of all types. It would be an integrated, open-ended, and collaborative research product with contributions by many students and faculty from various departments, disciplines, organizations, and institutions, especially ones outside of the conventional contours of the university. And it would potentially take scores and scores of researchers and participants decades to do well.

As new multidisciplinary fields such as environmental humanities, digital humanities, medical humanities, and urban humanities gain traction, we are starting to see research configurations in the humanities that are not based on, limited to, or derived from traditional departments. These configurations are not simply interdisciplinary by virtue of their subject matter or the descriptive modifiers attached to the humanities (as in doing the humanities digitally); instead, they introduce new conjugations of humanities research with the methods, tools, analytical techniques, and content of other disciplines. These configurations lead to different kinds of research questions, in terms of scale, method, content, participation, and output.

How can a single department or discipline possibly provide the range of expertise needed to investigate a phenomenon as complex, say, as the emergence of the Anthropocene and the impact of human activities on the earth's ecosystems, biodiversity, and climate? An emerging research configuration like environmental humanities responds by bringing climate scientists together with literary scholars, information architects, geographers, biologists, and historians. Other new configurations such as urban humanities are also needed to study the cultural, social, and architectural histories of megacities, where some 10 percent of the earth's population now resides. How can we respond to the grand challenge of designing and building a more just city without such a plurality of perspectives and expertise, not to mention partnerships beyond the walls of the university with nongovernmental organizations, city councils and regional governments, developers, museums, artists, schools, and countless other cultural and social constituencies? These are "big projects" that combine deep criticality, interpretation, and transhistorical, comparative perspectives with speculative, experimental, and projective problem-solving. And, more than that, they represent the "translational" public potential of the humanities, the applications of humanities knowledge far beyond the tiny group of specialists who typically encounter and care about humanities research.

It is clear that the old configurations of humanities departments as siloed entities—largely stratified by medium, period, and genre—make no sense at all for asking and answering these big urban questions. The conventional model not only is parochial but also facilitates a very narrow band of research questions that are ever more specialized rather than opening outward to comparative questions and real-world applications that cut across geography, period, language, medium, method, and institution. Our contention is that we typically expect humanities students to do siloed research and individual scholarship, on highly specialized topics, without putting these specializations together to form constellations or large-scale, collaborative projects. In contrast, we believe that we need to encourage the building of "aggregations" of knowledge that have broader application, involving partnerships with communities, with potentially global diffusion.

As we will argue here, a radical reimagining of the humanities has the potential to achieve a number of things: Foster integrated, collaborative research that embeds specializations and individual research into a significantly broader, multimodal, and interdisciplinary research context; create new paradigms for recruiting, mentoring, and training students; be a productive response to the "crisis of humanities" by providing a model for engaged, broad-based, collaborative, public humanities scholarship; and, finally, transform the scale, duration, impact, and public resonance of humanities scholarship by placing collaboration, co-creation, speculation, and experimentation at the core of the student experience.

Far from excusing the variety of disciplines outside of the humanities, which have had a history of looking at "big problems," our project seeks to breathe life into these spheres as well. We don't use this language metaphorically: while these disciplines—namely architecture, urban planning, and the social sciences—have a rich history of examining social ills and proposing bold solutions to these ills and can hardly be thought of as monolithic in any way, the past thirty or so years of social science research have tended toward the numerically quantifiable and the abstraction of human life. As the hegemony of econometrics has spread through planning, policy studies, and the gamut of social sciences to better interface with a global system of capital that translates human relations into an abstract economic calculus, fundamental questions regarding human existence, values, culture, and lived and sensed experiences have often taken a back seat.

Architecture, on the other hand, like the larger world of cultural production of which it is a part, fluctuates between an identification with avant-garde arts and its intrinsic connection to social concerns. While architecture has origins in the technical and applied arts, beginning in the 1970s and coincidental with the expansion of doctoral programs in architectural history and particularly theory, architecture sought to strengthen its roots in form-based logics. This led to a focus on internal or autonomous disciplinary questions like its critical history, its particular practices, the specific nature of architectural drawings, and the development of abstract form. Peter Eisenman's House VI (1975) (figure 1.1) was the "take no prisoners" primary object of architectural autonomy, with its demonstration that form did not emanate from function (for example, columns in House VI were not structural and didn't even meet the ground in one case).[9] Subsequent developments of architectural theory's impact on practice were varied, but tended toward abstraction, formalism, and discourse rather than social and political engagement. Thus, while the econometrics approach of the social sciences and the formal approach of architecture could not seem more distantly related, the two have striking similarities.

1.1 House VI by Peter Eisenman, 1975. Credit: Gerrit Oorthuys

There is, of course, a counter-history to these dominant narratives, and even more recent undertakings point toward a reversal of which urban humanities are also a part. A book that has received a lot of attention in urban planning and the social sciences is Matthew Desmond's *Evicted*, an intensely focused ethnography, which narrates the everyday struggles of those caught up in an increasingly broken housing system.[10] And the past few laureates of the Pritzker Prize have included Alejandro Aravena who has developed low-cost social housing in the Global South, and B. V. Doshi who has also worked on low-cost and sustainable housing in India. The field of urban humanities similarly turns its attention toward the aspects of human life that have long been the focus of the humanities, bringing the gaze of architecture, design, urban planning, and the social sciences with it. While attempts to address the "grand challenges" of our day should be celebrated, these efforts that often bring together so much of the quantified and abstracted world will be for naught if at the end of the day we forget about the person standing at the receiving end of some supposed "grand solution."

Urban humanities employ a set of practices and strategies to enter this bidirectional move—from the intensely focused humanities out toward the larger world, and from the bigness of architecture[11] versus the even more macroscopic view of the urban from the social sciences toward the micronarratives of embodied human beings. Our positionality within a university context necessarily forces us to contend with our biases, not the least of which is reproducing the tendency toward the very academic, abstract theorization, which we critique. Thus, while in our work and throughout this volume we return to sources of inspiration, which are often academic and theoretical, we also strive toward building urban humanities out of the projects of creative individuals such as political organizers, artists, and practitioners, but most of all through the on-the-ground practices that we have deployed— sometimes intentionally and other times unexpectedly—through a process of collaborative, iterative, and reflective inquiry. This "emplacement," or the operative frame that privileges knowledge, learning, experience, and creation, occurs in relation to specific places, and even *within* specific places, and is a fundamental driver of our particular formulation of urban humanities. As such, it is important to consider the specificity of our project as emanating from UCLA and Los Angeles, in particular.

Looking Out from Los Angeles

Urban humanities were born in Los Angeles. Our views emanate from an academic setting on the "Left Coast," at the University of California, Los Angeles (UCLA). But our work, however emplaced, is not focused only on our own backyard. We see contemporary urbanism shaped through processes of negotiation taking place in the settings of everyday life, which are plugged into a global network of cities, mediated through information and communication technologies, and constructed by flows of capital, but also by individuals, their collectivities, and cultural practices.[12] In fact, Los Angeles acts as a foil to consider cities around the globe. While we deem urban humanities useful and applicable for cities worldwide, this book describes our interconnected research projects, experiences, and collaborations in megacities of the Pacific Rim: Tokyo, Shanghai, Mexico City, and Los Angeles. It goes on, however, to elaborate those analyses in a broader array of cities.

These four Pacific Rim cities have their own identities and cultures, yet they also share what Lisa Lowe might term "intimacies" through curious linkages formed by migrations, investments, and interdependent histories. Urban humanities touch upon Lowe's notion of these intimacies across continents by "examining the dynamic relationship among the always present but differently manifest and available histories and social forces."[13] As such, transnational urban studies are enriched by transnational humanist perspectives, giving body to otherwise abstract flows. And, as a practice that aims not only to understand and interpret, but also to engage and intervene, urban humanities see these intimacies as a demonstration of the instability in definitions of "home" and "away": We often find ourselves at home in cities abroad and strangers in our own backyard, the vast landscape of Los Angeles.

The premise of urban humanities is that the city is a site of concrete connections and interactions in space. Therefore, the inquiries of urban humanities precipitate around the cultural artifacts of urban space and the micro-settings of everyday life—a housing project, a plaza, a six-lane boulevard, a gated community, a courthouse, a broken sidewalk, a mural-monument to life lost in a police operation—those are the spatial embodiments of histories, collective lives, intimacies, contestations, power relations, and social distinctions. These fragments of everyday life are influenced by larger forces, but also by subjective, human-scale realities that we as scholars, designers, planners, activists, and humanists have some capacity to affect.

This approach stands apart from the most recognized forms of urban study that precede it, in so far as it borrows from them all to produce a more powerful lens. Since time immemorial, authors have constructed remote locations for readers in literary narratives—from ancient Pausanias's portrayals of second-century Athens, to Baudelaire's and Benjamin's accounts of a changing nineteenth-century Paris. Over the last four decades, in response to critiques that such single-site urban biographies are too limited, parochial, and ethnocentric,[14] comparative urbanism has instead flourished, triggered by a desire to compare, contrast, or juxtapose parallel phenomena that happen in multiple socio-spatial contexts and likely influence one another.[15] But comparative studies also have been criticized as overly constrained by fixed entities and arbitrary divisions such as municipal or national boundaries. In reality, urban networks and influences are dynamic, diverse, and transcend such boundaries. The emphasis on comparison may also bring along the danger of homogenizing differences and disregarding local particularities in favor of extracting universal lessons to urban issues and problems.[16]

More recently over the past twenty years, a transnational perspective has gained favor in research on cities, responding to criticism that comparative urbanism suffers from a static perception of the urban.[17] In contrast, transnational approaches focus on interdependencies, movements, and flows across borders in regions and subregions. This transnational, transcultural, comparative approach is also reflected within the humanities, particularly in cultural criticism with its emphasis on mobility, migration, border crossing, and hybridity.[18] The human body—as national subject, traveler, migrant, refugee, or even as bare life[19]— stands at the center of such global abstractions and structures of power. By synthesizing these perspectives, of literary depictions of cities with comparative urbanisms from the social sciences, of global flows from transnationalism with the embodied emphases of the humanities, we find ourselves at urban humanities: studying global intimacies manifested in material culture and the human, everyday life interactions at urban settings.

With the expansion of global travel, the accumulation of digitally accessible foreign archives, the development of area studies in the university, and the wide circulation of international media, the study of places of "otherness" grows. The practices, pedagogies, and values of urban humanities arise from multi-pronged investigations in global cities of the Pacific Rim whose literatures, histories, geographies, and architectures do not lend themselves to Eurocentric cosmopolitan conventions, even under conditions of colonialism. Paradigmatic models of Paris, London, and New York are insufficient to grasp Los Angeles or Shanghai.

To illuminate urban humanities, the book features projects that come from our own research and teaching. These projects are the product of collaborations between scholars, community organizations, practitioners, and artists in the four aforementioned cities of the Pacific Rim. The projects are also theoretically founded upon and framed by work from other scholars, artists, and practitioners, often based in a range of other locales around the world. To provide a critical investigation of urban settings in cities, our projects focus on the spaces and artifacts of everyday life but also examine major themes found in contemporary urban settings, such as risk, resilience, spatial contestations of collective and individual identity, and the problematics of borders and migrations.

To study and interpret these complex issues situated in their socio-spatial contexts, urban humanities build a field of inquiry in which history, literature, architecture, art, and urban planning comingle to understand urban realities and respond to new urban challenges. These fused practices take place within scholarly settings of research and teaching, but also within contexts of shared experiences and community engagement beyond academia. These contexts occur in a wide range of urban social settings, from neighborhoods facing the threat of gentrification to streets and sidewalks upon which so much of daily life occurs.

Imagining a Future

In addition to the "situatedness" of our experiences and practices, two other values drive much of urban humanities: an acute attention toward the future and a drive to work toward spatial justice. Together, these values enable us, as the title of our volume suggests, to reimagine our collective life in the context of an increasingly globalized and urbanized world. Without spatial justice, attention toward the future, even with the best of intentions, has often resulted in disastrous consequences, such as the radical reimagining of urban cores that occurred during the middle of the twentieth century under the label of "urban renewal"—and this is but one narrative among countless others in the course of human history. While this vision of the future certainly held the promises of modernity for a select group, for others it was no future at all. Spatial justice demands that we ask why, how, and for whom? And the pursuit of spatial justice—the manifestations of a just world that often play out across spatial dimensions and within cities—with an eye only toward past injustices often leads to a hypercritical tendency to critique, deconstruct, and destroy those factors that have perpetuated these injustices. This pursuit is an important task, to be sure, yet one that all too often has left a void without consideration of reconstructing an alternative future, thus allowing further future injustices to happen. Jane Jacobs's appreciation for the city-as-it-is, calling out the destructive tendencies of modern urban planning, is an example that comes to mind; it certainly came out of a desire for a just city, yet its logical endpoint has landed us in our contemporary neoliberal city, with the seemingly universal traits of the lack of affordable housing, gentrification, and displacement. Only with both an attention toward the future and a desire for spatial justice can we truly and collectively imagine a future.

Most academic work engages with the past or the present through forms of historical and empirical inquiry. Yet by engaging with the city and by calling for spatial justice, we are necessarily thrust into the uncertain and unknown future. What kind of urban future might or ought to happen? What kind of future do we want, and for whom? What are the ways in which the future might be materialized, embodied, and spatialized? To engage with such questions, the urban humanist must gather data, narratives, and historical materials with the explicit mandate to imagine change and transformation. This is not a prescriptive practice mandating a specific future, but rather an expression of values and possibilities in the service of imagining a more democratic, equitable, and just future.

The few strains of scholarly work that engage the future systematically most often come from the professional disciplines of design, urban planning, and architecture, which envision projects and places to be built. Such work incorporates visions of urban futures such as Le Corbusier's *Ville Contemporaine* (1922), or Hugh Ferriss's depictions in *The Metropolis of Tomorrow* (1929), which Lewis Mumford called "utopias of reconstruction" (in contrast to utopias of escape).[20] While the historical, interpretive methods of the humanities do not, in general, pertain to investigations of the future or speculative design, the utopian imagination has a significant legacy that may be traced in works of literature, philosophy, art, and film. One need only mention Thomas More, Karl Marx, Vladimir Tatlin, and Fritz Lang, among many others. Lang's 1928 film *Metropolis*, for example, is a futuristic city marked not only by technology and speed but also by overcoming some of the greatest social and economic disparities.

Such total, utopian visions from the mid-1800s to the 1920s atrophied with the postwar retreat from cities to suburbs and the catastrophes of urban renewal in the 1960s and 1970s. Other strains of a future-oriented sensibility have found ground in creative fields, such as sci-fi artistic practices or speculative literature. The field of urban humanities calls for renewed scholarly attention toward the future, not as a totalizing, alternative regime but with an emphasis on spatial justice, and terms the necessity of such work "the generative imperative." This term also suggests the project-based orientation necessary for such work: urban humanities are organized around collaborative projects with material outcomes.

The initial foray into speculative work is one oriented toward setting agendas and framing questions, as well as outlining actionable projections. By engaging in fictions and narratives about what could possibly come, and by pushing these experiments to the edges of our imagination, we create the capacity to expand what is conceptualized as possible. This form of projection is akin to the exploratory artistic practices that Jacques Rancière has identified as providing fuel to expand the collective imagination.[21] We term this "immanent speculation" to preclude the decontextualized and ahistorical tendencies, which gave rise to the tabula rasa approach of 1960s urban renewal. These projects necessarily emerge from socio-spatial contexts, site specificity, and conditions immanent to the place in question. Thus, projective urban humanities work is always grounded in real places, interacting with the real people who inhabit them, in order to create engaged, responsible answers to the elusive questions about the future.

The value of spatial justice compels the urban humanist to act—action that defines an engaged scholarship and pedagogy of a different sort from those drawn from existing models of community-based research, service learning, and the like. Spatial justice is not necessarily a better form of justice; rather, it is a lens through which particular injustices are made visible in cities. So many of the greatest problems of cities, from environmental harms, to economic impoverishment and hunger have been chalked up not to any intrinsic and unalterable natural law, but merely to an inequitable distribution of resources and amenities. The urban humanist sees these problems as socio-politically constructed and spatially manifested.

While drawing upon the long literature regarding the "right to the city," as espoused by Henri Lefebvre and David Harvey,[22] our jumping off point is much closer to home: the critical geographer Edward Soja, who wrote one of his final volumes on the topic of spatial justice, grounding it in his experience of Los Angeles. In *Seeking Spatial Justice*, Soja describes the necessity for consideration of the spatiality of justice, not only because space acts as a political mechanism for the production of injustice, but also because a consideration of space opens up tools for social and political action.[23] To date, however, this effort has been grounded largely in the social sciences. By privileging actions and cultural artifacts of people in their urban settings, and working towards concrete spatial alternatives, urban humanities present a means for the incorporation of "other" marginalized topics and voices in order to expressively undertake new practices that work toward mending spatial injustices.

If urban humanists are to address the spatial injustices in cities, their locus of action will inherently transgress disciplinary, hierarchical, and geographical borders. Urban humanist scholars produce knowledge collaboratively not only across academic disciplines from the humanities, social sciences, and design, but also with other actors in the city, be they community members, policymakers, artists, or activists. In this regard, the research and pedagogical practices of the university are knit within a broader environment, not isolated from the city and outside organizations but, rather, in connection with them. This form of engaged scholarship and pedagogy introduces nonhierarchical, self-reflexive, and sited pedagogies to known practices of community-based research and learning, forming the basis for a series of new, exploratory research practices.

First, the researcher is a subject among subjects, in a nonhierarchical relationship in which collaborative practices contribute to a shared creation (e.g., a project, an event, a performance, a speculative design, or a report). The term "researcher" as deployed in community-based research may even be obsolete; terms such as "student" or "participant" may be more apt, but even these have their shortcomings. To play out one example, an urban humanist scholar might bring her research tools of mapping and ethnography to the community arts director who brings her practices of teaching and public relations, and together they collaborate with a community to concoct an appropriate plan for an arts center in the local park. Yet while the outcome of this plan is certainly beneficial, the process through which it was developed may have produced new networks of collaboration, experiences, and observations that would yield new knowledge of their own right, and reconfigured power relationships between expert and layperson, or between resident and visitor. Indeed, this example is based on several urban humanities projects undertaken in Mexico City and Los Angeles, which will be discussed in more detail in later chapters. Our current understanding of such engaged scholarship reflects this binational experience.

The commitment of urban humanities to academic scholarship suggests its own practices.[24] Prior to fieldwork or engagement, researchers study a place and its people through literature, film, arts, architecture, and history. The range of advance materials and experiences not only prepare, but *bias* researchers in self-aware and self-critical ways. Acknowledgment of our own subjectivity and positionality (in the context of collective, multidisciplinary teams) is fundamental to cultivating a generation of creative practitioners in urban humanities.[25] Further, attention to the positionality of others within a collaborative network, and the power relationships that define this network, are critical for producing work that can legitimately respond to spatial injustices. As such, an ongoing process of self-reflexive learning and project modification is necessary and, moreover, can yield creative insights into new project directions.

In addition to such traditional scholarly practices of reading, archival research, or formal analysis, new types of scholarship are evoked that are rooted in place, action, interaction, materiality, and community. Such sited engagement is important for grounding projects, and also for practices that demand spatial learning, reflection, and response. To extend Soja's arguments about the role of spatiality,[26] spatially specific engagement provides learning and tools that are capable of identifying and responding to those injustices arising from situated forms of injustice or oppression. This grounded learning emerges from site-specific practices such as fieldwork and spatial ethnography, which form the substance of urban humanities as developed *in situ*—a way of practice in the city, which we see as distinct from academic methodologies, as conventionally understood.

Practicing Urban Humanities

Urban humanities call for scholarship to be augmented by practices that directly engage with people and places, which in turn provokes questions about values. Why do we engage in these practices, and for whom? What assumptions lie behind them? The foundations of urban humanities rest upon three main values: spatial justice, an imperative to speculate about the future, and pedagogy supporting engaged scholarship. These values are expressed through a set of "fused" practices of scholarship, some of which we have developed in depth (and will be discussed later)—including thick mapping, spatial ethnography, and filmic sensing—while others remain in an experimental form, waiting for other interlocutors to take up their development. We identify these practices as "fused" because they are interdisciplinary, collaborative, and oscillate between process and output.

Given our transformed understanding of the contemporary city, and the values deemed necessary for ethical engagement with socio-spatial settings, existing disciplinary strategies for scholarly and professional work on cities often seem inadequate. For example, methods from urban planning and the social sciences generally rely on economic and quantitative analyses of neighborhood change, ignoring the symbolic, communicative, and cultural elements that also underlie change. Or a humanistic interpretation of changes in the same neighborhood may lack the data-driven evidence that may have the potential to influence policy changes. Moreover, urban understanding is grounded, sometimes tacitly, upon conventions emanating from the study of Eurocentric, postfordist models.

Our fused practices seek to address these shortcomings, though we would hardly claim that they have fully succeeded. Instead, they remain under constant modification, contextualization, and improvisation, given the particularities of a site and a circumstance. Their fusion is part of this process, occurring through the combination of researchers, collaborating across distinct positionalities. This connotes a networked and capacious formation of diverse individuals, who come together in common collaboration. These individuals come from a variety of disciplinary backgrounds with expertise in different research practices, from community-based organizations responsible for putting knowledge into action to disparate representational and communicative traditions that have the capacity to bridge scholarly, artistic, and practical media. Our work in urban humanities has brought together, for example, designers and architects, social scientists, literature and film scholars, and urban planners in collaboration with civic agencies, community groups, and nonprofit organizations. Communicating across such a diverse spectrum of individuals is helped by a grounded, action-oriented, site- and project-specific approach.

Fused practices of scholarship are necessary for understanding and intervening in the complexities of contemporary cities—no single discipline can fully claim ownership of a condition as vast and complex as the urban. This is overwhelmingly apparent in the megacities of the Pacific Rim. Therefore, a significant portion of this volume is dedicated to describing, unpacking, and demonstrating these practices. Fused practices deviate from past, exhausted discussions on interdisciplinarity and abstract conversations on how to bridge siloed scholarly work. Rather, they place emphasis on action-oriented, situated practices in order to engage with contemporary urbanism.

The term "practices" is more appropriate than "methods" for several reasons. First, grounded and exploratory, such practices are developed in situ, and lack the precedent and fixity that come with long-established disciplinary methods. This is not a problem, but rather allows for openness, flexibility, and responsiveness to the shifting goals of a project, or the surprises that arise amid new collaborations. Second, these practices are a fusion of research, representation, and action rather than fully instrumentalized methods that lead linearly from research questions to findings. Third, practice theory argues for the subject's agency in the contexts of broader, collective systems. The fused practices of urban humanities explicitly restore agency to engaged scholars and maintain the deep intersectionality of theory and practice.[27]

The practices introduced here (and examined in depth later in the volume) are not an exhaustive list but are representative and applicable beyond the particularities of our specific collaborators, projects, identities, skills, and places. These practices share several defining traits. First, and most clearly, they shift among research method, experimental scholarly output, and instrument for action; while they may manifest as more strongly one or the other, they are always much more than simply a data collection method. Second, they critically engage with forms of media, rethinking how we see, communicate, understand, and possibly transform the city. Third, they are fundamentally collaborative and project-based. And fourth, they are site-specific and embodied, examining practices of everyday life attuned to the positionality of the subject.

If we had to describe urban humanities with a single word, that word might be "thickness." Urban humanities "thickens" our understanding of the urban by unearthing the different layers that not only constitute its cultural and historical density, but, more importantly, also propel us into the future in ways that are grounded yet open-ended. Thickness goes beyond "more data" or "more layers" of information; it bespeaks a practice of adding complexity, voices, and perspectives, thereby eliciting productive tensions that enable new, speculative possibilities to emerge.

Contemporary cities like Los Angeles or Shanghai seem to elicit the construct of thickness because of their sheer size, complexity, and historicity. Building on the ideas developed for the Hyper-Cities digital mapping project by Todd Presner, David Shepard, and Yoh Kawano, "thick mapping" in the urban humanities is the process of composing a multilayered, multitemporal, and propositional spatial representation that foregrounds multiple voices, perspectives, and narratives.[28] Echoing Clifford Geertz's argument for the development of "thick description"[29] as an approach to ethnographic practices attuned to stratification and micro- and macro-level accounts and the construction of all narratives, so too is thick mapping an urban humanities practice for probing, narrating, and representing the city's spatial and temporal dynamics (figure 1.2).

Thickness is an attribute that is fundamental to all urban humanities practices. The central goal is to synthesize positivist and empirical modes of the social sciences with the embodied, speculative, critical, material, and ethical sensibilities of architecture and the humanities. Thickness moves beyond a singular or definitive reading, which is a "thin" approach to knowing and being. Rather, thick media incorporate—and perform—multiple readings and histories; they combine polyvocality and contestation in ways that create a greater whole without erasing what might be construed as conflictual or incongruent realities. Thick mapping, thus, takes the cartographic medium, long understood as an objective, scientific representation of the world based in geographic norms and state power, deconstructs it by exposing its assumptions and structuring epistemologies, and layers in the messy reality of humanity, culture, and history. The thick map takes on qualities of a spatial narrative to tell surprising stories of unfamiliar cities.

1.2 Students working on a thick map of the Chinese Massacre of Los Angeles in 1871.
Photo credit: Authors

We intentionally use the verb "mapping" to specify process, namely the incorporation of the range of practices involved in spatial data collection, visual representation, construction of narratives, and iteration, not to mention the deployment of a thick map in the service of political engagement, knowledge production, and policy development. Thick mapping is a practice not limited to the singular goal of a scholarly output, but also involves learning, teaching, and engaging. Thus, urban humanities work depends upon research as well as new pedagogical practices that incorporate collaborative and shared mapping in the classroom and in the field in order to see, create, and act anew. In the words of landscape architect James Corner, we pursue mapping to "emancipate potentials, enrich experiences, and diversify worlds."[30]

Spatial ethnography is another fused practice of urban humanities. It is grounded in the scholarly methods of spatial analysis (coming from geography, urban studies, and architecture), and in ethnography (primarily originating in anthropology and to a lesser extent, history). It merges these research methods with considerations of narrative, media, and fieldwork. The most central element of a spatial ethnographic practice, however, is the process of urban humanities fieldwork, construed in the liminal space between anthropological observation and the architectural site visit. Transnational metropolitan studies incorporate anthropological methods in which a researcher is immersed in an unfamiliar cultural setting in order to observe, experience, form thicker descriptions, and construct more compelling narratives.[31] At the other extreme is the site visit, common in architecture, planning, and urban design where an outsider relatively quickly assesses spatial and material qualities of an unfamiliar place. This location-specific investigation involves measurement and data gathering more often through immediate means such as mapping, sketching, and photography. Together, the practices of anthropological observation and the site visit inform the fieldwork undertaken by urban humanists. Fieldwork as defined in urban humanities quickly exposes suspect "othering" of geographies and communities, as well as cultures. Far from "parachuting in" to identify and fix a problem, the urban humanist engages communities, builds relationships of trust, and collaboratively generates possibilities.

At its most elemental, spatial ethnography is a practice of observing, describing, and analyzing situated cultures or people with particular regard to their spatial context. This can be as simple as georeferencing ethnographic information, allowing for anthropological investigations to identify spatial patterns. But spatial ethnography within urban humanities is laden with implications beyond this straightforward tweak to ethnography— and many of these implications stem directly from the fraught history of ethnography within anthropology. The "object" of analysis is never just "out there" but is very much constituted by the positionality of the subject who brings her worldviews, epistemologies, languages, sensitivities, and biases to any practice of representation. Moreover, "space" is hardly a fixed object or container for investigation, as spaces are always dynamic, fluid, mutable, and multiplying.[32]

Scholars from sociology and urban studies have deployed elements of spatial ethnography (without necessarily identifying it as such) to study the urban. William H. Whyte, for example, in his pioneering study of small urban spaces enacted practices of spatial ethnography, from a keen spatial observation, to placing importance on the embodied and everyday activities of individuals passing under the gaze of his cameras.[33] Yet Whyte did not push his spatial ethnography much beyond behavioral observation; without interviews the occupants of the plazas remained mute. What is the cultural context for the plaza users, and how does it relate to their use of space? What particular user narratives may enrich or even contest Whyte's reading and understanding of the plazas? What would it mean to focus on a few individuals rather than synthesizing their aggregate use of space? An urban humanities approach may have uncovered, beyond the formal and social patterns that can be directly observed, a "thick story" of the space.

What separates spatial ethnography from other forms of spatial analysis and GIS (geographic information system)-based social science is that spatial ethnography places the utmost importance on the embodied, everyday practices of people in their settings. Urban humanities aim to push this aspect further by making explicit the field's value claims, championing the importance of humanistic narratives and understandings of embodied spaces. One contemporary scholar who used spatial ethnography to analyze and document the vibrant streets of Ho Chi Minh City is Annette Kim, who merged macro-level socio-political analyses with direct observation of the micro-settings of everyday life (see figures 3.3 and 3.4). Her "critical cartography primer" is a collection of data about the activities taking place over the course of a full day on a single street in the city. She mapped down to the square foot observations of elderly residents playing games on the sidewalk with friends, shops with wares spilling out onto the street, or the rows of parked mopeds. Kim's practice emerges by taking a spatial ethnography sensibility and combining it with the recent, provocative literature on critical cartography.[34] In her words, these elements provide "the best hope for throwing off conceptual blinders."[35] Although Kim's methods can be used in a wide range of metropolitan settings, it is no coincidence that they have evolved outside Eurocentric urban conditions.

Filmic sensing is the third of our more developed practices of the urban humanities. Cinematographers, artists, and urbanists have long used the medium of film and video in order to represent cities, places, and spaces. In the process of developing and producing videos and films, the apparatuses used for capture (e.g., film cameras or cell phones) and editing (scissors or nonlinear editing software) become *sensing* devices through which our vision of the world around us can be transformed. Landscape architect Anne Spirn suggests that looking through the lens of a camera and capturing photographs not only senses the world but also allows us to *make sense* of it: "the practice of photography has long been a way of thinking and a method of discovery."[36] And just as these instruments allow us to see the world anew, they also allow for communication across linguistic, disciplinary, and cultural boundaries. In the twenty-first century, cinematic vision has become so transnational and normalized across cultural boundaries that it constitutes a de facto Esperanto of visual language, a common language through which disparate groups can comfortably communicate with one another. While highly specialized languages such as regression models, digital platforms of architecture representation, and textual exegesis tend to obscure understanding by the layperson, film and video have the particular capacity of allowing participation for those blessed with the "symmetry of ignorance,"[37] that is, all of us.

Filmic sensing has its intellectual origins in two spheres. It stems from work pursued under the auspices of visual and sensory anthropology and ethnographic film, where it is used to provide embodied and sensory information in ethnographic contexts. It also stems from the artistic and creative work produced under the rubric of essay filmmaking. In this sense, it implicates its author in a self-reflexive fashion, combining fiction and nonfiction in pursuit of truths that would have remained otherwise undisclosed. And, importantly, it explicitly engages the aesthetic realm, considering the formal, visual, and artistic elements that contribute toward these truths, effectively represented and communicated to different audiences.

For example, artist Neil Goldberg approaches his video art in precisely this way. One of his projects, titled *Surfacing* (2011), shows dozens of clips of individuals emerging from a New York City subway stop, stepping up into the brightly lit, midday bustle of a street corner (see figure 3.15). The camera acts as an extension of the human eye, framing and focusing the gaze onto microscopic facial expressions that might otherwise go unnoticed: anticipation, anxiety, exhaustion, resignation. And its database-like organization provides a rigor to this study of human reaction: each clip is precisely edited to capture an identical moment of emergence, so that we can note differences from one commuter to the next. This way, a larger picture emerges that would have otherwise remained opaque, capturing a moment of human universality in the shared act of locating oneself in the world, a split second of vulnerability before the commuter orients herself in the city. More than just a representational medium, filmic sensing becomes an observational and analytical tool for engaging with, probing, and denaturalizing the everyday life of the urban.

Urban Humanities: An Emergent Field

Urban humanities employ the aforementioned three creative practices of scholarship—thick mapping, spatial ethnography, filmic sensing—to study, understand, and transform the urban. They do so with particular attention toward the future and spatial justice. We will discuss each in more detail later in the book and illustrate them through a series of case study projects that use these practices to explore, compare, contrast, and propose interventions for settings of everyday life in Los Angeles, Mexico City, Tokyo, Shanghai, and beyond. These case studies (Projects A–H) are called out in the colored sections between chapters, which provide some visual and textual representation of the larger project, and a handful have been explicated at more length by their respective creators and authors in a series of "interludes" also located in between the primary chapters of the book.

The three practices of scholarship of urban humanities come from a fusion of established disciplines that, in our view, points to an emergent hybrid field for the study of the urban. This field blends a humanist understanding of the spaces and cultures of everyday life, as depicted in text, film, art, or spatial ethnography, with the projective and transformative interventions of urban planning and design. Like any field, urban humanities have an intellectual lineage. In chapter 2, we explore this lineage and the various scholarly influences and precedents that gave rise to urban humanities. These are partially derived from critical transnational urban theorists, but are also indebted to other writers, scholars, and artists who work within an urban humanist frame. In chapter 3, we explore the three practices in depth and touch upon a handful of other practices, which remain in experimental "beta testing." Chapter 4 brings the future to bear on all that we do, considering the implications of our reclaiming of the speculative, the projective, and the future within the context of academic and urban practice. Lastly, the penultimate chapter prior to the volume's conclusion dives deeper into the question of spatial justice, particularly as it informs our scholarly, pedagogical, and research practices within the contemporary university. In between chapters, we insert interludes—urban humanist projects undertaken by faculty, students and alumni of the program, or community-based collaborators at some cities of our intellectual investigations. These are paired with shorter descriptions of student projects, all indicated by the bright color assigned to each of the four cities (Mexico City: yellow; Tokyo and Fukushima: pink; Shanghai: red; and Los Angeles: blue). Both projects and interludes are included to help demonstrate or clarify our arguments.

Interlude 1:

Mexico City

Peatoniños:
Liberating the Streets
for Kids and for Play

Brenda Vértiz

with proofreading by Miguel Ángel Morales

Laboratorio para la Ciudad

1.3 Street closed to traffic for Peatoniños event, Mexico City, 2016. Photo credit: Laboratorio para la Ciudad

Mexico City is home to more than two million children that represent 26.7 percent of its total population. But despite their numbers, children remain a political minority due to their perceived limited capacity to influence their environment. Urban policies have been unsuccessful in considering children's needs and perspectives and have not integrated them in the urban planning process. Children, then, must adapt to existing urban conditions, whether or not they are appropriate. Mexico City's highly car-oriented urban form is a major challenge for children, as it negatively impacts their mobility and physical safety and also contributes to their exclusion from open spaces and streets, ultimately isolating them indoors.

Access to high-quality public and play spaces is one of the greatest challenges faced by children in Mexico City. Children living in marginalized areas are the most affected by the lack of open and outdoor spaces where they can rest, walk, or play—activities that are fundamental for their physical, emotional, and cognitive development. Thus, (re)claiming and (re)creating urban environments, for and with children, has become a central issue in urban development. The city's recently enacted Constitution includes "the right to the city" as a main precept. This is the right of all Mexico City residents, including children, to change the city as they change themselves; it is the right to imagine and create the city they live in.

The Peatoniños project focuses on the children's right to their city. The project was created and is led by the Laboratorio para la Ciudad (Lab for the City), which is Mexico City's creative and experimental office directly reporting to the mayor. *Peatoniños* is a wordplay in Spanish that means "child pedestrians" or "children that walk." The project is part of the Lab's Pedestrian and Playful city strategies initiative, whose objective is to understand how alternative, nonmotorized modes of travel and play can reconfigure urban imaginaries and encourage citizens to take an active role in the city-making process. Using "Liberating the streets for children and play" as its motto, the Peatoniños project consists of planning, designing, implementing, and evaluating streets that can accommodate play, in areas of the city with high levels of marginalization, large numbers of children, and few open play spaces (figure 1.3).

Peatoniños is a response to the general lack and uneven distribution of playful spaces in Mexico City. It seeks to expand and make more accessible play and playful spaces in the city through the use of existing streets. Peatoniños aims to produce physical manifestations of alternative street use, demonstrating the city's social fabric and community interactions beyond the spatial paradigm of the car-oriented model. The three guiding principles of Peatoniños are: 1) a community-centered design approach, 2) a spatial and urban analysis of street spaces and their adjacent neighborhoods, and 3) a pedagogical approach that promotes a child's right to the city, right to play, and knowledge of issues regarding road safety. The aim is to liberate and reappropriate the city streets through play, especially in neighborhoods where public space is scarce.

Instead of focusing on developing over-planned interventions, detached from already existing local practices and resources available on the streets, Peatoniños follows a process in which every street for play—its tools, activities, and methodologies used before, during, and after the intervention—is understood as a design iteration. The entire process of this project from start to finish emphasizes the social capacity of design. The purpose is to create an index of institutional and local knowledge, resources, and relationships that, ultimately, would help develop networks to scale up and sustain the implementation of the project, but also criteria by which one can assess the quality of each playstreet design.

Eight streets for play have been implemented throughout the city so far, through a variety of collaborations. The first collaboration, in March 2016, was with urban humanities students from UCLA and involved closing down a street in Mexico City's Doctores neighborhood and temporarily converting it into playspace for children. From this small experiment, Peatoniños has evolved into a project that is becoming an ongoing public program. Together with the local government of the Iztapalapa borough—where more than five hundred thousand children live—the merging of top-down and bottom-up approaches addressing the lack and uneven distribution of open play spaces for children is starting to happen. Collaboration with the local government in this area is helping to create a tool to measure the impact of Peatoniños playstreets and identify how play and playfulness influence public narratives and public policy. Furthermore, Peatoniños seeks to cooperate with civic programs that promote community participation in public decision-making (figure 1.4). Peatoniños is now focusing its efforts not only on closing streets and converting them into temporary playspaces, but also on forming a collective vision of how adults and children can shape the city in tangible ways. In its next stage, it also plans to create a new typology of permanent streets designed by and for the children.

1.4 Painting a zebra crossing and leaving a mark in the Obrera neighborhood of Mexico City. Photo credit: Laboratorio para la Ciudad

Figure 1.5 helps to visualize and communicate the overall spirit of the project, which is about considering children (Peatoniños) as active agents and city heroes with the capacity to join forces with "Peatonito"—a *luchador* (fighter) who defends the rights of pedestrians in Mexico City and changes the communities they live in (figure 1.6).

1.5 Luchador with children wearing masks and acting as city heroes in the Doctores neighborhood. Photo credit: Laboratorio para la Ciudad

1.6 Children wearing a luchador mask, in the Buenos Aires neighborhood of Mexico City. Photo credit: Laboratorio para la Ciudad

2
The Lineages of Urban Humanities

If we wish to understand diversity as constitutive of contested global processes we are required to pay attention to the criss-crossing, messy pathways through which ideas circulate, connecting cities in ways that can neither be ignored nor reduced to one-way traffic. The process of arriving at this idea conceptually and confronting the anxieties of dealing with the unpredictability of actual research requires building shared agendas and collaborative work practices among scholars at multiple locations.[1]

Understanding the urban and its diversity—how people imagine, interact, shape, and are shaped in different ways by the settings of their everyday lives—requires a nuanced look at cities, one that is not constrained by disciplinary silos or national borders. Such a lens reveals cities to be dynamic, fluid entities, partly defined by their own unique history, heritage, culture, and material and environmental conditions. But cities are also influenced in important ways by the ever-changing physical and virtual world outside their spatial boundaries, and the flows of people and ideas that transcend their borders.

To acquire such a complex perspective, the field of urban humanities relies on and is indebted to a number of intellectual influences and a loose association of ideas that have dominated in the last decades the intellectual discourse in critical urban studies as well as in the humanities and architecture. We consider these as the lineages of urban humanities, an intellectual heritage that comes from different disciplines and includes: architecture and material spaces; the spatial, cultural, and global "turns" in urban studies and the humanities; discourses around transnational urbanism, postcolonialism, and borderlands; investigations into the "micro-urban" landscapes of everyday life; and projects grounded in social and spatial justice and the right to the city.

Delirious Influence: Architecture and the City

Architecture, which itself straddles the humanities and the sciences, has always been concerned with the city, where buildings aggregate into socio-political, ecological artifacts.[2] Recent decades witnessed heightened attention to the urban as form, environment, and theory. Starting in the 1960s, a group of European architects, influenced by the writings of Jacques Derrida, advocated the deconstruction of the totality and universality of the Modern Movement in architecture, which sought to standardize diverse human needs, cultures, and settings, but also had the effect of homogenizing them. Against this, these architects began to consider the reading of the city as a text with many interpretations. Among them, Aldo Rossi in his highly influential book *The Architecture of the City* (first published in Italian in 1966) reemphasized the importance of the public realm and argued that the significance of place does not lie in its form or even its function, but rather in the human memories associated with it.[3]

On this side of the Atlantic, another particularly influential book was a series of documents and essays that came out of an architecture studio course taught at the Yale School of Architecture in 1968 by Robert Venturi, Denise Scott Brown, and

Steven Izenour. Published as *Learning from Las Vegas*,[4] the book stands out for two reasons that have been foundational for urban humanities: first, it documented not only a research method but also a teaching practice that was unusual for its time, using travel research, mapping, documentation through new media, and new combinatory forms of urban analysis; and second, it turned our attention away from the rarefied world of "academic architecture," then most often fixated on the products of high modernism, toward the ugly, mundane, and everyday forms of "low architecture" as reflected in the fluorescent signage and vast parking lots of Las Vegas.[5] This turn from great monuments to the everyday, material environment was also exemplified in contemporaneous studies of Los Angeles, such as those undertaken by architectural critic Reyner Banham.[6]

In the late 1970s, the New Urbanism movement also rejected modernism, and what were considered its dehumanizing characteristics, in favor of historical, nostalgic form, replacing the rhetoric of mechanized speed with that of walkability and livability. Andrés Duany and Elizabeth Plater-Zyberk's Seaside in the 1980s and Robert A. M. Stern's Celebration in the 1990s epitomize New Urbanist neo-traditional practices, which have, however, garnered critique for their social, ethnic, and economic hegemony. A series of other urbanisms followed in architecture and urban design, including infrastructural urbanism, everyday urbanism, ecological urbanism, and landscape urbanism. Each, to at least some degree, is an acknowledgement that architecture's larger context— the urban—demands that the discipline incorporate conditions emanating beyond its borders.

Arguably, the most influential contemporary architect writing about the city, and whose ideas have driven much of what we consider architectural urbanism and the city as a cultural object, has been Rem Koolhaas, who initially set up his firm Office for Metropolitan Architecture (OMA) in 1975 (along with Elia Zenghelis, Madelon Vriesendorp, and Zoe Zenghelis), as a discursive platform to visually analyze and unpack contemporary urbanism. His landmark book *Delirious New York* provided a "delirious" methodology of cross-wiring numerous historical snippets, elements of the built environment, and analysis of New York City to produce a theoretical manifesto of the contemporary city—one that we have used in urban humanities, despite coming to strikingly different conclusions regarding the agency and aims of individual people who live in and create urban space.[7] Koolhaas has also used a medium and practice of urban humanities, a form of filmic sensing, in an interactive documentary—*Lagos Wide and Close* (released in 2004)—that explores and details urbanity and informality, order and disorder in Lagos, Nigeria.

Strangely, however, only a handful of architecture's explicit turns toward the urban have been direct engagements with planning; and architecture has yet to explicitly engage with interpretive practices from the humanities (and vice versa). While professionally codified, the ways architects are educated tend to be remarkably circumscribed by the discipline and its methods. Even Vitruvius, some two thousand years ago, had the insight to incorporate the humanities into architectural education: "Let him be educated, skilful [*sic*] with the pencil, instructed in geometry, know much history, have followed the philosophers with attention, understand music, have some knowledge of medicine, know the opinions of the jurists, and be acquainted with astronomy and the theory of the heavens."[8] Not unlike Vitruvius, urban humanities emphasize the importance of history, the human sensorium (visual and auditory experiences), the centrality of the body, multidisciplinary perspectives on the world, speculative thought (philosophy and literature), and, finally, juridical knowledge that informs our orientation toward spatial justice and the right to the city. And to this list of useful knowledge we might add literature, film, planning, and cultural studies, as well as a set of new tools and new modes of working that depend upon collaborations among architects, urbanists, and humanists.

Urban Studies' Various Turns

A turn is a change in the road, an overhaul or a shift in a traveled and well-known intellectual route or disciplinary tradition. Starting from the 1970s, urban studies, the social sciences, and the humanities at large witnessed a number of such "turns" that have influenced profoundly the way we study and understand cities. The section that follows offers an overview of the spatial, cultural, and global turns and their protagonists.

The Spatial Turn: Reasserting the Importance of Space

Triggered by the work of French theorists Michel Foucault, Henri Lefebvre, and Michel de Certeau, a *spatial turn* emerged that emphasized the significance of space as at least an equally important factor as time in the understanding of the urban. Further articulations by Marxist and postmodern geographers in the 1980s and 1990s, such as David Harvey,[9] Doreen Massey,[10] and Edward Soja,[11] among others, were also critical of historicism and its suppression of the importance of space by the modern social sciences. That architecture did not undergo a spatial "turn" is due to its intrinsic spatiality. But the spatial turn of other disciplines brought heightened awareness to architecture that its practices were central to discussions of power, ideology, and cultural semantics.

The spatial turn considers space not as an "empty dimension"[12] but rather as the all-important foundation of social relations and the terrain for the manifestation of power relations. As such, according to Lefebvre, the production of space "should never be dissociated from an analysis of the production of time."[13] This intimate interrelationship between space and time was clearly expressed by Lefebvre:

> Space is nothing but the inscription of time in the world, spaces are the realizations, inscriptions in the simultaneity of the external world of a series of times, the rhythms of the city, the rhythms of the urban population, and in my opinion, as a sociologist, I suggest to you the idea that the city will only be rethought and reconstructed on its current ruins, when we have properly understood that the city is the deployment of time.[14]

The humanities became equally invested in the "spatial turn," and it was Mikhail Bakhtin, with his influential reflection on the "chronotope," who even before Lefebvre had suggested a very similar definition of space as a category inextricably intertwined with time. According to the Russian literary critic, and as described in his influential essay, "Forms of Time and of the Chronotope in the Novel. Notes toward a Historical Poetics," the novel (and literature in general) registers a number of elements or "spatial metaphors" where time and space come together.[15] Bakhtin calls these metaphors or spatial leitmotifs "chronotopoi" and defines them as the materialization of time in space. Here is the more detailed definition Bakhtin offers in his essay:

> We will give the name chronotope (literally, "time space") to the intrinsic connectedness of temporal and spatial relationships that are artistically expressed in literature. This term [space-time] is employed in mathematics, and was introduced as part of Einstein's Theory of Relativity. The special meaning it has in relativity theory is not important for our purposes; we are borrowing it for literary criticism almost (but not entirely) as a metaphor. What counts for us is the fact that it expresses the inseparability of space and time (time as the fourth dimension of space). We understand the chronotope as a formally constitutive category of literature; we will not deal with the chronotope in other areas of culture. In the literary artistic chronotope, spatial and temporal indicators are fused into one carefully thought-out, concrete whole. Time, as it were, thickens, takes on flesh, becomes artistically visible; likewise, space becomes charged and responsive to the movements of time, plot and history. This intersection of axes and fusion of indicators characterizes the artistic chronotope.[16]

A paradigmatic and semantically dense chronotope in late nineteenth-century European fiction is the train station for example, but there are other salient chronotopoi across literature according to Bakhtin, such as the road, the agora or public square or plaza, and even the Gothic castle.[17]

However, the spatial turn in the humanities and its essential contributions to urban theory and the study of the city as inhabited space go back to the mid-nineteenth century, with the industrialization of the modern metropolis and the development of new poetic and media strategies to represent its cultural, social, and urban forms. We find its true and most influential origin in French poet Charles Baudelaire's reflections on ephemerality and urban life in *Les Fleurs du mal* and the flâneur in *The Painter of*

Modern Life; in German philosopher-sociologist Georg Simmel's 1903 "The Metropolis and Mental Life," a paradigmatic analysis of the urban masses and the spiritual crisis of the city dweller; and, even more important, in Walter Benjamin's *Arcades Project* (1926–1940), an experimental study of the social and material history of nineteenth-century Paris that focused on everyday life and the built environment.

Baudelaire, Simmel, and Benjamin have arguably influenced humanistic inquiry as much as they have informed urban planning and architecture. The same goes for the main players of spatial turn-inflected postmodern thought, such as Jean Baudrillard, Jean-François Lyotard, and Fredric Jameson. It is fair to say that postmodern theory, postcolonial theory, and cultural studies are to a great extent responsible for the spatial turn, and that all these movements and theories have had a similar impact on the theory (and practice) of architecture, urban studies, the social sciences, and the humanities.

It is equally fair to say that prior to the spatial turn, the importance of place and spatiality was largely ignored and undertheorized in the humanities and social sciences. Doreen Massey attributes this to Heidegger's conceptualization of space/place as "being," and time as "becoming."[18] She finds this strictly dichotomous notion of time and space by Heidegger problematic because it fails to see their interrelationship; it also assumes that a place has singular essential identities that are constructed out of "an introverted, inward-looking history based on delving into the past for internalized origins," and seems to require the establishment of boundaries to define it.[19] In contrast, Massey argues, spaces and places are dynamic and ever transforming by the actions of their inhabitants, may acquire multiple identities and meanings for different users, and cannot often be defined by boundaries. In that sense, we can also argue that space/place is also "becoming," characterized by a myriad of overlapping, conflicting, or complementary parts and features, the presence of which entails the potential of transformation into different future spaces.[20] As we will discuss more extensively in later chapters, the urban humanities field is deeply invested in futurity by dint of its responsibility to help create just and inclusive places in cities, what Massey calls "a progressive concept of place."[21]

The dynamism and fluidity of space and its potential to transform are clearly underlined in Lefebvre's writings. He views cities as "oeuvres" or works in progress, and urban settings as "places of the possible."[22] Architectural historians, most notably Spiro Kostof, have likewise described the city as a process. Unlike buildings whose histories can be temporally located, the city is dynamic, ever-changing, and fluid.[23] And while Lefebvre (and Bakhtin) perceive spaces as "the inscription of time," and are certainly conditioned by their histories, Lefebvre also views them as common urban spaces "conditioned by anticipations of alternative futures."[24] In other words, while history and culture may influence the present socio-economic, physical, and political dynamics of cities, they do not completely dictate their future.

This simultaneous forward and backward examination of cities is a characteristic of the urban humanities project. For example, what are the different layers of history situated behind a busy intersection at Shanghai's famed former French Concession district, and how have these layers continued to shape its socio-spatial setting? Project A, which follows this chapter, details an urban humanities project that explores how the past meets the present at an intersection of Avenue Joffre in Shanghai.

Foucault's interest in space is in its relation to power, in the ways that it perpetuates or enhances power relations. According to him: "Space is fundamental in any form of communal life; space is fundamental in any exercise of power."[25] Foucault views the urban and its institutions (the prison, the university, the hospital, the factory) as the locus of power relations and oppressions. Thus, the "Panopticon," Jeremy Bentham's well-known nineteenth-century design for prisons, becomes the spatial metaphor for social control and surveillance, exercised in modern society by governments on their subjects. In contrast, Foucault's "heterotopia" (*hétéro-topie*) is a space layered with multiple meanings and sometimes hidden relationships that allows the presence of otherness and nonhegemonic conditions. In fact, Foucault's space becomes real because of the relations it produces and hosts,[26] or in his own words: "We do not live in a kind of void, inside of which we could place individuals and things. . . . We live inside a set of relations that delineates sites, which are irreducible to one another, and absolutely not superimposable on one another."[27]

Drawing on Foucault, the urban humanities project understands space not as a neutral container but rather as a political foundation of social relations in the city, one that can be bestowed with multiple, often complex and even contradictory meanings. How do we understand an urban setting such as the one of Shanghai's 1933 Slaughterhouse? Project D: 1933 presents the ways in which urban humanities students sought to make sense of a building that was a slaughterhouse for cattle in pre-communist Shanghai, a medicine factory during the city's communist era, a part of a creative cluster in postcommunist Shanghai, and a setting that served as the backdrop for the sale of Kobe Bryant shoes during the students' visit to the city. Not fortuitously, the building resembles a panopticon and has a long history of spatial control, but what can its diverse and multilayered history tell us about the city and the neighborhood that surround it?

If for Foucault the panopticon is the spatial metaphor for surveillance and control, exercised by society's powerful and reflected in the deterministic urban form of the modern city, Michel de Certeau, in contrast, is interested in everyday practices of engagement in the city. He considers how rigidity and oppressiveness may be confronted through "bricolage"—the tactic of common citizens making do, adapting, negotiating, and ultimately transforming the spaces of their everyday lives.[28] Like his fellow Situationists, de Certeau considers how a quotidian act as simple as walking in the city becomes empowering: we can choose our own "walking rhetoric"—cross, zig-zag, turn, slow down, or deviate from the city's orthogonal grid. In de Certeau's words:

> It is true that a spatial order organizes an ensemble of possibilities (e.g. be a place in which one can move) and interdictions (e.g. by a wall that prevents one from going further), then the walker actualizes these possibilities. In that way, he makes them exist as well as emerge. But he also moves them about and invents others, since the crossing, drifting away, or improvisation of walking privilege, transform or abandon spatial elements.[29]

For urban humanists, the urban is a juxtaposition of the formal and the bricolage, and following de Certeau, we are interested in accommodating alternative, informal, even counterintuitive uses of city space. How can a busy intersection in Mexico City that has been designed for drivers and their cars be reclaimed, reconceived, and repurposed to host children's play? Following what Nicholas Blomley refers to as "the traffic logic," cities have long privileged the automobile at the expense of pedestrians in the streets and sidewalks of most modernist cities.[30] Children's play has been largely banished from such streets and sidewalks, confined to specific, often sterile playgrounds and parks. But what if kids can reoccupy, even temporarily, a busy intersection for play? The interlude *Peatoniños: Liberating the Streets for Kids and for Play*, presented at the end of chapter 1, details how an urban humanities project worked toward this end.

While humanists like Foucault, de Certeau, and Benjamin were making space a central construct in their critical scholarship, architecture in the late 1970s and early 1980s was rethinking its relationship to history, or to time in the space-time dialectic. Space dominated architectural discourse, having been the central concept of modernism and the unquestioned essential element of modern architecture. Questioning the preeminence of space rekindled a neo-historical, that is temporal, fixation under the guise of postmodernism. Postmodernism's attraction began with Charles Jencks's 1977 book *The Language of Postmodernism*,[31] Charles Moore's building of Piazza d'Italia in New Orleans in 1978, and Michael Graves's Portland Building in 1982, which unleashed architecture's multidecade creative effort to reconnect to history. Citing modernism's failures, architects and architectural scholars sought temporal continuity for their discipline and historical grounding for their buildings just as other disciplines were exploring space. Loosely tied to postmodern theorists like Lyotard, Deleuze, and Derrida, architecture's postmodernity brought irony, humor, playfulness, and pastiche (among other things) into the built environment to replace modernism's ideological solemnity and moralizing social dimension. In some ways, this reciprocal turn toward time (without abandoning space) reinscribed history and theory into architecture. The persistence and hegemony of this dominant intellectual agenda pushed architecture further inward, creating both a powerful discourse of autonomy and destabilizing queries into the discipline's social relevance.

The Cultural Turn: Considering the Nuances of Culture

The first wave of theorists of the spatial turn, particularly those coming from geography, planning, and the humanities, never abandoned social relevance, but they examined the urban in terms of advanced capitalism, focusing on space, power, and control as exercised by the state and its institutions. Building on this work, a second wave of theorists focused on the intersections among gender, race, identity, and class and how they profoundly affect spatial and social relationships. It was impossible to ignore a growing body of work among cultural theorists, the most foundational of whom may have been Edward Said, who argued that "Western" scholarship about "The East"—Asia, North Africa, and the Middle East—subjugated and exoticized peoples and places through uneven relations of power and representational practices.[32] In response to this critique, a *cultural turn* emerged in the late 1980s and early 1990s, embedded in the wider debates around postmodernism and postcolonialism, that added the nuances of culture to the political and economic concerns that dominated urban theory in the 1970s and early 1980s.[33] Indeed, by the 1980s, the presence of the "other"—a heterogeneous mixture of social groups and cultures—had become impossible to ignore, "whiten," or metamorphose.[34] This was most clearly seen in cities and their urban settings, "where a multitude of other work cultures, cultural environments, and culturally inscribed bodies increasingly inhabit a built terrain that has its origins visibly in another culture; the culture lying behind the grid."[35]

Before the emergence of the cultural turn, the local was traditionally associated in the sociological tradition with the notion of a specific bounded space with shared social norms based on homogeneous cultural or ethnic identities.[36] But cultural theorists warned that such a view of contemporary urban landscapes is parochial, deceiving, and downright wrong. Homi Bhabha eloquently argued that culture has many locations, disabusing us of the presumption of singular or homogenous cultural spaces.[37] As Gupta and Ferguson further argued: "'Cultures' must be seen as less unitary and more fragmented, their boundaries more of a literary fiction."[38] And Rosaldo emphasized that the view of "an authentic culture as an autonomous, internally coherent universe no longer seems tenable, as the world is marked by borrowing and lending across porous cultural boundaries."[39] Architecture worked in two ways: following Rosaldo's observation, transnational sites of commerce were branded by homogeneous identities (think Starbucks or 7–Eleven convenience stores), while cities acquired unique landmarks by internationally recognized "starchitects" (with Gehry's Guggenheim Museum Bilbao being the most famous case). Perhaps both tendencies are part of an urban cultural turn.

In twenty-first-century cities, urban space is being transformed along the multidimensional axes of ethnicity, immigrant status, nationality, gender/sexuality, race, and other identities.[40] This affects the construction and representation of the urban, as a multiplicity of new cultures is producing a "fluid process of forming, expressing, and enforcing identities" on space.[41] These spatial effects of culture—widely construed—and variations in the patterns of use and appropriation of space are very much a focus of the urban humanities project as it tries to uncover, understand, and read the signs of local cultural specificity as they are contested, rehabilitated, and reaffirmed in fragmented urban spaces.[42]

The Global Turn: Studying Cities as Networks
Starting in the 1970s, a number of scholars began touting the need for comparative urban research that opens the eyes to broader urban phenomena that can be compared across municipal boundaries and national borders.[43] Underlying comparative approaches is the notion that urban imaginaries—namely, cities as they are imagined, contemplated, and written about—are "sites of encounters with other cities mediated through travel, migration and the circulation of images, goods, and ideas."[44] The reciprocal dialogue among cities is pervasive, and ranges from a neighborhood known as "Little Tokyo" in Los Angeles, to the

former French Concession in Shanghai, to New York's Solomon R. Guggenheim Museum expanding in Spain and Abu Dhabi.

Comparative studies require identification of similarities and differences of at least two entities and use the city or the nation-state as their unit of analysis. But they are also criticized as overly constrained by fixed entities and arbitrary divisions such as municipal or national boundaries. In reality, urban networks and influences are dynamic, diverse, and transcend such boundaries.[45] The emphasis on comparison may also bring along the danger of homogenizing differences and disregarding local particularities in favor of extracting universal lessons on urban issues and problems.[46]

At roughly the same time that cultural theorists were prompting us to confront the nuances of culture and the influences of a diversity of identities and bodies that constitute the urban, other urban theorists took interest in the ways global processes were shaping local outcomes.[47] In his seminal "World City Hypothesis," John Friedmann noted the interrelationships between urbanization processes and global economic forces, pointing to a hierarchical network of cities around the globe, spearheaded by a few "primary world cities" that constitute the "basing points of global capital."[48] While located in different geographic regions, these world cities[49] share some common spatial and economic characteristics and processes, as they constitute the "command and control" posts of the global economy.

In the decades that followed, the spatial dispersal of economic activities, an increasing international division of labor, the proliferation of agglomeration economies, and transnational corporations brought the era of globalization. In cities, socio-economic and political processes have brought the local much closer to the global and have increased and intensified the interactions and influences among different groups, between urban territories, and even within the same locale. As socio-spatial units distinct from nation-states, cities, according to sociologist Saskia Sassen, are intrinsically embedded in globalization processes, but are also being continuously transformed by these processes.[50]

An ensuing vast literature on globalization opened the door for multiple systematic comparative accounts and reflections of urban experiences across the globe. The most contemporary version of the global cities frame is the notion of planetary urbanization, popularized by Neil Brenner, which emphasizes a Lefebvrean attention to the *process* of urbanization as played out across disparate environments, which may be more or less "city-like."[51] This emphasis has allowed for both the nuanced analysis of global structural processes and the problematic omission of people at their most human scale. The overall contributions of this "global turn" in urban studies is the realization that urbanization processes should be largely examined within a wider and systemic context. As Jennifer Robinson remarked: "this has generated a new mode of comparative analysis, one which works with the connections amongst cities, the globalized conditions of production of the urban."[52]

Following this lineage, the urban humanities project analyzes cities less by their "similarities" or "differences" and more by seeking to emphasize their interconnections in discrete and important ways. Some of the cities that have been at the forefront of our academic inquiries—Los Angeles, Mexico City, Shanghai, and Tokyo—are indeed world cities at the forefront of the global world economy, but the connections are much deeper. These cities have affinities and interconnections with one another that include historical, cultural, social, and economic relationships, perhaps nowhere more visible than on the bodies that have and continue to migrate between the cities. To understand Los Angeles, you need to understand Mexico City, Shanghai, and Tokyo, among other cities. Historically and in the present, goods, ideas, architectures, as well as people circulate among these megacities.

These affinities are productively construed as intimacies, as American studies scholar Lisa Lowe writes in her groundbreaking text *The Intimacies of Four Continents*. Through this notion of political, historical, and geographic "intimacy," she argues for the "close connection in relation to a global geography that one more often conceives in terms of vast spatial distances."[53] Her examination of historical trade around slavery, colonialism, and labor interprets intimacy in a multivalent manner to critically reread conventional understandings of geographies, methods, and disciplines. Lowe opens new understandings by locating the formations of laboring peoples through their repressed spatial, historical, and political interconnections. According to her: "To write about the intimacies of four continents is thus intended to open an investigation, and to contribute a manner of reading and interpretation, and not to identify an empirical foundation or establish a new historical object."[54] Such a reimagining of transnational studies inspires the urban humanist's focus on cities on the Pacific Rim, not as independent objects but as deeply interwoven in terms of conflicts, collectivities, and engagements among different people and their socio-spatial-historical contexts.

Transnational Urbanism

Indeed, in more recent years, a transnational perspective has gained favor in urban studies. This arose in response to criticism that comparative urbanism suffers from a static perception of the urban.[55] In contrast, transnational approaches focus on interdependencies, movements, and flows across borders in regions and subregions.[56]

In the late 1980s, Manuel Castells was the first to conceptualize the urban not only as the "space of places"—material three-dimensional territories—but also as the "space of flows"—virtual relationships and linkages carried through the electronic circuits of a networked globe.[57] In the "Information Age," Castells argued that such flows enable dynamic interactions, social practices, shared actions, and meanings between distant locales.[58] Over the last two decades, the rapid advancement of new digital technologies, platforms, and applications and the proliferation of social media have strengthened even more the earlier observations of Castells, making the intimacies and interdependencies between distant places more potent.

The goal, then, of transnational approaches is to understand urban settings and experiences, not in isolation, but interactively, as they are composed by multiple regional, ethnic, or institutional identities and forces.[59] In other words, transnational urban studies wish to take down arbitrary divisions between entities so that both their interconnections as well as collisions become more apparent. Here is how Nicholas Kenny and Rebecca Madgin explain the need for a comparative/transnational perspective:

> To understand what makes the city, then, involves not just accounting for its various manifestations, but more probingly, requires us to think of cities as plural, in relation to one another, both comparatively and transnationally. . . . We cannot consider the story of one city without comparing it, even implicitly, to other cities, either within or outside the same national boundaries. Nor can we hope to know what cities are more generally unless we account for the exchange of information and ideas among them, and ground our understanding of processes and practices from within and across other urban centres.[60]

For transnational studies to build on the work of prior generations of scholars, previously collected urban data and ethnographic evidence that was limited by administrative borders must be reexamined in ways that reveal transnational forms and processes.[61] This requires employing multiple methodological lenses and traditional and nontraditional units of analysis to study the metropolis that may derive from different disciplinary fields. This is where the urban humanities project enters, with its blended trajectories and influences from urban studies, architecture, the social sciences, and the humanities.

If theories of globalization rest on constructs of the state, networks, economic flows, and data, transnationalism emphasizes human connections and their socio-spatial impacts, including migration, immigration, border crossings, political refugees, practices of economic exchange, as well as multicultural artistic influences and hybrid urban landscapes. Comparative urban studies lead, in the simplest sense, to ideas of same and different, while transnational urban humanities help to better understand past and presently linked practices between urban settings and culture. Take Los Angeles and Mexico City, for example. The United States and Mexico share borders, histories, migrations, economies, architectures, and cultures. Understanding the urban in Southern California, once part of Mexico and still quite Mexican, or in Tijuana, Mexican but also in many ways Americanized, requires a simultaneous transnational exploration of the past, present, and possible future of the two regions.

The Postcolonialist Critique

These different "turns" brought to the forefront issues of power and control as reflected in space, the interactions among cities, and influences of wider global processes and networks in shaping urban outcomes. But they also achieved this by privileging the study of certain cities and their histories and perspectives over others. With few exceptions, the body of work that developed in the late 1970s and 1980s had largely a core-periphery outlook, focusing primarily on core countries of the Global North and on studies of Western European and North American urbanism with little consideration of the remaining world.[62] A small number of world cities—in particular New York, Chicago, Los Angeles, London, and Paris—attracted the overwhelming attention of urban theorists, leading others to talk about the "metrocentricity" of urban studies—which casts light only on cities that represent the command and control posts of the global economy, while leaving completely in the dark "ordinary," "secondary," or "peripheral" cities, which are only examined insofar as they relate to the first category of cities.[63]

In the first decades of the twenty-first century, postcolonial theorists criticized this homogenous, static, and largely west-centric view of urban studies and the dominance of certain world cities in the prominent urban imaginary. They also argued that studies of non-western cities and their residents by western scholars lead to culturally inaccurate, and even exoticized, representations and understandings of those regions.[64] They criticized a patronizing view, for example, that may see Shanghai as the image of Los Angeles's future, which in turn points the way for the even more "undeveloped" Mexico City.[65]

Geographer Jennifer Robinson and urban planner Ananya Roy, in particular, have provided sharp critiques against the predominant narratives privileging global/world cities. Robinson accused such narratives of suffering from "asymmetrical ignorance" in their division of "First World" cities—generally viewed as paradigmatic examples of "cityness"—and "Third World" cities—widely perceived as failing.[66] She criticized the global/world cities narrative, which overconcentrates on centers and circuits of financial capital, and drops all other cities from consideration, and argued that urban models of both difference and similarity are inadequate: "The persistent incommensurability of different kinds of cities within the field of urban theory is out of step with the experiences of globalization, and the ambitions of postcolonialism suggest that simply universalizing western accounts of cities is inappropriate."[67]

Similarly, Roy has noted that such dominant theorizations of certain cities of the Global North do not take into account the long history of colonialism and imperialism that has shaped urbanization patterns of the Global South.[68] The construction of such narratives does not consider or explain other important cities of the Global South, such as Mexico City, Shanghai, Cairo, Mumbai, Rio de Janeiro, Dhaka, and Johannesburg, which also have crucial significance for the world economy. In contrast, Roy posits that "the distinctive experiences of the cities of the Global South can generate productive and provocative theoretical frameworks for all cities."[69] In terms of city form, transnational urbanization likewise reflects the *longue durée* of colonial history, where sixteenth-century Laws of the Indies, for example, came to the Americas via Spanish settlers, who themselves had borrowed from the Roman treatises of Vitruvius. In pre-Columbian Tenochtitlán, which would become Mexico City, those settlers confronted already gridded landscapes with sophisticated cosmopolitan architecture.

Thus, similar to cultural theorists, who a couple of decades ago injected the nuances of culture and intersectionality into the understanding of the urban, postcolonial theorists push back on the dominant urban studies paradigm indicating that: 1) local responses to global forces may diverge, as they are highly contingent on geographical location, local histories and cultures (including experiences with colonialism), regional frameworks, and types of governing regimes; 2) urban theory cannot rely only on insights from the Global North but should also seek to learn from the experiences of cities of the Global South; 3) contemporary urbanists cannot and should not imagine that global cities are converging to become more alike, nor exoticize their differences; and 4) cultural and political influences flow not just from colonizer to colonized, but with a recursive tension that renders all parties transformed.

Learning from the Borderlands

For us positioned in Los Angeles, fewer than 130 miles north of the Tijuana/San Diego divide, a particularly fruitful branch of transnational and postcolonial urban studies deals with the intricacies, intimacies, and conflicts of borderlands. As Gloria Anzaldúa eloquently writes:

> The U.S. Mexican border es una herida abierta where the Third World grates against the First and bleeds. And before a scab forms it hemorrhages again, the lifeblood of two worlds merging to form a third country—a border culture. Borders are set up to define the places that are safe and unsafe, to distinguish us from them. A border is a dividing line, a narrow strip along a steep edge. A borderland is a vague and undetermined place created by the emotional residue of an unnatural boundary. It is in a constant state of transition. The prohibited and forbidden are its inhabitants.[70]

Indeed, Anzaldúa demonstrated a form of urban humanities a quarter of a century before we started the urban humanities project. Her text blends poetry, fiction, and self-reflexive memoir with geography, history, and urban theory—an enlightened approach that has become a model for the humanistic urban project. The substance of her work on borderlands provides an intellectual lineage for urban humanities that is formed upon the scabs of one discipline grating against another discipline, within "the emotional residue of an unnatural boundary."[71] These contradictions operate on multiple levels: most obviously between our various academic disciplines, but also between our emotions of home and away, from Los Angeles to Mexico City and back again—and the route between the two, importantly including the U.S. Mexico border and the border cities of Tijuana and San Diego.[72]

We take from Anzaldúa's work that the "border" is not simply a linear divide that separates here from there and disconnects "us" from "them;" it is rather a wide socio-cultural and symbolic terrain that affects both its constituent parts. In fact, Anzaldúa in her conception of *mestizaje* challenges the binary thinking and "either–or" identities that have pervaded scholarly thought and geopolitics in the Global North. She then conceptualizes "borderlands" not only as the confluence of geographic territories but also as the confluence of identities, cultures, races, sexualities, and languages, and the ensuing collaborations, contradictions, and conflicts that characterize present-day urban settings.

The territories that borders delineate raise a question about the political relevance and meaning of different geographical entities, from nations to regions and cities. In Anzaldúa's writings, abstract national divides create visceral borderlands, but for sociologist Ulrich Beck, such borders are felt in the everyday life of cities. His discussions around risk and cosmopolitanism have been critical to urban humanities. Though beginning with a macro-scale, sociological look at the forces of modernity (rather than the deeply personal and intimate exploration of the borderlands as Anzaldúa undertook), Beck comes to at least one strikingly similar conclusion: given the problems we face, the national borders that divide us are hardly natural or sensible, and it is cosmopolitanism that compels us to see each other in one another—something that is necessary for our shared survival and prosperity. Beck frames this thesis as the "risk society," reasoning that our contemporary crises of global risk, spanning climate change and geopolitical instability, are precisely the phenomena that ought to drive us closer together than farther apart—and, particularly, that new forms of attention toward the future are required.[73]

More recently, architect, activist, and border scholar Teddy Cruz, who has lived and worked on both sides of the border, noted: "The border region has been one of the most productive zones for research in the last years, enabling the recoding of urban intervention by engaging the spatial, territorial, and environmental collisions across critical thresholds, whether global border zones or the local sectors of conflict generated by discriminating politics of zoning and economic development in the contemporary city."[74]

Over the last decade Cruz and Fonna Forman have initiated "The Political Equator," a comparative research project that examines radical disparities between the Global North and Global South along an imaginary line between the 28th and 33rd parallel. In multiple, thick mapping analyses, Cruz and Forman demonstrate that the existing border wall between Mexico and the United States is but one in a continuum of growing political divides between a northern geography of abundance and economic power and a southern geography of scarcity and conflict, which has an urgency that they believe is inspiring the most important thinking about urban transformation (figure 2.1).[75]

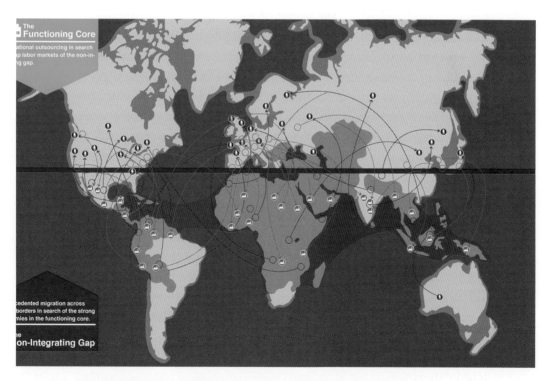

2.1 Illustration of the political equator, 2014. Credit: Estudio Teddy Cruz and Fonna Forman

Beginning in San Diego and Tijuana, the political equator is a corridor that extends around the world and includes the Strait of Gibraltar and North Africa, Israel/Palestine, India/Kashmir, and the Taiwan Strait. These geographies are among the most contested border zones in the world and bear witness to economic power, state surveillance, militarization, the politics of migration, and environmental catastrophes. Cruz and Forman bring together a wide range of stakeholders from border communities on both sides of the San Diego/Tijuana border to engage in "nomadic urban actions and dialogues" that denaturalize the political, economic, and social power of the border.[76] Through performances, design of public space improvements, and walks that traverse and unite these divided communities, the project seeks to "re-imagine citizenship beyond the nation-state" and build a common border identity around shared interests.[77]

Although the Mexico–United States border has long been a highly contested space, the violence and debate have intensified in recent years such that the border's ambiguity, porosity, and hybridity (not to mention historicity) have been overcome by a rhetoric of permanence, necessity, and radical closure, carried out by indefinite and ubiquitous policing. Many aspects of this transformation are captured in the politics of the proposed border wall's design and construction. The U.S. federal government commissioned eight "test walls" for the border in 2017 (figure 2.2). Architects partnered with contractors on these prototypes. Other architects designed critical, didactic border walls—like the Teeter Totter Wall by the studio Rael San Fratello described in chapter 3 (see figure 3.8)[78]—that seek to give embodied, human form to the distancing and abstraction of the wall itself and all that it represents. The substance of the work of Anzaldúa, Rael, and Cruz on borderlands provides a framework for urban humanities in action: contradiction, ambiguity, openness, but also knowledge exchange and speculative imaginings. The fusion of identities and collective capacities shows the way for an engaged pedagogy and scholarship.

2.2 Eight test walls on the U.S.-Mexico border commissioned by the U.S. government in 2017. Photo credit: Jonathan Banfill

Micro-urbanism and the Informal Landscapes of Everyday Life

An understanding of the urban is critically embedded in the relationships and interactions that frame our daily lives. The spatial manifestations of such interactions are a city's public spaces encompassing the sidewalks, streets, alleyways, bus stops, plazas, markets, shops, and offices—what Walter Benjamin calls "the dwelling place of the collective."[79] In his seminal *Arcades Project*, Benjamin succeeds in reconstructing "the prehistory of 19th century Paris" from scraps and fragments of the everyday world, signs, texts, and art.[80] In his urban exploits, Benjamin's flâneur views, senses, and comprehends the city by meandering through its boulevards and arcades. In the same manner, the urban humanities project privileges the "view from the street"—for example, spending one's time at Tokyo's Yoyogi Park and striking up conversations with its homeless denizens, or meandering through the narrow streets of

Tsukiji Market, talking to its fishmongers, and offering a counter-narrative to the official story about the city of Tokyo, promoted by the Tokyo 2020 Olympics (see also Project E).

In *The Practice of Everyday Life,* Michel de Certeau focuses on the anonymous city users who shape and transform the micro-spaces of their everyday lives by making "innumerable and infinitesimal transformations of and within the dominant cultural economy in order to adapt it to their own interests and their own rules."[81] They employ "tactics" to adapt, redefine, and renegotiate a city's public spaces according to their needs. Such tactics, uncoordinated and informal, are often in opposition to the formal, codified rules, ordinances, and plans that planning and municipal authorities employ to define, regulate, and brand prime city spaces.

More recently, scholars have coined the terms "everyday urbanism" and "informal urbanism" to describe the spatial settings of popular, unplanned, and spontaneous activities in cities.[82] Some of these activities are "informal" in that they take place beyond the regulations of official authorities and the state. And while informality has been primarily studied by a large body of "Third World" literature, informal activities and their spaces are abundant and relevant for cities of the Global North as well.[83] Despite this, planners, architects, and policymakers of the Global North typically have either ignored the settings of informality, or worse, have sought to shut them down. For example, urban design interventions traditionally focus on select prime spaces in the city—civic centers, corporate commercial districts, convention centers, plazas, transit hubs, and grand edifices of art and entertainment. Following neoliberal policies, many cities have employed commercialized urban design strategies to create city brands, attract the corporate world and its investments in "rejuvenated" downtowns, and bring tourists and conventioneers to prime spaces and iconic buildings.[84] Such interventions typically bypass poorer, ethnic, and generic urban areas and their myriad settings, where more ordinary activities of everyday life take place—the streets, alleys, sidewalks, bus stops, intersections, and neighborhood parks. The formal, large-scale design interventions neglect the widespread informal urbanism that occupies many domestic and public landscapes in cities of the Global North and the Global South.[85] In the last few decades, such neighborhoods have witnessed a resurgence of informality, defined as "the appropriation of public and private land for a range of purposes and activities that defy land use norms, zoning requirements, and the law."[86]

Inspired by de Certeau, the field of urban humanities finds transformative power and imaginative possibility in ordinary spaces and the informal activities that give rise to fundamental change in everyday tactics. Cognizant of the burgeoning informal urbanism that coexists, contrasts, and defies the formal cityscapes, urban humanities expand the scope and terrain of urban inquiries to encompass the ordinary and residual spaces of everyday life of a city's many neighborhoods. While everyday urbanism formulated its logic around residents to the exclusion of professional designers, the urban humanities approach, in contrast, seeks to create partnerships between the designers and the residents, to incorporate the expertise and day-to-day experiences of both.

Spatial Justice and the Right to the City

This more expansive urban inquiry of the formal and informal cityscapes of everyday life comes with an ethical aspiration that the urban humanists' scholarship contributes toward a more just city. Lefebvre has written extensively about the "right to the city," which he perceived as nothing less than a "right to urban life,"[87] and which is spatially construed:

> The right to the city is not a natural right, nor a contractual one. In the most "positive" of terms it signifies the right of citizens and city dwellers, and of groups they (on the basis of social relations) constitute, to appear on all the networks and circuits of communication, information and exchange. This depends neither upon an urbanistic ideology, nor upon an architectural intervention, but upon an essential quality or property of urban space: centrality. Here and elsewhere we assert that there is no urban reality without a centre, without a gathering together of all that can be born in space and can be produced in it, without an encounter, actual or possible, of all "objects" and "subjects."[88]

David Harvey in his *Social Justice and the City* also explored how social inequalities are expressed in space and perpetuated by locational patterns, such as, for example, the mismatch between jobs (often located in the suburbs) and affordable housing (often located in the inner city). Harvey put his faith in political processes to avert "moving towards a state of greater inequality and greater injustice."[89] Nearly thirty years later, Harvey modified his ideas about how cities would grow more just, by retrieving the construct of utopia, not as a totalizing social order, but specifically as a "dialectical utopia" in which our urban material culture can be reimagined: "And it is here that the case for a non-miraculous dialectical utopianism becomes compelling, not as a total solution but as a moment in which we gather our intellectual, critical, and imaginative powers together to give possibility a much grander press than currently exists."[90]

Following Lefebvre's and Harvey's leads, Edward Soja articulated the concept of "spatial justice," arguing that justice has a geography, and the equitable distribution and access to city resources, services, and amenities is a basic human right. In his book *Seeking Spatial Justice*, Soja encourages us to think spatially about justice.[91] He articulates the ways injustices are manifested and perpetuated spatially, noting the same "socio-spatial dialectic" first identified by Lefebvre—that society shapes space and, in turn, space shapes society. Citing Edward Said's observation that seeking spatial justice entails a "struggle over geography," Soja demonstrates that there are particular forms of injustice that are intertwined with and perpetuated by spatiality: the long history of exclusionary zoning and redlining, the lack of investment in public transportation infrastructure (in contrast, for instance, to highway systems, which tear apart neighborhoods and displace residents), the unequal distribution of healthy sustenance as demonstrated by food deserts, and the enforcement of unwanted spatial conditions such as the siting of a garbage dumpster or a prison, to name only a few examples.[92] While Soja admits that "perfectly even development, complete socio-spatial equality, pure distributional justice, as well as universal human rights are never achievable," he encourages us, nonetheless, to develop "spatial strategies" to counteract injustices and disparities in cities.[93] Susan Fainstein has also written about the "just city," laying out three criteria to ensure that the goal of spatial justice manifests in the context of the contemporary, capitalist city: diversity, democracy, and equity.[94] Her practical analysis is intended primarily for urban planners, but is situated in a longer lineage of political theory by the likes of Rawls, Nussbaum, and others, and is relevant for urban humanist pursuits that cross over the boundaries and thresholds of planning practice.

Urban humanities projects seek not only to uphold this moral imperative of spatial justice and the right to the city, but also to expand upon it. Consider two studies, one in Mexico City and the other in Los Angeles. Both cities erode notions of "here" and "there" that underlie conventional comparative urban studies, because like other polyvalent locales they comprise multiplicities on nearly every dimension of analysis. Their intimate interconnections extend through centuries, connections made literal through conquests, immigration, environmental issues, and economies, to name a few. That connective tissue sets the context for two activist studies of spatial justice in specific urban streets: the already discussed Peatoniños project in Mexico City reclaiming neighborhood streets for children's play (see Interlude 1), and in Los Angeles, the En Movimiento project heightening awareness of bike commuters of necessity, for workers whose primary means of transportation is biking (see Project B).

Looking from Los Angeles: The Los Angeles School and Beyond

We will be remiss if we do not include as a lineage of urban humanities the legacy of the Los Angeles School, which inserted Los Angeles into the lexicon of urbanism not as an oddity or aberration but as a paradigm. As mentioned earlier, urban history in the United States looked longingly across the Atlantic toward the European "motherland"—ancient Greece, Rome, and the Medieval and Renaissance cities of Europe—as the cradle of its own roots and civilization. Within the United States, New York and especially Chicago have defined our urban imaginaries; the latter provided the dominant model of the city with a singular commercial-industrial core surrounded by concentric residential rings of decreasing density and increasing socio-economic status. This model was held to be true even though the twentieth-century cities of the Southwest bore little resemblance to Chicago or other earlier gridiron economies and cultures.

Not until the mid-1980s did a group of academics from the West Coast codify a new approach. Building on the work of a number of Los Angeles-based geographers and urban historians,[95] as well as Reyner Banham's famous "four ecologies," the Los Angeles School counterposed a new polycentric suburban/exurban logic in which the hinterland organized the center, against the bull's-eye urban form forwarded by the Chicago School.[96] The Los Angeles School considered the sprawling Southern California metropolis as paradigmatic. "Los Angeles," Ed Soja used to quip, "is like a window, through which one can see processes and patterns that are likely to be experienced by other North American cities." Whether neo-Marxist or postmodern in terms of theoretical bent, the future anticipated by Los Angeles School scholars involved further racial and ethnic segregation, advancing environmental degradation, fragmented governance, and technology-driven spatial and class divides, with little hope for more optimistic urbanities. Mike Davis's opus *City of Quartz: Excavating the Future in Los Angeles* (1990) captured a bleak future (also depicted in the noir images of *Blade Runner*) that stemmed from surrounding trauma at the time, from Rodney King and the 1992 LA uprising to the Northridge Quake, to ballooning homelessness and Reaganomics.[97]

The Los Angeles School did not, however, have much input from architecture or the humanities. Over time, Los Angeles scholarship has increasingly emphasized the region's pervasive links to the Pacific Rim, along with its cultural hybridity, artistic effervescence, and openness to transgressive identities. Humanists contributed to this regional understanding, with the emergence of the digital humanities generating broad (if controversial) interest in big data and multimedia visualization for creating narratives of place and the formation of urban identities.[98] At the same time, the rise of Silicon Valley and the Bay Area's techno-youth culture (which has now aggressively expanded into Southern California and found firm ground in Venice and Playa Vista as "Silicon Beach") is shaping academic ideas about urban futures in a context of deepening inequality, gentrification, and worries about the region's drought from climate change. Drawing on the public arts, creative placemaking, design innovation, the do-it-yourself (DIY) "maker" movement, and digital technology powered by big data, speculative ideas about the city have become more nuanced, tactical, political, and material.[99] Thus, the urban humanities field builds on the lineage of the Los Angeles School and its understanding of an alternative urbanism, but enriches it through a multidisciplinary confluence of ideas that come not only from urban studies but also from the humanities and design, and do not focus only on Los Angeles but also on the interrelationships, networks, and flows that connect this city to other cities of the Pacific Rim.

Beyond the Los Angeles School, our situatedness within the context of Los Angeles has most certainly defined, circumscribed, and influenced our work in ways that we may not even realize. Our thinking through the meaning, form, and processes of contemporary urbanism is largely framed by our understanding of Los Angeles, and our research and teaching almost always begin with Los Angeles, even when it is in relationship to other places throughout the Pacific Rim and the world. As such, several additional urban theorists and historians who have focused their attention on Los Angeles must also be mentioned. Beyond Banham, Kevin Lynch whose landmark *Image of the City* was fundamental for shaping how we understand urban morphology did some of his work in Los Angeles, though it was a city from a different time.[100] One of the most notable authors whose work redefined how we understood Los Angeles within its sociopolitical context was Carey McWilliams, whose prescient *Southern California: An Island on the Land* published in 1946 examined the city from the view of its radicals, its overlooked residents, its larger-than-life denizens.[101] McWilliams, influenced another major Los Angeles author, whose work has defined how we understand the city: in his book *City of Quartz*, Mike Davis unpacked the city's historic conservatism, which in its neoliberal version has since spread to other cities across the United States, even as Los Angeles itself has moved on.[102] More recently, historian William Deverell in his *Whitewashed Adobe* (2004) directed particular focus onto the area's Mexican past and the numerous histories of those in power attempting to erase or transform that past—especially relevant given the attention that the urban humanities cast on culture and spatial justice.[103]

Beyond the grand urban narratives of Los Angeles so often written by white male historians, journalists, and theorists, a number of female or nonwhite authors are creating and focusing new lenses on the city of Los Angeles. These authors have expanded their engagement with the city beyond book writing to include activism, counter-mapping (mapping of settings and histories overlooked in traditional cartographic representations), and multimedia interventions—all practices that we enthusiastically take up within the context of urban humanities, as well. Dolores Hayden's *The Power of Place* provides an important set of theories about place in the built environment and also details the history of Biddy Mason (a former slave who became the first African American woman to own real estate properties in Los Angeles); Hayden also provides a practice and example of intervening in urban space to actually create public monuments and memorials to such overlooked and invisible histories.[104] Dana Cuff's *The Provisional City* explores a number of "Los Angeles stories of architecture and urbanism," most notably the history of Chavez Ravine, a Latino neighborhood that was erased to give space to Dodgers stadium, and became the inspiration for a variety of other recuperations of this history in other media, such as Ry Cooder's album of the same name.[105] Eric Avila's *Popular Culture in the Age of White Flight: Fear and Fantasy in Suburban Los Angeles* casts a critical race lens on the City of the Angels that resulted in "chocolate cities and vanilla suburbs,"[106] while Laura Pulido's *Black, Brown, Yellow, and Left: Radical Activism in Los Angeles* details histories of the new activism in the city after the 1970s to inspire a younger generation of students and activists on how to engage with their city.[107] Pulido's collaborative volume *A People's*

Guide to Los Angeles further engages aspects of LA's erased or ignored histories, providing a set of counter-memories and counter-mappings aimed at recovering the layers of indigenous histories, multiethnic and class narratives, and environmental histories, which are embedded—but all too often ignored—in the urban spaces of the city.[108]

In conclusion, urban humanities as an emergent epistemology and practice finds its lineage in the ideas and theories described in this chapter. The field draws from this rich intellectual content to encourage new historical narratives, new contemporary interpretations of culture and everyday life that transcend borders, and transitions from past traditions to future transformations that compose a more just city. The influences described in this chapter, however, are only a start—numerous other authors, artists, and activists have shaped not only the way we think, but also the way in which we operate in our urban humanities practices. Many of these authors we return to in the following chapter on the practices of urban humanities, especially as they relate to art, media, mapping, ethnography, and film.

Project A: Intersections
Shanghai

"The past is never dead. It's not even the past."
—*Requiem for a Nun*, William Faulkner

2.3 Collage mapping of commercial imagery at the intersection of Huaihai and Maoming streets, Shanghai 2015. Credit: Authors

Humberto Castro, Andre Comandon, and Insky Chen

There are thousands of intersections in Shanghai. The one mapped in this study was conceived by the French imperial urban project in 1901. While the original name of the intersection's main street was Rue Sikiang, this central avenue of the former French Concession would be remembered by its new 1915 name: Avenue Joffre (figure 2.3).

Since the French Concession was founded, many layers of history have accumulated at this site, creating overlapping temporal topographies. The intersection between Avenue Joffre and Rue Cardinal Mercier is different than the intersection of Huaihai Zhong Lu and Maoming Nan Lu, despite the fact that these are names of the same streets. While an intersection presupposed the existence of a plane in which two lines can cross, here there are multiple planes.

The physical form of the intersection, including the buildings at each of the corners, is fixed in space—a reality that is the same for all who pass through it. One corner is occupied by the grand Cathay Theater; diagonally opposite is the largest Uniqlo clothing store in the world; on the other diagonal are the Line 1 metro station and the flagship store of the Gujin Underwear Company.

How each observer perceives (or chooses to perceive) this space is infinitely variable. One person may see a space shaped by global capitalism while another may be overwhelmed by nostalgia for a time when the Cathay Theater played only state-sponsored movies. Yet another may remember having to flee their childhood home in 1937 during the Battle of Shanghai. These histories coexist. They shaped, and continue to shape, the intersection.

As visiting scholars to this intersection, we developed a typology to make sense of its multiple layers. We focus on four topographies— Nostalgia, Capitalism, Colonialism, and Globalism—as forces that have shaped the built environment. In doing so, we juxtapose the empirical and the imaginary, the past and present to suggest connections that span the intersection's history.

The intersection of the two streets forms four corners. Each corner reveals as much as the audience wants to see. In the northeast corner, we see the number of films produced each year in China and the United States. As the movie industry in China became more globalized, the number of Chinese movies grew on par with the Hollywood powerhouse. During this same time period, China vastly expanded the metro network as evidenced in the northwest corner. This was executed almost directly proportionally to the tremendous rise of the Shanghai stock exchange, shown in the bottom half of the map's intersection.

This intersection dwells on the dreams of a future past. But for how long? The theater has survived for more than eighty years, through wars, revolutions, and reinventions. Can it survive in this intersection, where ambition is measured and posed, where forces blend and merge? Can we find the past, or only the future?

Project B:

En Movimiento
Los Angeles

2.4 Urban humanities students and advocacy group members mapping cycling routes through Boyle Heights, Los Angeles. Photo credit: Authors

Angélica Becerra, Peter Chesney, Paul Kurek, Lucy Seena K Lin, Jeannette Mundy, and Teo Wickland

The *Boyle Heights en Movimiento (BHM)* project was developed collaboratively by the advocacy group Multicultural Communities for Mobility, the art collective Self-Help Graphics and Art, and UCLA urban humanities students (figure 2.4). The working-class Latinx neighborhoods east of downtown Los Angeles are the setting for the project. Part of the work involved the production of a series of life-size cutouts to be placed in public places along sidewalks and even on streets. Local artists and residents created posters and stencils of bike commuters of color who live in and pass through Boyle Heights and its surrounding areas (figure 2.5). By capturing the moment in time when low-income cyclists of color occupy the street, we make them visible in a manner similar to what artist Ramiro Gomez did with his cardboard cutouts of domestic workers.

Commuting by bicycle, often to city districts and ethnic enclaves with spotty or unreliable transit service, bike commuters of color use the best transportation option available to them. Bike commuting is far less expensive than driving or riding transit. However, it is dangerous in Los Angeles. The city's streetscape has few markers and legal barriers wholly separating and protecting bicyclists from car, truck, and bus traffic. In practice, motorists often callously disregard the safety of bicyclists; at the same time, bike commuters willingly risk harm. Fearing death under the wheels of a speeding motorist does not prevent them from riding to work. Such a notion of a future at stake does not constrain their agency. Instead, they ride and put on public display the radically different futures for urban mobility embedded in their experiences. Making such a future possible means inserting both bike commuters and their representations into the streetscape. Motorists can easily ignore a bike commuter rushing by in the dark, but *BHM* cutouts seize their gaze, operating comparably to the ubiquitous "eye-catching" billboard advertisements that litter the streetscape.

BHM cutouts present bike commuting as something more than a dangerous lifestyle choice or regrettable situation. Inspiration derives from the everyday actions of working-class commuters of color who are forced to use many modes of urban transportation. LA bike commuters seek to thwart the city's dominant motorist-centric, high-speed mobility regime.

Positioning art as a tool for representation of bike commuters on certain streets or even freeways and, moreover, as a means for participation and engagement ushers in a new imagination for civic life. It seeks to shift the narratives and culture that have come to publicly dominate Los Angeles, from "the car capital of the world," to a space where flows of bike commuters, pedestrians, and bus riders can also lay claim to the public imagination. Or as Chicana philosopher Gloria Anzaldúa says in her 1987 book *Borderlands/La Frontera*: "I am cultured because I am participating in the creation of yet another culture, a new story to explain the world."

2.5 Bicyclists of East Los Angeles. Photo credit: Authors

Interlude 2:

Tokyo
Common Matters

Christian Dimmer and Keigo Kobayashi

2.6 A community café project acts as a commons in the Yanaka neighborhood of Tokyo.
Photo credit: C. Dimmer and K. Kobayashi

While the growth-obsessed Japan of the 1980s and 1990s was synonymous with an insatiable hunger for individualized consumerism and commodification, today some of its neighborhoods, including Tokyo's historic Yanaka district, have transformed into flourishing social laboratories, with community innovators, civic-minded entrepreneurs, local decision makers, socially engaged artists, and local residents experimenting with alternative practices and lifestyles.

Everywhere in urban Japan communities are similarly experimenting with new economic and spatial models that are needed to deal with the country's shrinking and rapidly greying population. Local innovators search for uses to fill the empty buildings and vacant spaces that open up in an age of depopulation and postgrowth. Everywhere in Japan and beyond, communities are searching for more sustainable and fulfilling forms of life.

Often the producers of these community projects are unaware of, or not explicit about the larger (political) implications of providing new social and economic models for Japan's nascent postgrowth society. But where people explore new forms of social relations, collaboration, decision-making, cultural practices, or human experience beyond the state and market logic, they prefigure a more democratic, pluralistic and sustainable society.

Community innovators are often motivated individuals with high levels of social capital, who seek to enrich their personal lives beyond the constraints of corporate Japan and to find individual happiness and meaning. What often starts from a personal impulse and a strong commitment to a locality leads to individual empowerment and creates intersections with other similarly socially engaged producers. At these meeting points new common worlds emerge.

Having been invited to participate in the Seoul Biennale of Architecture and Urbanism 2017 under the theme of "Imminent Commons," we began an extensive field research with our students to address a simple question, "How are commons (community-shared spaces) formed and for whom?" Over a period of several months, we conducted interviews with local residents to identify social and communal activities in the Yanaka neighborhood. With repeated visits, the invisible barrier separating us from the locals began to melt away, and the answer to our question slowly took shape.

The Yanaka neighborhood cuts across the borders of three different Tokyo boroughs. Somehow at the margins of three local governments a vacuum was created that allowed civic activism to flourish. This area—also known as "YaNeSen" (**Ya**naka, **Ne**zu, **Sen**dagi)—has a new spatial identity that was assembled through one of Japan's first place-based citizen magazines, launched in 1984 by community activist and housewife Mayumi Mori and two of her friends. In a time of skyrocketing land prices and a seemingly unstoppable redevelopment frenzy, the activists sought to create common interests by rediscovering local histories and cultures and mobilizing against outside pressures. As the timeline of the area suggests, the social activities and projects increased as economic growth intensified.

Few other places in central Tokyo escaped direct destruction during the Great Kanto Earthquake of 1923 and later the Allied bombings of 1945. The extensive greenery of temples and cemeteries—concentrated here after a large fire devastated the overcrowded city center in the seventeenth century—had protected the area and preserved its fine-grained spatial structure. The dense web of narrow back alleys and micro-open spaces prevented extensive redevelopment activities and led to the existence of a large stock of older buildings, which would later become a common cause for preservationists.

Mr. Mitsuyoshi Miyazaki, a former student living in the area and now an architect, convinced the owner of an old student residence to renovate the building rather than demolish it. He proposed to turn it into a hotel with a variation: the hotel's typical functions, such as the lobby, bathroom, and guestrooms, are all dispersed within the existing neighborhood, either using abandoned buildings or designated existing facilities. Mr. Masami Shiraishi, an art producer, saved one of the local public bathhouse buildings, which had gone out of business, by turning it into an art gallery for area residents. Mr. Toshiyuki Makizumi, a local resident and an architect, decided to rent out one of the vacant lots he owns to the neighbors; more than five hundred events have taken place there over the last ten years, gathering and connecting residents together in what had been a barren, unused space. Mr. Keiji Sawada, a headmaster of the local nursery school, has been working on turning a local road into a temporary park during weekends for the children living in the area. A local artist, Mrs. Setsuko Murayama, started a yearly event called Geiko-ten, which turns an entire neighborhood into a big gallery. Mr. Yoshiki Mishima, former resident of the area and landscape architect, works to promote street gardening using private individual pots. He calls it the "green infrastructure."

As an installation for an exhibition at the Seoul Biennale, we presented twenty-one elements (see figure 2.9) that represented the wide and rich spectrum of community projects and commons within the YaNeSen neighborhood (figures 2.6–2.8). The elements represent ordinary, everyday matters that show the people's diverse motivations and strong individual aspirations, as well as the desire to collaborate with others, which are the vital prerequisites to

2.7 A community commons on a Yanaka neighborhood sidewalk in Tokyo. Photo credit: C. Dimmer and K. Kobayashi

2.8 Empty land activated by community use in Tokyo.
Photo credit: C. Dimmer and K. Kobayashi

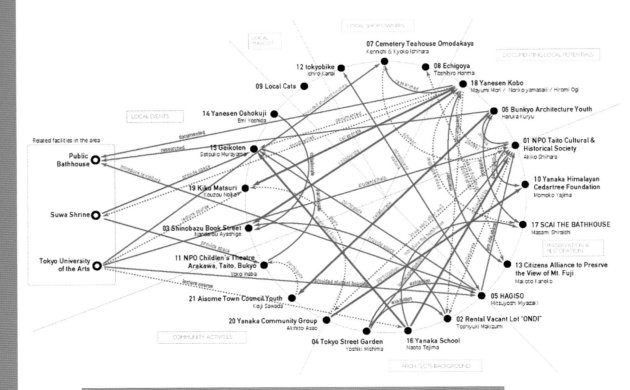

create and maintain the multiple commons. At the exhibition, each of the elements was laid out on the grid, independent from each other, and yet as the viewers began to gather around them, the elements began to merge, turning dots into a field.

Mrs. Akiko Shiihara, who leads an effort to protect old buildings and the ordinary daily lives of the Yanaka neighborhood, believes in "My town before Our town," and says "My town" can and should be created by people's own initiatives. Community and commons don't exist *a priori*, nor are commoners born as such. They co-emerge with common matters that connect people and places. While historical processes and the spatial setting make YaNeSen unique and help to bring about a very distinct local culture, the neighborhood has many matters in common with other parts of Tokyo. What the YaNeSen area and other neighborhoods suggest to us is that it is not necessary to coerce everyone into a unified *common* mindset, but rather allow and embrace the coexistence of a variety of motives, loosely connected to each other by small and big common matters. In pluralistic societies a collection of independent actions with self-empowered, strong, intrinsic motivations has the power to create sustainable projects and foster creativity.

3
Fused Scholarship: Practices of Urban Humanities

The urban humanities field is grounded in an evolving set of experimental practices aimed at creating and opening up possibilities for engagement and inquiry in urban settings, rather than systematic and rigid procedures or conceptual models often associated with conventional scholarly methodologies.

We consider methods and practices of understanding the urban to exist in a recursive relationship: Experimental and experiential practices (ranging from walking in the city and the contingency of encounters with others to urban interventions, community-academic partnerships, artistic and performative engagements, and interactive exhibitions) give rise to new ways of interpretation, such as spatial ethnographies, thick mapping, and filmic sensing. For example, the ongoing development of video practices gives rise to collaborative filming practices that aim to break down the distinction between the documentarian and the subject.[1] Urban humanities offer a praxis of engagement with the city at different levels, starting from the micro-facets of everyday life and the built environment to the cultural expressions of communities, to the spatial outcomes of urban policies and municipal regulations. While the scales of engagement may vary tremendously, the urban humanities project always begins with the embodied positionality of the researcher and the specificity of location, in conversation with and in relationship to people on the ground.

As discussed in chapter 2, Michel de Certeau in his book *The Practice of Everyday Life* identifies "walking in the city" as a practice for apprehending the variances, rhythms, and significance of everyday life. He contrasts this experience of the city "down below" to that of the desire for the panoptic view of the city as a whole realized from above (often depicted in the maps of cartographers and city planners). According to de Certeau, everyday practices of city dwellers in lived spaces contain possibilities for engagement, resistance, disquiet, improvisation, and transformation. He calls these practices "tactics" in order to emphasize how—in contrast to the strategies put in place by those who represent and benefit by systems of power—they operate through movements or interventions in time that "can change the very organization of space."[2] As we mentioned in chapter 2, urban humanities draw knowledge from such tactics, which expand the scope and terrain of urban inquiries.

In this chapter, we discuss three fused practices that can help us understand diverse experiences of the city, bringing together different types of knowledge and varied representational approaches to apprehending the significance of the everyday: spatial ethnography, thick mapping, and filmic sensing. We also discuss two practices that can provide a more experimental form of urban inquiry and intervention: socially engaged art and mixed-media installations. Each of these practices can be undertaken individually or fused together, in collaborative milieus inside and outside the university, with input from different disciplines, using media, new and old, which act as both the content and form of representation. We emphasize the tactical dimensions of making, application, and performance of these methods and practices, while also underscoring their experimental, creative, improvisational, and even playful qualities.

Spatial Ethnography

While it could be argued that ethnography—as an academic discipline and method of study—has always had a spatial dimension (after all, the researcher has to travel to observe another culture on site, in its own place), the term "spatial ethnography" is a relatively new coinage.[3] The conjunction of the term "spatial" with "ethnography" connotes a specific appreciation of the decisive role that space and spatial relations play in the cultural and social construction of meaning in cities. Ethnographers such as Clifford Geertz analyzed the semiotic systems that comprised cultural expression while inadvertently conducting spatial ethnographic studies (just where the stolen sheep end up or the cockfight takes place is in fact central to Geertz's reading of events). An explicit spatial ethnography analyzes the role of space—built, represented, and symbolic—and how it gives rise to various kinds of cultural meanings, expressions, and stratifications (social, cultural, economic, or political). Spatial ethnography also takes into account the material culture of the city, teeming with artifacts worthy of interpretation and embedded with significance. Adjacencies, spatial relations, personalization of the built environment, furnishings, forms of ornament, types of debris, evidence of maintenance or wear-and-tear, and, not least, signage, are open to ethnographic readings. Goods sold on the sidewalk are important to Annette Kim's work (as discussed below), while Yoh Kawano locates multisensory clues for his spatial ethnography of postdisaster Fukushima (see Interlude 3). And since space is often connected with structures of power and possibilities for both disempowerment and empowerment, questions of spatial justice come to the foreground of spatial ethnography.

At least since anthropologist George Marcus identified "multi-sited ethnography" in 1995, as a method of inquiry that follows a group through different field sites geographically and socially, ethnography's explicit spatiality became widely available for use by urban planners, architects, geographers, and humanists who critically examine the sociality of space rather than relegate it to a backdrop or understand it as merely a "setting."[4] In 2005, geographers Sharad Chari and Vinay Gidwani edited a special issue of *Ethnography,* titled "Grounds for a Spatial Ethnography of Labor," which introduced the "spatial turn" to ethnographies of work.[5] Articles in this issue employed the spatial analytics introduced by Henri Lefebvre in *The Production of Space* and the work of David Harvey, Edward Soja, and other critical urban geographers who built on and extended Lefebvre's theories to bear on ethnography.[6] While the work of critical geographers was foundational to the spatial turn and the introduction of space to a variety of fields of inquiry including anthropology and ethnography, their frame rarely focused on the intimate, lived scales that are explored by architects and humanists in specific places and buildings.

More recently, historian Lisa Silverman and architect Arijit Sen in the introduction to their edited volume *Making Place* name spatial ethnography as a "comprehensive methodological approach."[7] They see a critical engagement with space as the mechanism by which analyses can move across scales with attention to the micro-scale, lived, and embodied realities that are so vividly captured through ethnography, but with the added capacity of identifying linkages to larger meso- and macro-scale phenomena, which operate in larger geographic spaces or across multiple spaces. And, in contrast to much of the earlier spatial ethnography work, they discuss the necessity of visual materials, noting that spatial phenomena can be represented with far more nuance, clarity, and richness in a visualized form as opposed to text alone.

Prehistory of Spatial Ethnography

Some of the earliest and notable "proto"-spatial ethnographies are the works of Kevin Lynch and William H. Whyte, even though the term "spatial ethnography" was not used by them. Their backgrounds were in architecture and urban planning, which helps explain their invention of new methods for documenting, analyzing, and visualizing social-spatial relations. Kevin Lynch's landmark book *The Image of the City* (1960) is a study of how perceptions of the spatial organization of the city organize how it is imagined.[8] Visuality played an important role not only in how Lynch understood cities, but also in the methodology by which he conducted his research and urban design practice. He deployed a new graphic practice, cognitive mapping, in order to explore as well as document his new concepts. Not coincidentally, Lynch's work was carried out in collaboration with the visual artist Gyorgy Kepes. Summarizing the ambitions of the project, Lynch connects visuality with the legibility and identity of cityscapes: "This book will consider the visual quality of the American city by studying the mental image of that city which is held by its citizens. It will concentrate especially on one particular visual quality: the apparent clarity or "legibility" of the cityscape. By this we mean the ease with which its parts can be recognized and can be organized into a coherent pattern."[9]

Lynch's study culminates in the finding that inhabitants of a city produce mental images and comprehend their city on the basis of five basic spatial elements: paths, edges, districts, nodes, and landmarks (figure 3.1). But the striking component of his project that has been revisited more often by subsequent researchers is the process by which Lynch came to these conclusions. He fused multiple practices into a unique mashup of social scientific and spatial analysis with interviews, observations, and most important, the exploration of numerous cognitive maps produced by individuals who lived in and moved through the cities he examined. A few of the more unusual practices included observing participants interacting with photographs taken of the city he studied, asking them to essentially lead and narrate a walk around a city block, and interviewing motorists who might have a different perspective on the form of the city than pedestrians—all creative and useful means one might use as complements to a larger spatial ethnography.

The single method that has lived on in a wide range of disciplines is the systematic production and analysis of cognitive maps—and, indeed, this is the key piece that transforms Lynch's

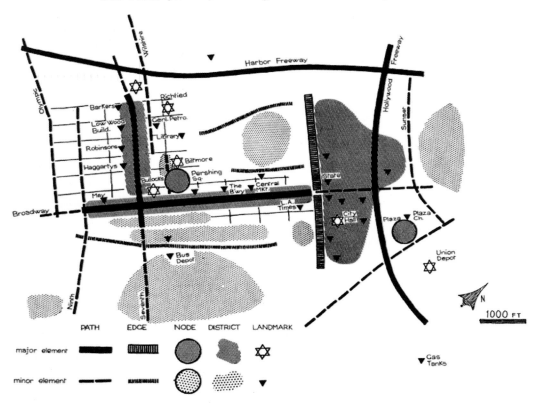

3.1 Kevin Lynch's analysis of the "visual form" of Los Angeles as produced by his team of "experts." Source: K. Lynch, *The Image of the City* (Cambridge, MA: MIT Press, 1960), 33, figure 14

rich study into a proto-spatial ethnography.[10] Explorations of cognitive mapping, especially as they relate to discourses around critical cartography and critical GIS continue to this day.[11] Lynch would ask his subjects to draw a map of their city from memory, and then study the map's distortions, omissions, and emphases. "Imageable" cities contain multiple sites that command attention and figure strongly into the subjects' perceptions of the urban form, while areas left off the map indicate that subjects have little experience with or memory of that space.

a)  b)

c)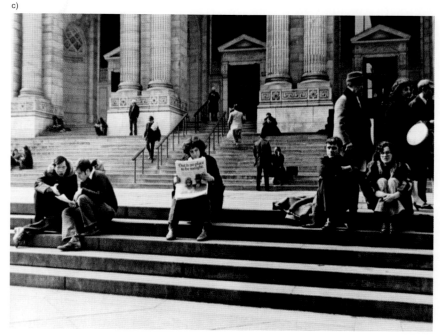

3.2 Images from W. H. Whyte, The Social Life of Small Urban Spaces (New York: Project for Public Spaces, 1980). Reproduced in Michael Miller, "Social Performance: Prototyping User Behavior," Scenario Journal 2 (Spring 2012). Credit: Project for Public Spaces

Another pioneer of spatial ethnography was William H. Whyte whose "Street Life Project" examined the urban life of New York City, and is well represented by his team's study of the plaza in front of Mies van der Rohe's Seagram Building, along with Paley Park in Midtown Manhattan, both examples of the privately owned public spaces common to American cities (figure 3.2). As if to signal his awareness of the unusual nature of his inquiry, Whyte begins his book *The Social Life of Small Urban Spaces* with an explanation of method: "We started by studying how people use plazas. We mounted time-lapse cameras overlooking the plazas and recorded daily patterns. We talked to people to find where they came from, where they worked, how frequently they used the place and what they thought of it. But, mostly, we watched people to see what they did."[12] Georeferenced observation, data visualization, and most prominently, film and photography all played key roles in this quasi-ethnographic study. "With the growth of a mass market for Super-8 photography, a by-product has been just such an [ideal] device—small, light, excellent, and inexpensive. With it you can multiply yourself as an observer, study many areas simultaneously, and do it with an accuracy and stamina few humans could match," Whyte wrote.[13] His experiments raised a host of methodological considerations from camera placement, to time-noting considerations (such as including a clock in the frame), to equipment selection, filming at night or in slow motion, and safety, among other things.

The substantive conclusions that Whyte draws cover topics ranging from environmental concerns such as sun and trees (shade is nice, but not too much), to architectural issues such as seating and capacity (more seating is better), to social issues such as the shunning of "undesirables" by other public space occupants or the positive phenomenon of what he calls "triangulation," wherein strangers find cause for conversation and interaction.[14] More directly than Lynch, Whyte's research also incorporated the futurity we will discuss as an attribute of urban humanities in chapter 4. His policy recommendations were adopted by city government, setting design standards and redevelopment strategies for New York's small urban spaces.

In both of these proto-spatial ethnographies, we see the merging of large-scale, abstracted, social-scientific spatial analysis with micro-level detail and attention to people as they move through or mentally comprehend space. The oft-cited maxim appears to hold true that we shape space and in turn, it shapes us—whether on the basis of our cognition and perception, or in our everyday interactions in public spaces. We also see in both projects an openness to fusing new practices, new methods, creative strategies, and novel technologies to capture the dynamism and vitality of urban space, which is often simply too complex, multiplicitous, and fast-moving for conventional observation by the human eye. Multiple media and media technologies are deployed not only in the methodology, but also in the representation and output produced from the research.

Injecting Spatial Justice in Spatial Ethnography

Kevin Lynch and William H. Whyte sought to capture the socio-spatial interactions in the quotidian spaces of everyday life, which Annette Kim builds upon by introducing attention to power, conflict, agency, and resistance. Influenced by Manuel Castells's examination of urban social movements and landscape architect Jeffrey Hou's work on "insurgent public space," Kim weaves together a new, more engaged form of spatial ethnography wedded to spatial justice.[15]

In her book *Sidewalk City*, Kim sought to capture the city on the ground, particularly the embodied, everyday experiences of Ho Chi Minh City's lively streets and sidewalks.[16] In attempting to represent this dynamism, she found that fixed, Euclidean mapping was insufficient and even complicit in certain forms of spatial injustice. Temporality, contingency, and lived experience were key ingredients in the vitality she was trying to depict, yet these elements are consistently omitted from the abstracted space of a two-dimensional map. Kim developed new strategies of data collection, new forms of data visualization, and new approaches to mapping in order to capture these phenomena. The sidewalks of Ho Chi Minh City were not just sidewalks: they were lived spaces, occupied by a dizzying array of uses, social relations, and materialities, which indicated not only local realities, but also the national, historical, and global forces at play. Spatial ethnography emerged as a "comprehensive methodological approach," to use Sen and Silverman's language,[17] which could encapsulate all of these disparate forms of knowledge, while also providing a multimodal means of visual and scholarly expression for the data.

One of Kim's maps, for example, is a time-based study of sidewalk use over the course of sixteen hours. Realized on a base map of the city, the vaguely anthropomorphic shapes that arise from the sidewalk are color coded by use over time, giving rise to a form of counter-mapping that puts missing or overlooked people back on the map, but also endows the map with a sense of fluidity and temporality, rather than a static ontology (figure 3.3). Another narrative map captures the daily life of a coconut water vendor who spends the bulk of her day tactically poised on the administrative boundary between two districts with separate police jurisdictions. When her illegal vending meets the ire of the police, she merely crosses the street: the police avoid the messy

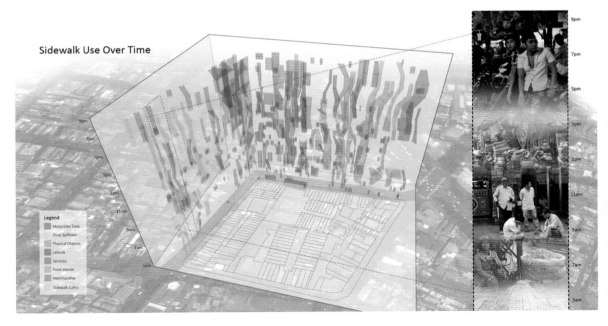

3.3 Space-time map of different sidewalk uses over the course of a day in Ho Chi Minh City. Credit: Annette Miae Kim

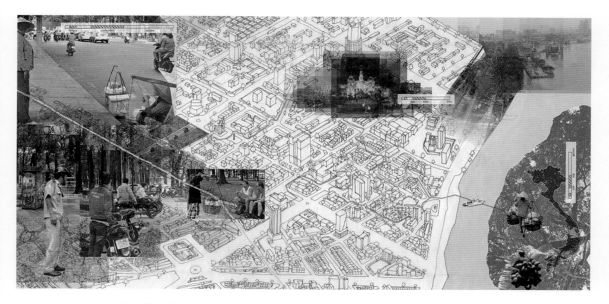

3.4 Narrative map, tracing a street vendor through Ho Chi Minh City. Credit: Annette Miae Kim

business of enforcement in the neighboring district and the vendor is free to continue selling her wares (figure 3.4).

This points to larger issues at play within this micro-scale dance of everyday life: policies aim at eliminating street vending from Vietnam's cities, long a beloved, culturally specific activity of urban life. These policies, in turn, stem from a national push to replicate the "pristine" forms of urbanism and street life found in the former colonial powers of the Global North. As such, the map is a form of counter-mapping[18] since it foregrounds people who are typically not included in traditional cartographic representations (which tend to highlight monuments, great leaders, and aggregated data of the state), while it also undermines fundamental epistemologies of cartographic reason (which tend to reduce mapmaking to rational grids, external coordinate systems, and objective realities with one-to-one correspondences with representational strategies). Counter-mapping, as we shall see, figures large in the urban humanist's toolkit. In Kim's work, the stacked photographs, blurred images, meandering routes, and hand-drawn base map offer a humanistic approach to spatial ethnography. They present a critical cartographic practice that we term "thick mapping."

When spatial ethnography and inventive mapping practices come together, they add contour to what visualization expert and political scientist Edward Tufte calls the flatlands of conventional depictions:

> Even though we navigate daily through a perceptual world of three spatial dimensions and reason occasionally about higher dimensional arenas with mathematical ease, the world portrayed on our information displays is caught up in the two-dimensionality of the endless flatlands of paper and video screen. . . . Escaping this flatland is the essential task of envisioning information—for all the interesting worlds (physical, biological, imaginary, human) that we seek to understand are inevitably and happily multivariate in nature. Not flatlands.[19]

Urban humanities rely upon spatial ethnography as a practice to interrogate the urban not only because it permits spatial analysis at macro- and micro-scales, but because it also deploys new sensory tools for capturing and representing our lived reality, blends together disparate methods, or even because it provides a means to see what has been overlooked. Spatial ethnography is especially appropriate to urban humanities because it has embedded within it a process for exposing inequities, power structures, and forms of dispossession and thus presents a key approach to the transformative possibilities of realizing spatial justice. The site specificity of an ethnography conducted in Tokyo's Golden Gai neighborhood became an intrinsic component of one urban humanities project that identified the unique phenomenon of "intimate publics" that were formed in the neighborhood's minute spatial configurations (see Project C: Intimate Publics in Golden Gai).

Thick Mapping

Thick mapping starts with "critical cartography" in order to deconstruct the idea of "the map" as a truthful representation or reflection of a reality "out there." Using maps and mapmaking practices, critical cartographers show how mapping is a contingent, constructive practice imbued with histories; ways of seeing, knowing, and controlling; epistemological assumptions, ideological worldviews, and political languages. Maps are not "natural" or "objective," but rather are knowledge constructs harboring ways of knowing and being. They propose worlds and tend toward the prescriptive rather than the descriptive. As processual, dialectical practices, mapping and counter-mapping (the activist use of maps and mapping to resist or critique dominant power structures)—can enable critical perspectives, speculative thought, and the pursuit of spatial justice. Mapmaking can be deconstructed and thought anew by bringing in elements of "thickness" that problematize single narratives, monocular perspectives, and totalizing claims. This is the deconstructive ambition of thick mapping.

The theoretical and disciplinary basis of critical cartography was established by geographers such as J. B. Harley, Denis Cosgrove, Denis Wood, Doreen Massey, and others who denaturalized "the map" as an objective representation of an external reality.[20] They did this by historicizing mapmaking practices on a global scale, showing how mapmaking not only has a millennia-long history but also its representational practices vary tremendously across cultural and social situations.[21] Maps are contingent formations linked with certain political, social, economic, cultural, and epistemological investments; they often—but not always—serve to extend the power of a sovereign over a territory and thus have a deep linkage with imperial and colonial histories.[22] Building on critical theory, Marxist social criticism, and feminist theory, critical cartography unpacks this nexus of power and spatial representation by deconstructing the map's claims to objectivity, naturalness, and necessity.

But critical cartography also has another dimension, namely the consideration of the map as an aesthetic object, as a work of visualization and artmaking. When Buckminster Fuller published his Dymaxion Map in *Life Magazine* in 1943, it provocatively visualized the earth as one interconnected landmass in a powerful political, aesthetic expression (figure 3.5).

Far from the claims of objectivity or science, the map as a work of art moves perspective, framing, annotation, symbology,

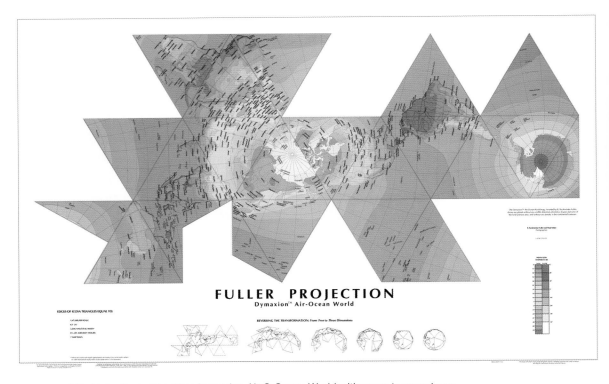

3.5 Fuller Projection Map Dymaxion Air © Ocean World with mean temperatures.
Credit: The Fuller Dymaxion Map design is a trademark of the Buckminster Fuller
Institute. ©1938, 1967, 1992. All rights reserved, www.bfi.org

and iconography to the foreground, underlining the fundamental
subjectivity at the heart of this artmaking practice.[23] In so doing,
the visual dimensions of the map as a media artifact operating
in multiple contexts are made explicit. For cartographers such as
Rebecca Solnit, this nexus between the map as an object of power
and the map as the object of visual play becomes a productive
site for unmasking the seductiveness of the whole enterprise of
cartography while also imagining new, place-based possibilities
for making the invisible visible once again.[24] In this respect,
her maps in the *Infinite City: A San Francisco Atlas* begin with
a seemingly standard base map of the city of San Francisco but
bring together new datasets, testimonies, archival materials,
and personal perspectives that have—for various institutional,
political, economic, and social reasons—been effectively left off the
map and erased from representation. Her map of San Francisco's

Mission District, for instance, contains the streets and blocks that are familiar in the public imaginary, but with new symbology, color-coding, borders, and annotations. She denaturalizes the map to reveal the hidden histories of immigration, day laborers, gang violence, and personal histories of border crossings and struggle at the heart of this community. In so doing, the map functions as a complex archive of testimony, an object of empowerment, and an aesthetic object of placemaking that tarries with the history of

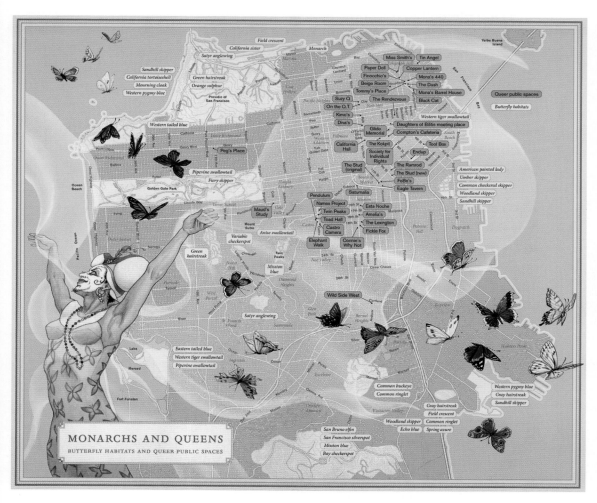

3.6 Mapping butterfly habitats and queer public spaces in San Francisco. Credit: R. Solnit, *Infinite City: A San Francisco Atlas* (Berkeley: University of California Press, 2010), 46–47

immigration at both a local and an international level. In another map (figure 3.6), Solnit brings together two seemingly disparate geographies—butterfly habitats and queer public spaces—as a poetic rumination on their obliquely related nomenclature: "monarchs" and "queens." Her capacious approach to mapping is nevertheless grounded in visual standards of cartography: the purported objectivity of the cartographic frame suggesting that these two phenomena might have some important conceptual link, forcing us to contemplate their interconnected spatiality.

The tradition of critical cartography also carries over into the realm of digital mapping. Because of their ubiquitous integration into the everyday, we might assume that Google Maps (and other digital mapping and wayfinding platforms) are somehow objective systems, free of ideology, strictly utilitarian, and open to everyone. But we must not forget the military infrastructure that supports the Global Positioning System (GPS) upon which such platforms rely for satellite imagery, data collection, and real-time reporting. The history of remote sensing satellites stretches back to the 1960s with the launching of the first military spy satellites and the research to build the GPS. Completed in 1993, the twenty-four satellites and five ground stations provide signals that allow receivers to accurately calculate and potentially target any point on the planet according to latitude, longitude, altitude, and time. These technologies were invented, deployed, and are maintained by military and corporate infrastructures of targeting.[25] While place data can be indicated at many levels (from point data and address to city or country), the most granular mark-up gives location in terms of latitude and longitude based on a standard coordinate system, usually World Geodetic System 84 (WGS:84), a reference system derived from the Mercator projection and developed by the U.S. Department of Defense for the Global Positioning System.[26] As such, the viewing technologies of Google have to be recognized as the product of the Cold War and the mode of seeing made possible by aerial war, precision guided missile systems, global surveillance, and GPS infrastructures. An open question remains: What might a postcolonial, postimperial practice of counter-mapping look like?

3.7 Transborder Immigrant Tool, 2009. Credit: Ricardo Dominguez with Brett Stalbaum, Amy Sara Carroll, Micha Cárdenas, and Elle Mehrmand

To begin to answer this question, it is worth examining some of the profound ways in which GPS and GIS have been repurposed to destabilize physical borders and facilitate critical forms of counter-mapping, subversion, and hacktivism. For example, Ricardo Dominguez, founder of the Electronic Disturbance Theater, developed the "transborder immigrant tool," a recycled phone equipped with a GPS receiver, basic GIS maps, and a digital compass to guide immigrants to water caches and safety in the desert between Mexico and Southern California (figure 3.7). The device relies on the very infrastructure of the imperial imaginary precisely to destabilize it, if only for a moment, by providing a life-saving hack for the people that the United States seeks to expel and keep out. As Dominguez explains, the tool allows new forms of agency and activism to emerge, which make use of and "offer access to this emerging total map economy." He adds: "With the rise of multiple distributed geospatial information systems (such as the Google Earth Project for example), GPS (Global Positioning System) and the developing Virtual Hiker Algorithm . . . it is now possible to develop . . . Transborder Tools for Immigrants to be implemented and distributed on cracked Nextel cell phones. This will allow a virtual geography to mark new trails and potentially safer routes across this desert of the real."[27] Dominguez further reworks GPS into what he calls a "Geo-Poetic System," sending poetry and maps to immigrants in an effort to produce a "counter-aesthetic" and "counter-map" to the borderlands, the borderwall, and the technologies of surveillance and opacity that characterize the seemingly all-pervasive power of the U.S. Border Patrol.[28]

Expanding on the practice of interventionist mapping with regard to the U.S.-Mexican border, architect Ronald Rael has recently published the manifesto *Borderwall as Architecture* that provides a set of speculative propositions and imaginative possibilities for rethinking the border as a physical construct that operates as a kind of "third space" of both division and potential unity.[29] Rael's intervention is to historicize and denaturalize the border, to show it as a politically contingent formation that has, in effect, given rise to various kinds of hybrid identities, intimacies, and possibilities for thinking across ethnic, cultural, economic, environmental, and even political divisions. Inspired by the work of Gloria Anzaldúa among others, he proposes a series of architecturally poetic speculations that rethink the "borderlands" without forgetting its traumatic histories or repressing the violence and death that it produces. As he writes: "The wall, like the scar it will leave, must be accepted—not only as a political symbol of security but also as the latent connective tissue between the United Mexican States and Los Estados Unidos de América."[30] In proposing a series of ludic (but also deeply engaged) design alternatives to the wall—including imagining it as a climbing wall, a cactus wall, a theater wall, a teeter-totter wall (figure 3.8), and a communion wall—Rael seizes upon the speculative possibilities of architectural practice. His proposes that the wall collects solar power for adjacent Mexican households or the water needed by border-crossers who die from dehydration, thus envisioning a counter-narrative for the border wall as supportive, open, and life-affirming.

Also working with digital spatial technologies in order to reclaim and politicize mapping practices, Laura Kurgan seeks to pry apart "their opacities, their assumptions, and intended aims" through critical, activist modes of creativity.[31] Working between

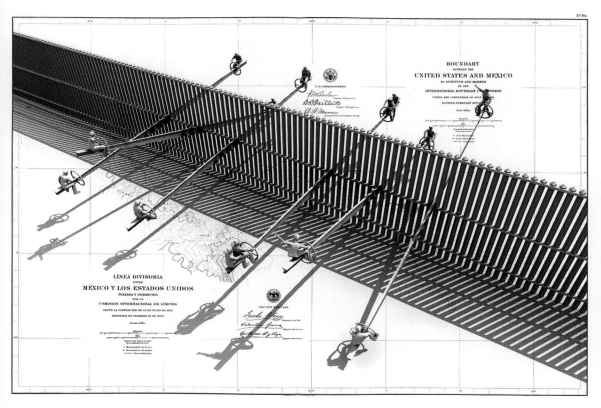

3.8 Conversations about the problematics of the wall in R. Rael, *Borderwall as Architecture* (Berkeley: University of California Press, 2017). Photo Credit: Rael San Fratello

the arts, design, and GIS, Kurgan turns the very technologies against themselves, offering a kind of deconstruction of their underlying assumptions and "truths." One such project, Million Dollar Blocks (figure 3.9), for example, uses data from the criminal justice system to map the city-to-prison migration flow in five major U.S. cities in order to show how much the state is spending, by block, to incarcerate people annually. The most egregious results display "million dollar blocks" that have radically evacuated civic infrastructure and community investment in favor of exorbitant prison spending.[32] Using GIS to map the data at the block level, she makes visible the unseen dimensions of incarceration and the criminal justice system. Kurgan calls this work "justice mapping"

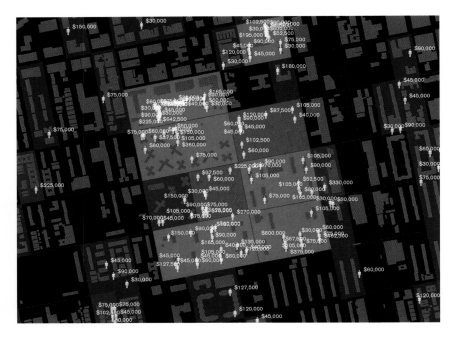

3.9 Million Dollar Blocks project. Credit: Laura Kurgan, Eric Cadora, David Reinfurt, and Sarah Williams

and connects it to a broader set of concerns around spatial justice. In this sense, she uses the technologies and the data to politicize mapping and evince its subversive power. In Los Angeles, the historian Kelly Lytle Hernandez has worked with data about the ongoing incarceration of brown and black bodies in "million dollar 'hoods'" around the city, creating an online, interactive map. Lytle Hernandez wants to empower residents in those neighborhoods as well as make the wider public aware of deeply discriminatory policing (see Interlude 5).

While Kurgan makes use of police data to analyze and expose the pervasiveness and fundamental inequities of policing practices to the public, a final dimension of critical cartography places both the tools of mapmaking and the data creation itself in the hands of the public. Participatory mapping is a community-based approach that empowers people living in the neighborhoods to create their own maps and forms of self-representation. While participatory mapping practices vary tremendously, the collective mapping

3.10 Collective mapping from the Eco Museum workshop in Mexico City by the Iconoclasistas (2012). Credit: Iconoclasistas

projects of the Argentina-based group *Iconoclasistas* and their "Manual of Collective Mapping" are inspiring approaches for what we call "thick mapping" in the urban humanities.[33] Bringing together a range of collaborative mapmaking devices, experiences, and projects, the Iconoclasistas consider "collective mapping [to be] a creation process subverting the place of enunciation to challenge dominant narratives on territories."[34] The approach draws from everyday knowledge and the experiences of participants to create graphical forms of representation that generate new kinds of knowledge, viewpoints, and perspectives. Crucially, the knowledge created is embodied, processual, and differential, not abstracted, transcendental, or totalizing. It subverts dominant narratives created by structures and institutions of power by placing the tools of representation, narrative, data creation, and interpretation in the hands of the people (figure 3.10).

What we earlier described as "counter-mapping" includes such strategies of participation and deconstruction. These strategies have roots stretching back to the critical urbanism and psychogeography practices of the Situationists in the 1950s and 1960s that gave rise to a broader orientation around spatial justice through the work of Marxist geographers in the following decades. Far from the Apollonian eye looking down from a transcendental view, "participatory mapping," "counter-mapping," and "thick mapping" betray the contingency of looking, the groundedness of any perspective, and the embodied relationality inherent to any locative investigation. Such mapping is never simply mimetic (a one-to-one correspondence between representation and reality), but rather motivated by a deconstructive impulse, one that unmasks assumptions, uses the technologies against themselves, and exposes their conditions of possibility. At the same time, it uses the affordances of GIS and the history of mapping and spatial visualization practices to ask new questions, by putting datasets in dialogue with one another; by revealing correlations, patterns, and knowledge that would not be visible otherwise; and by opening up participation to new collectives and collaborations. As such, it brings mapmaking practices out of the esoteric and elite world of Geographic Information Sciences and into the everyday life of the city and the public writ large. Thick mapping emerges in this productive tension out of the traditions of critical cartographies.

Thick Mapping in Theory

"Thickness"—as a method, epistemology, and practice of urban humanities—connotes a multiplicity of interpretive, interconnected layers: layers of meaning, layers of time, layers of data, layers of history, and layers of voices and experiences. While we may think primarily of GIS layers, the term comes from the German philosopher of history, Reinhart Koselleck, to connote, first and foremost, *Zeitschichten*, or time-layers.[35] The German word *Schicht* is not only a layer but also stratum referring to both sedimentary strata and social constructs, as in class strata or social divisions. It is also the root of the German word for history (*Geschichte*), which could be translated—very loosely—as "that which is layered." But even the concept of *Geschichte* (history) is itself layered because the term means both things that happened and the narrative or representational means of making sense of those happenings or occurrences (*das Geschehen*): in other words, events and the compositional work of turning those events into narratives, stories, films, maps, or other media objects. As such, thickness refers to layers of time; various kinds of social, economic, linguistic, and cultural stratifications; events and occurrences; and the narrative means and representational practices of composing those layers into histories and cartographies. A thick map is attuned to all of these permutations of meaning.[36]

Such complex formulations of layers or strata provide thick mapping with its foundations. For thinkers such as Walter Benjamin, who has played a central role in forming our approach to urban humanities (not least because his magnum opus, *The Arcades Project*, is an urban-historical investigation of the city of Paris in the nineteenth century and a study of the idea of modernity), "history" does not break down into stories because events are not homologous with the story-like structures of linear narratives; instead, Benjamin suggests, history breaks down into images: "*Geschichte zerfällt in Bilder, nicht in Geschichten.*"[37] If history breaks down into images, we must also confront those images as images, which would require us to consider things such as perspective, framing, media formats, legibility, recognizability, reproducibility, and simultaneity—other key concepts in Benjamin's historiographic lexicon. Legibility and recognizability (*Lesbarkeit* and *Erkennbarkeit*, respectively) are both *potentialities*, possibilities that are contingent upon many things, including one's point of view, the needs and desires of a viewer, a socio-political moment, our ethical orientation, and the structures of power that variously highlight or occlude certain things. Not everything is legible or recognizable by everyone; not everything will be legible or recognizable all the time; not everyone will care; and some things will be lost forever. Why, for example, have indigenous mapping practices been ignored for so long and only recently been taken seriously by scholars interested in differential ways of knowing and imagining the world "out there"?

If a thick map presents "images" of history, it does so in the plural: not a single, static image of the past or a definitive story, but rather many images, layered upon one another, perhaps bleeding into one another. Benjamin explicitly called his historiographic method "literary montage,"[38] an assembly of many cacophonous voices, stories, images, and citations that, together, fashioned not the past, but a precarious relationship between that which is past and that which is present. This eschewal of positivism or objectivism (that "the past" can be definitively known and resurrected) in favor of an ethical form of social construction is a cornerstone of urban humanities' approach to thick mapping. Maps are never "true" or "singular" images, and the mapmaker is always implicated in the contingent process of mapping.

Beyond thickness as layers and pluralities, thickness also connotes an approach to visualization, translation, narrative, and the representational work of thick description. Clifford Geertz, of course, popularized the term "thick description."[39] Thick mapping is a practice that, perhaps somewhat surprisingly, is arrayed against conventional hermeneutical approaches that privilege depth or models that claim a certain purchase on "truth" or the "representation of reality" by way of their deep analysis. For these reasons, we prefer "thick maps" over "deep maps" since the latter implies hermeneutical models of digging deeper to get to an underlying truth.[40] Urban humanists do not imagine getting to *the* truth by digging deeper or mapping better; instead, we foreground the accrual of multiply contested meanings, some rising, some falling, some visible, some erased, some legible, some no longer extant. Thickness allows us to foreground ongoing processes of contestation, tension, mapping, counter-mapping, and incommensurability. Thick mapping is never finished.

As such, mapping (like filming, translating, describing, and narrating) is processual, and maps are hardly stable objects that simply reference, reflect, or correspond to an external reality. Mapping is a verb that bespeaks an ongoing process of picturing, narrating, symbolizing, contesting, repicturing, renarrating, re-symbolizing, erasing, and reinscribing relations. Maps are visual arguments that tell stories; they make claims and harbor ideals, hopes, desires, biases, prejudices, and violence. They are always relational, in dialogue or in contact with someone or something. Even when they attempt to reference, reflect, or represent an "external reality" (however one defines that), they remain, fundamentally, propositions (as Denis Wood argues[41]), suffused with worldviews, structuring epistemologies, and ways of seeing. Urban humanities pursue "thick mapping" as a practice that foregrounds multitemporal layers of representations that enter into and out of legibility at a given time. And just as important, thick maps betray their conditions of possibility, their authorship and contingency, without naturalizing or imposing a singular worldview. In essence, thick maps give rise to forms of counter-mapping, alternative maps, multiple voices, and ongoing contestations. Thick maps speak back.

In this respect, we might contrast thick maps to "thin maps": The former are relational, multivoiced, situated, and contingent; the latter are ontological objects that declare (tacitly or openly) their truth, neutrality, or objectivity, as if they are somehow devoid of time and place. A thin map masquerades as a state of being, an objective worldview that has overcome its specificity, potentiality, contingency, and conditions of possibility. Thin maps are the maps of power, control, and the imperial imaginary; thick maps, on the other hand, deconstruct those dynamics of power, sometimes using and overturning the very tools of the imperial imaginary, to speak back, speak against, speak up, and speak together. Thin mapping is about ontology, while thick mapping is about ethics.

When Geertz developed the notion of thick description, the term functioned retrospectively and prospectively to articulate his "position"[42] more generally with regard to ethnographic description. Since the publication of his programmatic essay "Thick Description: Toward an Interpretive Theory of Culture" in 1973, thick description has been widely adopted and deployed in countless fields beyond anthropology and ethnography, such as sociology, architecture, literary studies, and art history, as a way of describing complex cultural phenomena. We have thick descriptions of works of art, thick descriptions of urban environments, but also thick translations, thick urbanism, thick media, and, now, thick mapping.

Thick mapping, to apply Geertz's articulation of thick description in ethnography, is both grounded (or we might say, "emplaced") and fictive—not in the sense of false or nonfactual but in the original meaning of *fictiō*, as something made or fashioned.[43] Thick maps, like thick descriptions, are fashioned not as definitive and deep but as projective, possible layers that enter into and out of legibility or recognizability at a given time, in a given place, in a given language, and in a given socio-political and cultural-historical context. Part of the reason for the thickness, according to Geertz, is that cultural analysis is "intrinsically incomplete;" we don't "get . . . to the bottom of it"—"it is turtles all the way down."[44] In fact, he argues, a cultural analysis fixated on digging deeper can sometimes "lose touch with the hard surfaces of life—with the political, economic, stratificatory realities within which men [*sic*] are everywhere contained—and with the biological and physical necessities on which those surfaces rest."[45] This approach to cultural analysis remains incomplete (and, therefore, always extensible in multiple ways). Not unlike Benjamin's thoughts on history, it does not follow "a rising curve of cumulative findings"[46] as a march toward progress; rather, it is a disconnected, partial, perspectival, contingent, situated, and time-bound representational practice.

Twenty years after Geertz published the essay on "thick description," the philosopher and literary scholar, Kwame Anthony Appiah, published a seminal essay called "Thick Translation," explicitly referencing Geertz's notion in order to highlight the importance of incommensurabilities between languages and cultures.[47] According to Appiah, translation is not about the "attempt to find ways of saying in one language something that means the same as what has been said in another" but rather the commentary of honestly presenting the points of failure, difference, and even disconnectedness between languages and cultures.[48] Translation, in Appiah's view, should aim to present ever thicker "contextualization"[49] and understandings for a given text and, thus, Appiah advocates for a kind of "thick translation" that "seeks with its annotations and its accompanying glosses to locate the text in a rich cultural and linguistic context."[50]

Essentially, good translations should explain why translations are also sometimes impossible. He later says that one reason for thick translation is to preserve cultural and linguistic differences (rather than level them or presume equivalencies can always be found), which is ultimately "a project of a genuinely informed respect for others"[51] and a situated awareness of the perspectives, assumptions, and ways of knowing that we bring to the study of cultures (and we might say, cities) that are different from our own. In essence, thick translation honestly respects difference, since not every concept, utterance, and perspective can simply be carried across different cultural and linguistic contexts.

Thus, moving between cities calls for thick mapping as a form of thick translation, highlighting the cultural, social, and linguistic specificity of our entire enterprise. For urban humanists to study, experience, map, and speculate about different cities is not a matter of turning over every stone, as it were, but a respectful awareness of others and their spatial contexts. In addition to linguistic incommensurability and the call for "thick translations," we might also interrogate methodological and epistemological incommensurabilities, asking whether local contexts might give rise to specific methods and ways of knowing that don't "translate" universally. It allows us to raise a fundamental question: What would a practice of postcolonial mapping look like? Our spatial ethnographies in the urban humanities have privileged thick compositional processes of mapping, filming, translating, and describing as ways to investigate cities at varying scales, through various tempos and in various media, attuned to the persistent dialectic of legibility and erasure, inclusion and exclusion, that which is past, present, and yet to come. We essentially compose the thickly layered city through mapping that is a multimediated, propositional, choreographic, and experimental practice aimed at both designing knowledge and undoing power.

Thick Mapping in Practice

What might a thick map of the Chinese Massacre of 1871 in Los Angeles look like and what might be the process of creating it? This is precisely the question that has guided a classroom exercise each year in UCLA's Summer Institute for Urban Humanities. The Summer Institute is an intensive, graduate-level workshop that introduces twenty-four students from architecture, urban planning, and the humanities to the practices of urban humanities. In preparation, the students spend a week studying the area around the mythical birthplace of the city, *El Pueblo de Los Angeles*; they complete fieldwork in its vicinity and learn about the multiple, contested histories embedded in the buildings and streets radiating out from *La Placita*, the plaza at the city's historic core. The students read a series of articles about the Chinese Massacre, which draw on primary and secondary materials including eyewitness testimonies, police reports, newspaper reports, oral histories, census and building records, maps, and photographs. They are asked to extract a number of "data layers" from the articles in order to make a collaboratively produced "thick map" of the event, to bring together multiple contexts (historical, social, economic, racial), a broad set of agents and actors, multiperspectival narratives, and a thoughtful approach to symbology and epistemology in rendering the data into graphical form. As a starting point, we also provided part of a base map derived from a mid-nineteenth-century map of the key streets around La Placita. The rest of the map was to be created by the students (figure 3.11).

The Chinese Massacre itself is considered one of the largest mass lynchings in American history, in which a mob of 500 Angelenos, mainly men, tortured and hung between seventeen and twenty Chinese immigrants over the course of a single day on October 24, 1871.[52] While the basic facts are not contested, much about the spatial and temporal contours of the event is incomplete so that its mapping is not a straightforward exercise but instead, a form of inquiry. Moreover, the inquiry raises important ethical questions about responsibility and sensitivity in mapping practices, making the process of mapping as important as the final product. The students work in teams to determine what data is available, what stories they want to tell, and how those data and stories could be graphically presented. It is a collaborative undertaking in which the students negotiate among themselves about what to map and how to present it. Working over a large base map on the floor

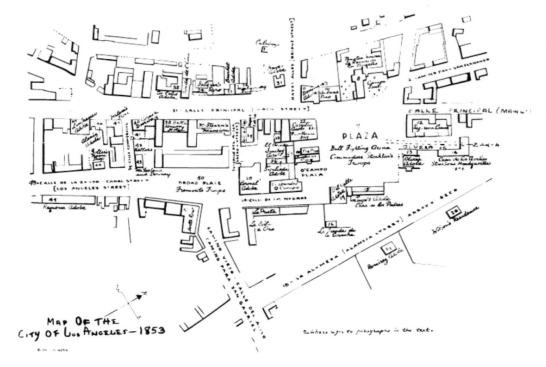

3.11 Base map of El Pueblo and the Plaza in Los Angeles derived from a map of 1853. Credit: Ana Begue de Packman, "Landmarks and Pioneers of Los Angeles in 1853," *Historical Society of Southern California Quarterly* 26, no. 2/3 (June–September 1944); map by Ruth Saunders

of the classroom (about twelve by eight feet), students use colored pens, pencils, sheets of paper, and other materials to construct their map, annotate it, and augment it.

Fundamental questions about the ethics of representation inform the process of mapping. In whose name is the map being created? How is the map also, potentially, a memorial? How could it embody many different perspectives, not only of the eyewitnesses but also of varied historical practices of representation and occlusion? What kinds of comparisons and frameworks of interpretation ("layers") should inform the representational process? How should students position themselves and their varied positionalities with regard to racial, economic, social, and political violence?

Students begin by annotating the base map with the relevant streets and buildings in relationship to the lynchings, essentially putting the victims of the mob violence on the map (figure 3.12). Even here, significant ethical questions arise about how to inscribe the humanity of those who were lynched. Depicting the temporality of the event hinges on a series of micro-events that occurred on October 24, starting according to some accounts with the killing of Robert Thompson, a white rancher, caught in a battle between two groups of Chinese men. The mappers attempt to incorporate the uncertainties, contradictions, and biases that characterize accounts of that day. Routes of the police, the lynch mob, business owners, and victims are incompletely known and charted. Students expand the temporal boundedness of the event backward and forward, relating it to the history of anti-Chinese legislation like the Anti-Coolie Act of 1862 and the Chinese Exclusion Act of 1882; other students connect these anti-immigration laws up to the Patriot Act of 2001 and more recent anti-immigrant legislation. The nearby Los Angeles jail, where disproportionate numbers of black and brown bodies are incarcerated, is sometimes mapped, as are the many spaces dedicated to policing in the downtown area. Students further expand the spatial boundedness of the event beyond the streets around La Placita to include Mexico where in the 1930s Chinese residents were discriminated against, expelled, and killed, or Birmingham, Alabama, which sits along the 34th parallel with Los Angeles, in order to show that such racial violence was hardly bound to Los Angeles or to a remote history.

Students include the names of the victims on the maps and, where possible, provide brief biographical entries about who they were and the circumstances of their killing. For example, a widely known Chinese doctor was among those lynched; the men's hair or queues (called pigtails in the newspaper) were cut off; rope and clothesline were provided by local business owners to the lynch mob. The edges of the map provide space to render a timeline of Chinese immigration to the United States, a history of anti-immigrant legislation, and contemporaneous events like the Chicago fire that had occurred two weeks prior. Finally, students create visualizations of the demographics of Los Angeles in 1871, finding ways to show that from its population of 5,000 people, a full 10 percent was involved in the mass lynching (though not

3.12 Urban humanities graduate students creating a thick map of the Chinese Massacre of 1871. Photo credit: Authors

a single person was convicted or served time for murder). This would help to scale the event and appreciate its significance in 1871, and its ongoing significance in the context of contemporary struggles for justice and reform.

Although thick mapping is intrinsically open to continued inquiry, a deadline is set for the end of the exercise when we literally sit around the map to discuss the decision-making process, the data collection and design process, and the ethical questions raised. We consider what was mapped, how it was mapped, whether the map constitutes a "thick map," what layers of meaning might still be added, and how the map speaks back. In what ways does such a seemingly "bound" historical event that happened on a single night have reverberations for understanding the city of Los Angeles in the past, the present, and the future? What does thick mapping offer in terms of understanding the city and approaching its contested— and sometimes erased—histories? In what ways is memory linked with history and how might these be given spatial dimensionality? Questions such as these continue to inform our practices of engaging with the city throughout the year.

Filmic Sensing

Another urban humanities practice is filmic sensing, which entails the creation of moving images and, more specifically, the use of the mobile phone video camera as a sensory extension of our bodies in urban space. Like spatial ethnography and thick mapping, filmic sensing is an experimental way of being in and perceiving urban space and also a means of interpretation and representation for that experience. Like thick mapping, filmic sensing can be considered a form of spatial ethnography that has a specific medium associated with the practice—in this case, rather than the map we have the moving picture. This specific medium—now manifest almost entirely in digital video[53]—is embedded with particular experiential, practical, and conceptual implications that enable forms of interpretation more closely resembling the city. That is, the temporality, spatiality, and sensorial qualities of urban life are better captured through video than through many other media. Our use and understanding of video within the urban humanities has more in common than one might think with spatial ethnography and thick mapping. For example, a completed moving picture resulting from a process of filmic sensing ideally performs as a sort of cinematic map, connecting conceptual threads across the space and time of many frames.

Why is filmic sensing a practice of urban humanities? A look into the origins of cinema demonstrates the latent qualities and histories that make it a fundamentally urban humanist medium. These histories are here exemplified through "city symphony film" (an explanation follows) and the ways in which the technology and medium of moving images have evolved in parallel with changing formations of the city. Conceptually and methodologically, filmic sensing is a mashup of essay film and sensory ethnography, two different but well-established forms and practices found within the medium. To provide examples, we will discuss works by filmmakers that portray various forms of filmic sensing, as well as a handful of projects from our work and experience in urban humanities.

Sensing Urban Space: From City Symphony to YouTube

During the nineteenth century, the development of the technologies of photography and, subsequently, moving pictures was coincident with the later stages of the Industrial Revolution, a period that ignited urbanization, as workers migrated to factories and jobs. When Eadweard Muybridge created what many have called the first movie in 1878, splicing together twenty-four images of Leland Stanford's horse Sallie Gardner, about two-thirds of his fellow Britons lived in a city. In one of the most famous myths of cinema, moviegoers leapt out of their seats at the sight of an approaching train during an 1896 screening of the Lumière brothers' *L'Arrivée d'un train en gare de La Ciotat*, suggesting the cinema was a dramatically new way of seeing at the time of its creation, yet one that has become utterly normalized within our contemporary moment of livecast reality. Both cinema and urban spaces are products of a modernity that such cultural artifacts can help us understand. So it is unsurprising that cinema, long intertwined with urbanism, has come to play a critical role in urban humanities. Its methodological function is not only one of sensing the present but also of tracing the city's changing nature over time.

One genre that has proven to be a useful starting point is "city symphony," an avant-garde and experimental form that began in the 1920s as artists explored the trappings of modernity that were transforming daily life: industrialization, urbanization, mechanization, and new technologies. The film that most clearly represents the genre is Walter Ruttmann's 1927 *Berlin: Symphony of a Metropolis*, the title reflecting its organization into an overture and five acts, whose filmic rhythms match the unfolding rhythms of the day depicted. For example, fades, jump cuts, and montage are deployed—as in many other city symphony films—in a relatively calm fashion during Act I, which shows the city in the early hours before its inhabitants have awoken, while Act V uses those techniques more frenetically to represent the city's nightlife, replete with neon lights and burlesque dancers. Time speeds and slows, space expands and contracts, reflecting the delirium of the modern city. Just as we might produce a thick map that layers, confuses, and elucidates the multiplicity of contemporary urbanism, so too we might use city symphony as a template for how to produce a cinematic map, which foregrounds the dynamic temporalities of urban life.

But perhaps even more germane to urban humanities is Dziga Vertov's 1929 film *Man with a Movie Camera*, another quintessential city symphony film (figure 3.13). Like Ruttmann's *Berlin*, the film's montage of modern urban life spans the time of a single day. It is also known for a range of novel cinematic techniques such as double exposure, reflected images, and self-reflexively showing the movie camera as a character within the film. As the architectural scholars Stavros Alifragkis and François Penz have documented in their analysis of the film, its novel techniques embody an exploratory futurity common to avant-garde artists of the time; its prosaic content of everyday life is more akin to the realist art that predated the avant-garde, and its organization serves to extol a Marxist political economy.[54] In other words, the temporality and polyvocality of cinema enables a kind of thickness through multiple registers that interlink aesthetics, politics, and everyday life—perfect for the aspirations of urban humanities.

Media scholar Lev Manovich goes so far as to name *Man with a Movie Camera* emblematic of new media—computationally enhanced media that ostensibly could only emerge during and after the 1980s—because of its demonstration of so many of the qualities that define digital media.[55] In *The Language of New Media*, he describes a "transcoding" that occurs between a "cultural layer" and a "computer layer" in the production of digital media—a phenomenon that occurs in Vertov's film between an urban layer and a cinematic layer. Manovich is also known for proposing the "database" as a way of understanding the cultural shift away from the linear narratives found in novels and movies toward the nonlinear and hyperlinked structures found in new media and on the internet. Here too he cites Vertov, claiming that "*Man with a Movie Camera* is perhaps the most important example of a database imagination in modern media art."[56]

The database, too, functions methodologically in its capacity for archiving, retrieving, and mixing the infinite datapoints one

3.13 Scene from Vertov's 1929 film *Man with a Movie Camera*

might find in urban space. Manovich's overarching argument is that the cinematic eye has become so dominant that when used in new technologies such as digital interfaces, our ability to use those interfaces is second nature. When he wrote at the start of the new millennium, Manovich could not have predicted the ubiquitous emergence of the camera phone, enabling not only the understanding and consumption of new media, but also, in a dizzying recursive loop, a digital interface predicated on the cinematic eye, which almost universally enables the production of new video.

A final element of *Man with a Movie Camera* worth discussing is its self-reflexive inclusion of the movie camera itself as a character within the film. Cultural critic Malcolm Turvey has explored the anthropomorphizing of the movie camera: "Emerging on its own onto a bare stage, the camera proceeds to walk about on its tripod *like a human being*, carefully displaying its limbs to the appreciative audience within the film and almost bowing to the audience in the process."[57] He goes on to suggest that Vertov does this to exalt the superiority of the camera eye to the human eye, quoting Vertov:

> The mechanical eye, the camera, rejecting the human eye as crib sheet, gropes its way through the chaos of visual events, letting itself be drawn or repelled by movement, probing, as it goes, the path of its own movement. It experiments, distending time, dissecting movement, or, in contrary fashion, absorbing time within itself, swallowing years, thus schematizing processes of long duration inaccessible to the normal eye.[58]

Thus, the camera more than merely duplicates the work that the eye performs. It goes beyond to create new ways of sensing its surroundings, interpreting time and space, and ordering and making sense of the world. In other words, it is an apparatus that can be used as a spatio-temporal research tool. It is this same thinking that undergirds the practice we call filmic sensing.

The fact that the cinematic eye has become a universal way of seeing levels the methodological playing field, since all the disparate disciplines that comprise the urban humanities come together in using video as a kind of lingua franca. Perhaps most important has been the recent emergence of new media, enhanced through digital and networked means, allowing for the rapid use of the camera as an urban sensing device, and enabling footage to be transcoded into database formats for rapid organizing, recalling, remixing, georeferencing, and disseminating. As user-generated, networked, and social-media-shared, video has become ubiquitous, and its use has become a novel method for comprehending the spatio-temporal realities of contemporary urban life.

Filmic Sensing: An Essay Film and Sensory Ethnography Mashup

If the history of the medium of motion pictures already demonstrates the latent qualities that make it ripe for scholarly use, then what are the practices making these qualities extant, transforming a broad field into the specific practice of filmic sensing? We propose that the answer lies, in part, in the combination of an experimental film genre and an experimental scholarly methodology, namely, essay film and sensory ethnography. Filmic sensing pulls methods, values, concepts, forms, aesthetic qualities, and practical considerations from these two realms to produce a uniquely urban humanist practice.

The essay film is an ill-defined genre, often floating somewhere between documentary and a cinematic autobiography, where the filmmaker (often an auteur) creates a voice-over that reads like an essay. Essay films often include experimental and fictive qualities, typified by the already discussed *Man with a Movie Camera*, as well as *Los Angeles Plays Itself*, in which director Thom Andersen narrates a history of the city and of cinema entirely through clips of Los Angeles as represented in film. Another essay film relevant to urban humanities is Chris Marker's 1983 *Sans Soleil*. The 100-minute film splices between footage of disparate locations, focusing on scenes from Japan and Guinea-Bissau, but also including Iceland, San Francisco, and other locales. Over the beautiful and often dizzying visuals is the voice-over of a disembodied woman reading letters that reflect on the nature of time and space, of the interwoven nature of human existence between places we may be seeing, but also within the maze-like quality of our minds and memories. All the film's sound is asynchronous, including the narration, the ambient sounds, and the Mussorgsky composition after which the film is named.

Film critic Andrew Tracy has noted that while cinema, like many artistic media, has sought pure autonomy, the essay film returns the medium to the ground of our world at large: "What will distinguish the essay film . . . is not only its ability to make the image but also its ability to interrogate it, to dispel the illusion of its sovereignty and see it as part of a matrix of meaning that extends beyond the screen."[59] The film is at once a rigorously constructed database of places and ideas, and a poetic, impressionistic filter. It offers an example for the exploration of space/time by urban humanists, layering text, sound, and image.

Cultural theorist Eric Cazdyn has identified an additional critical element that endears *Sans Soleil*, essay film, and video to urban humanist work: its ability to incorporate reflection on the future, on the generative, the unimagined, and the impossible. He describes how Marker's film begins provocatively with light (a white image of children in Iceland) but yields to black. He writes:

The condition of cinema, not only in terms of narrative development (the black before the beginning (or as beginning) and the black after the ending (or as ending), but the black theatre (the historical space of consumption) and the materiality of the film stock (the black separating each frame). Black is the absent cause of all film and, more self-consciously, is the absent cause of *Sans Soleil*.[60]

The black-without-light in Marker's film represents the starting point for urban humanities, which seek to open unknown possibilities through fused practices. This radical openness is a critical component of making scholarly work speak toward the future.

If the essay film brings a logic of self-reflexive futurity, sensory ethnography brings the foundations of experiential knowledge to filmic sensing. Sensory ethnography charts a path through the evolution of ethnography, geographic theories of space and place, notions of the mind and embodiment, and the politics of the self and the other, according to cultural and media scholar Sarah Pink. Firmly embedded within the norms of academic work, sensory ethnographers reach into the filmmaker's toolkit to deploy the affordances provided by sound and moving picture media. Attention to experience also offers a theoretical frame for understanding why these media are so fruitful for urban and spatio-temporal studies. Pink explains why the experiential and the sensorium, as well as the use of media that can capture these elements, are critical:

> The implication of understanding knowing as situated in practice is that it implies that to "know" as others do, we need to engage in practices with them, making participation central to this task. The idea can be extended to seeing "knowing in practice" as being an embodied and multisensorial way of knowing that is inextricable from our sensorial and material engagements with the environment and is as such an emplaced knowing. Although it is possible to speak or write about it, such knowing might be difficult to express in words. This is one of the challenges faced by the sensory ethnographer seeking to access and represent other people's emplacement.[61]

In other words, sensory ethnography provides a lens through which we can see the sensory and material realities of contemporary society, which often go ignored. Perhaps even more important, it offers scholars a means to engage, blurring or erasing problematic boundaries between "researcher" and "subject." Since these insights are difficult to convey through conventionally written texts, they demand alternative media such as video for their documentation and conveyance.

Many of the practitioners who have shaped sensory ethnography have emerged from Harvard's Sensory Ethnography Lab, including filmmaker J. P. Sniadecki, whose experimental videos explore and document the dynamic landscape of contemporary China. One of his films, *People's Park*, codirected with Libbie Cohn, consists of a single, continuous long shot as the two sensory ethnographers wind their way through Chengdu's central, eponymous public space. Their only piece of equipment is a jerry-rigged mobile tripod, a wheelchair with filmmaker, camera, and protruding microphones. The seventy-eight-minute video has no apparent plot, but it has a clear rhythm that ebbs and flows as the camera moves through the park among flora, architecture, cicadas (heard but not seen), park visitors exercising, old men playing board games, and elderly dancers. As viewers of the video, we find ourselves, inexplicably, on the edge of our seats in this slow-moving web, as our mind struggles to build connections and identify patterns, as we spot a repeat character or determine the source of some audio feature. The movie comes to a climax as we weave our way through older retirees dancing to a throbbing beat in the middle of the park, a large crowd gathered to watch them, and by extension, to watch us (figure 3.14). Most of the dancers are women, many of whom dance with each other, but one silver-haired man sensually moves his body to the beat and begins to lean backward, bending over impossibly as the camera rotates around him, and just as he makes eye contact with us through the lens of the camera, we cut to black.

People's Park asks us to do some of the work, placing us within an immersive audiovisual and sensorial experience that we must process, decode, and interpret, rather than handing us precooked "findings" as might be typical in an academic article. In this way, it subverts typical understandings of scholarly media, and even of the distinctions between expert and layperson, providing us here with Eric Cazdyn's black screen, an open space where both

3.14 Still from *People's Park*, dir. J. P. Sniadecki, showing the "dancing grannies" of Chengdu, 2012. Credit: Libbie D. Cohn and J. P. Sniadecki

endings and new futures can be imagined. It situates the viewer as first person, moving through the space of the park, interacting and even building a rapport with the figures we see on the screen. The interaction between the filmmakers and the camera, the people in the park, and the park as place creates a discursive space, where embodied and emplaced knowledge become manifest: *we* dance with the silver-haired gentleman. The film provides us with a platform for what Pink calls "knowing in practice."[62]

If essay film provides us with a formal strategy for creating Clifford Geertz's thickness, layering datapoints of image, sound, and text; and if sensory ethnography provides us with a means to point scholarly attention to capturing and conveying a full, embodied ethnographic sensorium, the urban humanities ask what a fusion of these two genres would look like. How can the apparatus of the camera be used as a scholarly tool for sensing the spatio-temporal intricacies of urban life? Its product, like these genres, would serve in many ways to unite the long distinction held between abstract, mental, conceptual space with material, embodied, sensorial space. As art and architecture theorist Caroline Jones suggests, such sensorially and scholarly synthetic practice "dreams that we can come to feel the body pulsing in tandem with its prosthetic extensions and microscopic addenda, that we can learn to partner our proliferating technologies in increasingly coordinated, supple, and critically conscious ways."[63] Filmic sensing is the extension of the eye, the ear, and in turn, the mind, enabled through a video camera, so that we might document, interpret, and convey our contemporary urban surroundings anew.

Hallelujah Anyway: Sensing Life in the City

To find an example of a protofilmic sensing, we might look to New York-based artist Neil Goldberg. His oeuvre spans many media and decades, but his video work over the past twenty years demonstrates a profound sensitivity to place, embodiment, and self-reflexivity, which are indicative of filmic sensing practices. There is also a peculiarly dark optimism that runs through Goldberg's work, typified within an early series of video projects titled *Hallelujah Anyway*—a title that Goldberg notes came from a poem whose content didn't quite live up to the yearning promise of its title. In *Hallelujah Anyway No. 2*, we see a series of short video clips of New York City shopkeepers rolling up the protective metal grilles that protect their glass windows from vandals; the roll-up doors themselves are covered in graffiti. *Hallelujah Anyway No. 4* maintains the same structure, short clip after short clip of elderly New Yorkers struggling up the few yet epic stairs onto a public bus. Each clip has a database-like quality: the collection and repetition of a particular phenomenon in urban space, a demonstration of temerity, and the continuity of everyday life despite hardship and frailty.

In many of Goldberg's projects, the video camera zoom is used to capture nuances that observation by the unaided eye might not capture, similar to the way in which a professional golfer might use a video camera to record a swing. In *Salad Bar*, Goldberg captures the facial expressions of New Yorkers who decide to get a carry-out lunch from a salad bar, noting that he "found their expressions tender, a little sorrowful, and also somehow brutal, reflecting both the vulnerability created by our need for food and also the ruthlessness required to attain it." In *Ten Minutes with X02180-A*, he follows the facial expressions of visitors to the

Brooklyn Botanic Garden, who lean in for a sniff of plant number X02180-A—in this case, translating the elusive olfactory sense into video form. And in another project, *Missing the Train (Uptown F at West 4th Street)*, Goldberg abandons moving images, opting instead for the intensive focus of video stills that capture facial close-ups of subway commuters who missed their train.

Perhaps Goldberg's work is best exemplified by his project *Surfacing*, which demonstrates all of these qualities. In this aggregate database of serial video clips, each shows a close-up of an urban commuter's face, one after another, as they climb from the subway below to surface on the street (figure 3.15). We see diversity yet universality, as their faces convey a shared pattern: a stone-cold expression, which lets up for the shortest of moments with a squint into the sun and a confused turn of the head, left and right, giving way to reorientation. The urban demeanor, a fighter's face, returns as each person steps off into the city. It is a shared moment of everyday experience that, apart from Goldberg's careful documentation and video work, would never have been noticed and named—yet upon seeing the third "surfacer" in the video, we immediately gather what is happening, we immediately recognize the pattern to which we too have belonged.

Our filmic sensing work in urban humanities has been informed by Goldberg, his projects, as well as other moving-image theorists and videographers. Sending researchers into the field with cameras and video recorders to document, sense, and experience a uniquely mediated urban landscape has been as important as processing, discussing, and editing captured footage to produce ethnographic and analytic videos on specific sites. In one student project titled "1寰9格3核3," for example, researchers blended sensorial and ethnographic footage captured at the site of a historic abattoir turned cultural cluster in Shanghai with fictional interpretations of the lacunae in the building's history and development, producing a video that is partway between scholarship and video art that gets at many of the spatial and experiential qualities so often left uncaptured in academic literature (see Project D: 1寰9格3核3).

Filmic sensing also provides the performative conveyance of documentation and analysis, which otherwise might be transmitted

a)

b)

c)

3.15 Stills from *Surfacing*, 2010–2011. Credit: Neil Goldberg

through dry texts that fail to reach a wider public audience. Moving image documentation can combine spatial ethnographies, thick maps, historical footage, data, and narratives. One of the most compelling aspects of video methods is that practically all students are experienced with the technology, given social media practices. And like maps, videos are a common format to so many fields that they serve interdisciplinary scholars well.

Experimental Urban Humanities Practices

While we have presented three of the most well-developed, utilized, and productive practices of the urban humanities—spatial ethnography, thick mapping, and filmic sensing—there is also a range of more experimental practices that remain only partially developed yet promising in what they have to offer. We describe these experimental practices here as in-progress, incomplete, and extensible experiments that we invite others to take on, refine further, or even discard in efforts to explore as yet uncharted experimental practices. The idiosyncratic nature of urban humanities—so dependent on the specific site and city, the particular collaborators with their strengths and interests, and a constantly changing point in time—demands that the field's practices are tailored to the work at hand, and that new practices are always being explored.

Socially Engaged Art and Artistic Research

Artistic projects have served as useful precedent studies for urban humanities from Ron Rael's border walls to Neil Goldberg's videos and Rebecca Solnit's maps. Mentally and conceptually framing urban humanities work as "art" is a useful way of liberating our practices from fixed academic methodologies, opening them up to rigorous yet more creative, fluid experiments. Indeed, the history and typological diversity of artistic work provides a theoretical starting point for various explorations in urban humanities. Socially engaged art—at times referred to as social practice or participatory art—and artistic research are but two types of art that have proven particularly fruitful.

Socially engaged art is a field that has long existed at the fringes of the art world, since the "happenings" of the group Fluxus or the installation of a fully functioning restaurant in New York's SoHo neighborhood by artist Gordon Matta-Clark and others, all in the 1970s. Art theorist Grant Kester has described such projects as existing in a liminal space between art and activism: the aesthetics of socially engaged art demand not only visual considerations but also an ethics of interpersonal action, often occurring through conversation but also through protest, political action, or even projects that might appear as though they are an urban planning undertaking.[64] Claire Bishop has also staked a claim in this theoretical terrain, arguing for the importance of agonistic action for socially engaged art to retain its political potency. She cites artists such as Santiago Sierra who is known for several pieces in which he hires local marginalized individuals from wherever the current art biennial is, and pays them to perform meaningless tasks, such as having a line tattooed on their back, or sitting underneath cardboard boxes.[65] Such actions are seen as ethically problematic, yet for Bishop and Sierra it is precisely this ambivalence that is able to dramatically highlight the problematic nature of work, pay, and capitalism.

The use of socially engaged art in urban humanities aligns more neatly with Kester's notion of the practice that sees action as art and aesthetics as ethics, exploring the multiplicity of ways in which human interaction can simultaneously operate on symbolic and material registers. Art has the capacity for producing new means of communication and action between individuals, and for framing political action or everyday urban space in poetic and symbolic terms. These two capacities are useful when difference encounters difference, as is so often the case when a scholar enters a new space with the best of intentions toward some political action or end. Socially engaged and participatory art requires a reciprocal interaction and engagement in the same way that urban research ought to operate in more porous and multidirectional terms, as we discuss later in chapter 5. We reject Bishop's version of participatory art as useful for urban humanities because of the way in which it requires an "art world" to function.[66] Her commanding analysis is certainly valuable for framing a particular genre of art, yet it is one that largely isolates art from other aspects of the social and material world.

The work of social practice artist Suzanne Lacy is instructive in demonstrating the possibilities that socially engaged art provides to urban humanist inquiry and intervention. Lacy conducted a series of projects in Oakland, California, over the course of ten years from 1991 to 2001, each of which explored youth politics and culture through the practice of her art. The artworks' boundaries with regard to authorship, form, and audience, however, cannot be easily identified. In one project, over one hundred cars, half red "youth" cars and half black-and-white police cars, were arranged on the roof of Oakland's City Center West Garage along with discussion circles where youth, police, and community members discussed youth needs, ways to address police hostilities toward youth, while painting a broader understanding of safety and fear in the neighborhood. Numerous video production teams live-produced videos of the event that streamed through some thirty monitors, and the entire performance culminated with forty teenage dancers who drew together the whole crowd in music and movement as everyone filtered down from the roof.

This project, *Code 33: Emergency Clear the Air!* (figure 3.16), was framed as an art performance and has been written about in art publications and presented in art galleries and museums. Yet its presentation was largely after the fact: *documentation* of the actual artwork is what was presented and collected, while the performance, participation, and experience are what constituted the work. What is the medium—the students? The cars parked on the rooftop? The students and the police? The conversation? The project, like all successful socially engaged art projects, lacks easy definition. The project was aesthetically and visually scripted; however, it was also important that the conversations were meaningful and educational. Putting time and effort into constructing a valuable "lesson plan" with the use of distinguished faculty and teachers constituted an important artistic "technique" for the work. And the project also demonstrates the way in which a socially engaged artwork can make a real political intervention,

3.16 Art and politics performed in *Code 33: Emergency Clear the Air!* (1997–1999) Suzanne Lacy, Unique Holland, and Julio Morales. Photo credit: Kelli Yon

while also—or perhaps even because of—its framing as art allowed for the construction of a new space where conversations and interactions could unfold, and which would have otherwise been off limits.

Networked Mixed-Media Installations

Another experimental practice involves two distinct yet interrelated elements: material installations and web-enabled platforms. These are particularly apt for urban humanities, since they intervene in the world and simultaneously connect to virtual audiences, narratives, and databases. Physical installations use the tangible, disparate media and materials of urban humanities—mappings, histories, objects, architectures—and put them into conversation with one another by curating space within the city itself or in the context of a gallery exhibition. There are considerations of materiality, so often underappreciated within the textual emphasis of scholarship, as well as of the relationship between "scholar" and "public." New discursive spaces are created as installations are built and as the public interacts with both the material objects and the scholars face to face. Web-enabled platforms, on the other hand, act as a kind of installation in virtual space, deploying the capabilities afforded by information and computer technologies, networked cultures, and social media to produce audiovisual interventions in the discursive and public spheres, and often making a meaningful social impact.

The possibilities embedded within digital and especially networked space allow for a mixing of media, producing thickness through the layering of text, sound, image, and interaction. Web-enabled platforms provide yet another means for scholarly work to engage new publics and to experiment with alternative—albeit digital—materialities. Here, too, new discursive spaces are formed. By returning to Lev Manovich's idea that Vertov's *Man with a Movie Camera* was an early exemplar of the database in new media, we find the genealogy of networked new media installations currently being explored in urban humanities. Their ability to visualize a database, their experimental and experiential capacities, and their newly participatory and networked nature, reflective of our contemporary social and urban life, are mediated in unique ways through projects.

Two groundbreaking projects that capitalize on new networked technologies and computing power available through big data include *The Real Face of White Australia* and *YAMP* (the Yale AIDS Memorial Project). In *The Real Face*, Kate Bagnall and Tim Sherratt explore the intimate and real human effects of White Australia Policy, a group of laws implemented in the early twentieth century, which restricted immigration and targeted the human rights of Asian Australians. Bagnall and Sherratt used a computer to extract portraits and retain original documents of those individuals targeted from the National Archives of Australia, producing a haunting digital archive and exhibition of portraiture. Many of the faces are from documents related to "dictation tests," which evaluated one's English accent and were used to bar unwanted migrants from entering the country (figure 3.17).

Similarly, the Yale AIDS Memorial Project is a collaborative and hypertextual memorial to those who died during the AIDS epidemic. Established as a nonprofit led by Yale University alumni, the memorial seeks to recuperate the memory and history of the

the real face of white australia

home · about

3.17 *The Real Face of White Australia.* Credit: National Archives of Australia

hundreds of students, faculty, and staff who were often outcast and erased through the progression of the disease. The memorial's design is hyperlinked, organizing a variety of narratives, which are interwoven on the basis of place, time, and activity (either major or occupation). Individuals are also linked with others that they knew, and the project is extensible and participatory, allowing friends and loved ones to submit photos, ephemera, and remembrances (figure 3.18). Both projects exemplify the potential of this experimental practice.

In an urban humanities project, students explored the sport of sumo as one of nine *Ghost Guides to the 2020 Tokyo Olympics* (see Project E). Student teams created guidebooks to reveal an alternative view of Tokyo, in contrast to the promotion of the city that was being deployed for the gaze of the global tourist and Olympics media audience. In this project, students mapped

Poet
Artist
Architect
Writer
Journalist
Musician
Professor
Philanthropist
Banker
Activist
Lawyer
Accountant
Teacher
Playwright
City Planner
Scholar
Art Historian
Museum
Administrator
Psychologist
Administrator
Diplomat

the Frank O'Hara of his generation" according to poet Ted Berrigan. **Frank Moore** was a painter and founding member of **Visual AIDS**, one of the most important groups of AIDS activists in the art world. In all, **Harry Kondoleon** published 18 plays, two novels and two books of poetry. **Jim Brudner** established a prize at Yale that honors individuals who have "made significant contributions to the understanding of LGBT issues or furthered the tolerance of LGBT issues." Architect **James Terrell's** innovative department store designs won the Store of the Year Award four times. **Leonard Raver** created dozens of influential works in a range of modern styles, many of which mixed the organ with electronic sounds and percussion instruments. A talented scholar, **John Boswell** utilized his knowledge of 17 languages in his studies, including Ancient Greek, Catalan, Latin, Church Slavonic, Old Icelandic, classical Armenian

3.18 Screen capture from *YAMP*, the Yale AIDS Memorial Project. Credit: Yale AIDS Memorial Project, yamp.org

a counternarrative to Tokyo's promotional campaign in support of the massive urban change sparked by the Olympics, instead seeking to instate sumo wrestling in the 2020 games. By locating the neighborhood where sumo culture thrives in the city, students designed wooden signage installations to memorialize important histories at specific sites, akin to cultural wayfinding and public history signage. Each sign also incorporated a QR (machine readable) code that linked to a longer story of the wrestlers, the traditions, and the current sumo culture told through a digital platform. For example, in the neighborhood where nearly all sumo wrestlers live and arduously train, a wooden marker might stand at a local café that specializes in the particular diet wrestlers must follow. The digital platform tells about the sumo diet, how it has changed over the years, and which famous wrestlers have dined at the café. The project's intent was to open the possibility of sumo's inclusion in future Olympics by demonstrating its current absence and omission. It marked the sport's significant past and presence in Tokyo, by installing a networked system of both physical and tangible components linked with a digital and web-based platform, which expanded its breadth and potential educational use.

Conclusion

All these practices, from spatial ethnography to the production of digital platforms, share a number of features. First, they are practice and project oriented, encouraging collaborators from disparate backgrounds to come together in the common cause of exploring and understanding the city. Second, they are both process and output, recursively incorporating the methods by which one gathers and processes information, as well as the medium by which one shares and conveys information. Third, they are creative, experimental, and extensible—that is, they skirt the line between scholarship and art, proposing new ways of learning, teaching, and being, just as they also make no claims to be definitive but, instead, allow for change, improvement, and modification. In many cases, we also experiment with flattening hierarchies between students, faculty, public, and audience, uphold rigor as a standard for creative scholarship, and seek small and large means to forward a spatial justice agenda. Urban humanities work, far from being a defined, siloed discipline or specified field, is an ongoing, iterative, in-process, mutating set of projects, methods, and practices. And, finally, these fused practices all share a form of experimental openness to allow engagement by viewers and participants, along with engagement of the future, itself.

The next chapter focuses on this critical quality of urban humanist work, what we term "the generative imperative." It discusses why this quality is so important for scholarship in and on the contemporary city, and how one goes about achieving it.

Project C: Intimate Publics in Golden Gai
Tokyo

3.19   Rendering of typical micro-bar in the Golden Gai neighborhood of Tokyo. Credit: Authors

Brady Collins, Morgan Currie, and Stephanie Odenheimer

Golden Gai, a neighborhood of about one city block, hides within Shinjuku, one of Tokyo's busiest business districts. Golden Gai's unique array of narrow passageways and two- and three-story wooden structures house over 250 tiny bars and restaurants. A haven for criminals and illicit activity in the past, *yokochō* areas like Golden Gai were once considered old fashioned and unsafe, but today are tourist attractions. Though Golden Gai is now a recognized cultural hub and low-key drinking spot, the neighborhood is continuously under threat for redevelopment, with the city citing its structural instability and vulnerability to fire as the key concerns.

We refer to Golden Gai as an "intimate public," a term first coined by Lauren Berlant, who described a collective intimacy based upon common consumption of a commodified culture.

An intimate public challenges prevailing notions of what is private and public to reconsider the relationship between intimate and communal.

Resistance is at the core of an intimate public's identity, serving as the foundation from which it evolves and adapts. In 1960, massive protests took place in Tokyo in opposition to the U.S.-Japan Security Treaty, eventually leading the University of Tokyo to ban student protestors from university grounds. A group of activists transformed several stalls in Golden Gai into small bars, creating a space for suspended students and other protesters to meet and further organize their political resistance. In another form of resistance, urban development has been thwarted thus far in Golden Gai by the highly complex nature of property rights in the neighborhood. According to local bar manager

3.20 Maintenance worker in the Golden Gai neighborhood. Photo credit: Authors

3.21 Visual survey of doorways in the Golden Gai neighborhood. Photo credit: Authors

Mama-san Michiko, Golden Gai's resilience owes much to this condition: "Golden Gai won't disappear easily. In the past there has been pressure, with people trying to force the owners out. The Tokyo government wants this place gone, but there is complexity in the ownership of each building, and it would be hard to track everyone down to get them to leave."

Other key elements of Golden Gai's intimate public identity include routine maintenance as well as caretaking. Plants outside must be watered, trash must be taken out, ice is delivered to each bar in the morning, alcohol must be available to be delivered to a bartender within five minutes, sometimes until 5 a.m. The social atmosphere also requires care. According to one bartender, "My job is to maintain relationships with the clients here. If there's any trouble I mediate conflicts. I've learned to manage people." Whether jazz, punk rock, manga, avant garde film, literature, or sports, often the bar's particular theme not only dictates the interior decor, but the clientele and topic of conversation as well.

This combination of resistance and mainte–nance transforms urban and private commercial space so that individuals can engage one another in a way that is not possible in the public realm. In this sense, the intimacy of an intimate public is a product of these two components and its most desired characteristic.

Project D:

Shanghai

3.22 Stills from student essay film about a former slaughterhouse building in Shanghai. Credit: Authors

Jonathan Banfill, Fang-Ru Lin, and Cameron Robertson

This project is an investigation into the history and memory of Shanghai through the lens of one of its most iconic buildings, the former slaughterhouse that is now simply called 1933 (老场坊) (since it was first built in 1933). It consists of a cross-disciplinary series of inter-linked projects, including visual diagrams, a short fictive narrative piece, as well as a unifying fifteen-minute "essay film." In them, we imagine 1933 (老场坊) acting as magical machine that is able to render different fragmented pieces of the city—images, memories, historical moments, dreams, fantasies, nightmares, and so on—into something new, just as a film projector takes singular images and sutures them together into movement.

How do you understand a building such as 1933 (老场坊)? It is a place whose very structure is experientially confusing and hard to grasp at first entry, with its ramps, curves, and multiple levels. Adding to this is the building's layered history and different incarnations (slaughterhouse, medicine factory, creative cluster) stretching back nearly a century and into multiple eras of Shanghai. Trying to understand this unique building, and the unique city around it, was our group's assignment and challenge.

At the beginning we had to approach building 1933 from afar, virtually researching from Los Angeles. We scoured the web for images, travel articles, and blog posts. From these we found a range of different takes on the building. Some views presented it as fashionable and trendy, a site of Shanghai's new creative culture, while others portrayed it as cold and creepy, full of imagined ghosts and empty spaces. We found historical records, architectural sketches, and academic articles that recounted the building's transformations, as well as other theoretical pieces that added dimensions to our analysis. We also watched multiple films in preparation for our own filmmaking, working through Shanghai's urban cinema and selections from China's New Documentary Film movement, as well as other "essay films."

All these sources combined to give us an initial sense of the place, from which we could start generating larger ideas. We made a list of possible themes we were interested in—for instance, 1933 (老场坊) being a building that collected different fragments of the city and processed them into something new just as it once had processed meat—and worked them out in an early theoretical essay. Though highly speculative, as we had not actually been to Shanghai yet, that essay provided an initial set of ideas that would guide our working process when we arrived in the city, guiding and filtering our group vision.

One lesson that we took from Chinese documentary film was the concept of realistic encounter (xianchang), where rather than controlled direction, the unpredictable spontaneity of reality guides your inquiry. The week we spent working inside 1933 (老场坊) we attempted this, as we engaged with the "reality" of the space through a method of encounter: wandering, talking to people, capturing senses, feelings, and representative images. Most of all, we relied on trusting the synchronicity that occurs from being somewhere and letting a collective intuition, gained through rigorous research, open our eyes to experience.

3.23 Interior of a former slaughterhouse building in Shanghai. Photo credit: Authors

Project E:

Ghost Guides to Tokyo
2020, Ryogoku
Tokyo

3.24　Nine ghost guides created by students in Tokyo, 2017. Credit: Authors

Nick Bruni, Cate Carlson, Pradeep Kannan, and Takashi Obase

In March 2017, urban humanities faculty and students headed to Tokyo in search of past and future Olympics, turning up a host of ghosts and monsters. Of the three Olympic games sited in Tokyo, the first (1940) never fully materialized, the second (1964) went far beyond sports to radically transfigure the city and even the nation, while the third (2020) was taking shape during our year of study. We prepared for fieldwork in Tokyo in traditional academic fashion: we read histories of Tokyo, studied urban transformations that were tied to international events, and watched Japanese films that described city life through moving images. *Gojira/Godzilla* (1954), the best known of these films, opened the door to a long tradition of ghosts and monsters in Japanese folk literature that became a productive metaphor for urban studies.

We collaborated with an impressive, diverse group of Japanese colleagues in Tokyo: a poet, an anarchist woodblock print collective, two different urban research collectives, a renowned author and performer, as well as an architect and an urban studies academic along with their students (see Interlude 2). The chief results from our side of the Pacific were enduring relationships, but also the creation of nine Ghost Guides to Tokyo 2020. Through maps, imagery, data, and narrative, the guides trace itineraries around sites and render the voices of communities that are already and will be further affected by the international event, from homeless groups in Yoyogi Park to fishmongers and operators at the historic Tsukiji Market. The nine projects unfold as chapters of a collective project, a counter-guidebook that offers alternative narratives of the city that the Olympics might otherwise bury. The guides identify the ghosts that will continue to haunt Tokyo after 2020 has passed.

One of the nine ghost guides, the one for Ryogoku, documents the centuries-old sport of sumo in the Ryogoku neighborhood, where wrestlers have lived, trained, dined, and competed for generations. Since sumo was denied entry to the Olympic games (though it was officially proposed and other new sports were added), our team sought to include it in the unofficial Tokyo 2020 games.

For this project, we coordinated our experiences of walking in the neighborhood's public places with digital media, thick mapping, and in situ interventions. For various points of interest in Ryogoku, traditional wooden signage inspired a new design that hosts a QR code, visual icon, and short site explanation. Together a series of signs, a paper map, and a website give visitors interactive, immediate stories of sumo wrestlers and sumo life that would otherwise be inaccessible to outsiders. The QR code links to a website where the provocative, politicized history of wrestling and wrestlers opens another lens on Japan and marks the significance of that history through memorialization. The website entices the viewer deeper into the stories with a wealth of information that includes newspaper reports, biographies, and photographs. The project is a model of craft, storytelling, and urban humanities practices.

3.25 Traditional wooden signage in Ryogoku neighborhood of Tokyo. Photo credit: Authors

3.26 Student project emulating traditional wooden signage in Tokyo. Photo credit: Authors

Interlude 3:

Fukushima

Narratives of a
Nonurban Humanity

Yoh Kawano

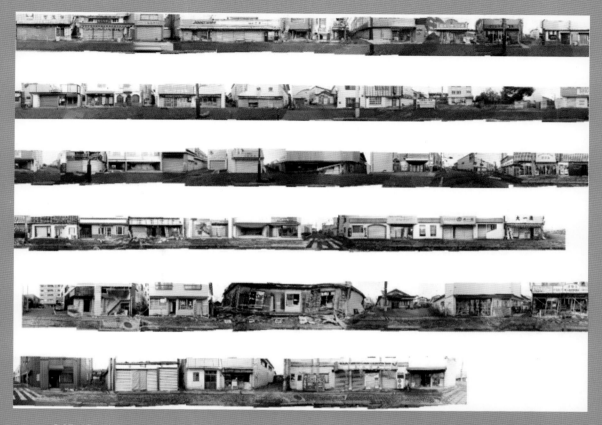

3.27 Visual survey of postdisaster Fukushima. Credit: Authors

In one of the most perilous environments on Earth, an invisible dome encapsulates a twenty-kilometer zone around a crippled nuclear power plant in Fukushima, Japan. The zone is accentuated by its abandonment—long gone are the 150,000 residents who used to live here—and a visit inside this zone reveals a landscape that bears little semblance of the thriving agriculture and fishermen culture that was once the pride of Fukushima (figure 3.27). A small sector at the epicenter of this catastrophe continues to employ as many as six thousand workers a day, mostly men, working feverishly to undo what was supposed to never happen (figure 3.28). The radiation contained within the power plant is so powerful that operators have yet to find a way to remove the melted fuel rods. News footage reveals remote-controlled robots "dying" in their vain attempts to clean up nuclear debris, as well as the seemingly preposterous implementation of the world's largest "ice wall," an underground refrigerator system that consists of 1,500 pillars, each measuring thirty meters in height, plunged into the earth to preemptively freeze any natural groundwater that passes through the nuclear reactors. Each undertaking is pushing scientific boundaries to the limit in its effort to prevent further

3.28 Workers in a postdisaster zone in Fukushima. Photo credit: Authors

radiation leaks, at the same time evoking feelings of a dystopian future bereft of reason. And yet, what is noticeably missing in this spectral place are any other signs of humanity.

When I first set foot in Fukushima's evacuation zone in the summer of 2012, I held a white device with gauges and measurements I couldn't understand at the time. I was in the midst of an otherwise tranquil countryside, a vast expanse of mountains, rivers, rice paddies, shrines, and traditional Japanese homes that quaintly dotted the oceanside. I was also just a few miles away from the Daiichi Fukushima Nuclear Power Plant, site of the world's worst nuclear disaster since Chernobyl. What I did recognize were the audible and visual cues: the high-pitched beeping noises and the oscillating needle moving from left to right, eventually hitting the right edge (thirty microsieverts/hour). The digital screen displayed the word **OVER**, signaling that whatever invisible matter it was monitoring had exceeded the capacity of the device. I was struck by these thoughts: How could something so dangerous be invisible to the human eye? Why have we, as rational human beings supposed to pursue a more desirable livelihood, instead subjected ourselves to such a tragedy? More important, how has this disaster affected the people who were forced to evacuate? And what are the narratives of humanity in this "nonurban" environment?

It would take a tremendous multiyear undertaking that involved a transnational, interdisciplinary academic team to start answering these questions. A collaboration between UCLA and Niigata University was established, and scholars from a variety of fields got together: nuclear science, engineering, medicine, nursing, urban planning, architecture, public health, and agronomy. Our fieldwork inside the evacuation zone would help formulate a comprehensive, multiperspectival understanding of the scientific, political, social, and physical fabrics that emanate from these postdisaster spaces.

Our agenda included multiple visits inside the stricken nuclear power plant, as well as the surrounding communities within the evacuation zone. One of our missions was to test the effectiveness of using spatial ethnography as a method to conduct societal monitoring through a multisensorial depiction of the affected and transformed urban spaces. We coordinated extensive ground-level excursions on predefined paths to scientifically measure radiation levels, collecting millions of datapoints (figure 3.29). We simultaneously photographed, filmed, and recorded sounds to capture and map the visual, sonic, and spatial environment. Data were later correlated with existing and historical airborne radiation levels, creating a visual interaction between at-risk geographies and radiation's impact on human life. The convergence of science (radiation data), coupled with a visual ethnography (photography, video) and verified through cartography (transect routes and GPS receivers) eventually created a layering of interlinked "rich" objects, or a "thick map" that merged transdisciplinary perspectives, prompting an intellectual discourse on the meaning of postdisaster spaces.

But our inquiry does not end here. Frequent visits to Fukushima put us in contact with government officials, nuclear industry leaders, displaced citizens, priests, farmers, teachers, community leaders and children. We discovered a simple way of life that was in an instant transformed by the aftereffects of radiation exposure (figure 3.30). These wounds run deep and linger on many years after the disaster zone's collective abandonment. While the nation's leadership pro-

3.29 Measuring radiation levels amid the rubble in Fukushima.
Photo credit: Authors

claims that "everything is under control," displaced citizens are forced to come to terms with their fragmented lives, while lamenting the loss of human relations that will never be restored.

Our focus is shifted to the social, political, and sensorial aspects of postdisaster spaces: how are the people affected, how are spaces redefined, and how are those held culpable asked to undo what they have done? As much as some disasters are based on human error, so too, must the road to recovery be based on a humane response that brings the voices of contesting parties onto the same platform. The approach of using visual ethnography forces each party to confront the realities of the others, where therapeutic planning can plant the seeds for mutual learning and understanding. Such knowledge can offer valuable insights into the recovery process, elucidate the impact of prolonged trauma, and bring forth the narratives of survival and reconciliation, exposing the issues needed to set new policy agendas, and persuading the global community to reevaluate the hidden perils and consequences of human-made disasters.

3.30 Former sea wall in Fukushima breached by the tsunami. Photo credit: Authors

4
The Practical Future

For urban humanities, to imagine spatial justice in the city means to undertake historical analysis, contemporary cultural and social interpretation, and speculative thinking. This is a generative practice, in which past and present inform speculations about the future.

While the demarcations of disciplines such as history and cultural studies may be productively contested, the disciplinary terrain of the future is decidedly more ambiguous, without a shared theoretical or methodological foundation. The past not only has its own field—history—it also has a piece of many other fields (such as art history, history of philosophy, history of science, and so forth). Similarly, the present is studied in a wide range of fields such as cultural studies, sociology, psychology, and anthropology. The future has no such purchase or reciprocity, although a number of professional fields—from architecture and planning to social welfare and public policy—certainly aim to intervene in the present for the sake of creating a more just, equitable, and better future.

While the disciplines of urban planning and architecture incorporate historical knowledge and social science methodologies, their intrinsically forward-looking perspectives give rise to valid, critical questioning within the humanities. If architecture is, in some sense, always trying to reimagine a better world, it does so through design practices that embed tacit assumptions about the occupants of its plans. Similarly, planning and its subspecialties translate metrics into plans and policy that will inevitably have both intended and unintended consequences for diverse populations. These virtual proclamations about how daily life should unfold produce genuine disciplinary friction, especially among humanists, who interrogate the justification for making such claims, the grounds for the designer's or planner's agency, and most vociferously, the assumptions regarding the users. Who, exactly, are these designs and plans for? As a result, imagining future implications for the city is one of the urban humanities' most challenging—but potentially most constructive—components, producing explicit terms, positions, and frames for debate. What we call the "generative imperative" signals the importance of experimental, studio-based work that is propositional rather than merely critical, prioritizes interdisciplinarity over specialization, and pursues a project orientation as the avenue to a broader understanding of the urban.

Urban humanities contend that we engage with speculation about the future in a way that can withstand substantive critical inquiry. Yet this perspective of engaging with, designing for, and speculating about the future is so underdeveloped within the humanities that it can be difficult to move from well-articulated debate to rigorous, creative, forward-moving thinking. Perhaps this is because the hallmark of academic work is mainly a critique that often remains within scholarly discourse when, as we argue here, it could be more productive if pushed into the public sphere. This is not to say that there aren't already many compelling examples that link intellectual scholarship with activism. Philosopher Angela Davis, for example, not only stands against the prison-industrial complex but imagines a world without prisons;[1] sociologist Manuel Castells lends power to his substantive critique of neoliberal urbanism through studies of alternative, cooperative communities;[2] writer Octavia Butler builds worlds with alternative forms of humanity, kinship, and social structures—forms that move beyond racial violence and economic stratification.[3] These future-oriented projects advance what is currently "unthinkable," precisely so that it can be thought out.

Widely accepted models of futurity exist even in architecture and planning; theories and methods for speculative thought range from utopianism to participatory planning. Relatively recently, voices from literature and history have articulated new logics intended to incite greater social and political agency within their fields. Building on Hannah Arendt's concepts of "natality" and "insertion,"[4] for example, literary scholar Amir Eshel argues for the importance of human agency linked with poetic language in his explorations of postwar and contemporary world literature and visual arts. The possibility of a "new beginning" points to the importance of human action and an open horizon of possibilities for change in the wake of the catastrophes wrought by the totalitarian regimes of the twentieth century.[5] As Eshel writes, futurity is "the potential of literature to widen the language and to expand the pool of idioms we employ in making sense of what has occurred while imagining who we may become."[6]

In this chapter, we will explore a handful of such practices to demonstrate that engaging with the future may be fraught but is not without precedent. To act by proposing even a fragment of the world we want to live in means we must inspect the spatial justice and injustice embedded in future designs, asking not only who we might be planning for, but also who is involved in the planning itself. Such scrutiny intrinsically involves checking our own privilege and assumptions. The power dynamics underlying speculations about the future are dangerous in so far as they remain tacit and raising them to the surface is a necessary starting point. Healthy, pervasive skepticism, a hallmark of modernity's criticality, however, can also serve as a roadblock to constructive agency. Scholars, in contrast to professional practitioners, can more readily take refuge in astute critique that reveals flaws in every potential action. And professions like architecture and urban planning have sometimes advanced futures that were numb to or had entirely misread social issues, as the history of urban renewal shows, or that serve the status quo without concern for equity or inclusivity.

For urban humanists, both postures are problematic, precipitating the "generative imperative" as a call to action or, put more strongly, a responsibility to speculate.[7] Academics and creative professionals are urged to engage with the future in a particularly imaginative way, a practice that engenders open, creative potentials in place of critical dystopias thrust at a weary society. In what follows, we pose several practices by which one might fulfill this generative imperative, including the idea of "immanent speculation," or drawing out from the fabric of already existing reality the futures that should and could happen, linking speculation to discourses on imagination and ethics. Such practices can be found in unexpected territories, from utopian proposals and science fiction to environmental or other highly politicized art installations. We continue by applying Hayden White's notion of the "practical past" to discuss the notion of the "practical future," a rigorous imagining of "what might come" that applies practical knowledge to our present moment and draws on the wealth of historical knowledge to shape and enlighten contemporary action. We conclude by discussing what speculation about the future, or futurity, may mean within the context of the urban.

Thinking Ahead, across Fields

The creative potential of an urban humanist to engage with the future is not reliant upon innate talent, empathetic capacity, or prophetic vision. Instead, it needs something that can come from anyone: the commitment to practice the future, a willingness to systematically engage with imaginative possibilities and tactics to effect changes. But before we delve more deeply into a practice that might be claimed as especially urban humanistic, what are the related ways of engaging with the future found in other disciplines?

Perhaps the most established practice of urban speculative thinking is the utopian tradition, which began with Thomas More in the early sixteenth century and most recently flourished in the postwar period among neo-avant garde conceptual architects like Archigram (figure 4.1), Constant, Kikutake, and Yona Friedman. Narrative utopias put forward imaginaries that served to critique the present more than act as a blueprint for a place that was meant to manifest in reality—as the very etymology of the term "utopia," or "no place" suggests. By contrast, material utopias, or what urban scholar Lewis Mumford referred to as "utopias of construction," seemed shackled with intrinsic problems.[8] These problems include the need to isolate the utopian community from the rest of society, a concomitant disregard for the existing city, the tendency toward totalitarianism, and a guiding ideological singular purpose (e.g., leisure, equality, adaptability, education), to name a few. If and when a utopia is built, those same problems return with a vengeance.

Architecture's experiments to create better worlds often followed the logic of modernism, which posited that a new city,

4.1 "A Walking City" by Ron Herron for Archigram, 1964. Credit: The Museum of Modern Art, Licensed by SCALA, Art Resource, NY

one started from scratch and dominated by speed, technology, flexibility, and functionalism, could produce social transformation. The top-down organization of these schemes enabled the sites' repressive character. As architectural theorist Reinhold Martin notes:

> As so much critical social thought has demonstrated, state-based programs for the care and management of populations were notorious disciplinary sites. From housing to prisons to schools to hospitals, such sites were recognized as arenas for the reproduction of institutionalized norms that managed desire, suppressed dissent, and propagated a whole host of unfreedoms. Still all of these institutions . . . remain contested sites for the enactment of social justice.[9]

Modernist experiments took place in cities across the globe, from Tripoli and Chandigarh (figure 4.2) to Mexico City and St. Louis. These material utopias were variously flawed, which led to wide-ranging critiques of modernism as well as its utopian aspirations. The critical backlash remains so vehement that it has been difficult to separate modern architecture from utopian thought, to recuperate what might be of value from the latter (or the former). In a range between trivial and profound, all architectural work seeks to make the world a better place, or as Rem Koolhaas said, "every architect carries the utopian gene."[10]

Reimagining the future has also emanated from environmentalism most notably demonstrated in Ian McHarg's optimistic ecological approach for landscape architecture beginning in the 1960s (figure 4.3). Another direction for postmodernist utopian thinking is taken by intentional alternative communities such as Christianopolis in Denmark or Burning Man in the Nevada desert. From the perspective of urban humanities, both environmental and communitarian utopian thought hold valuable lessons, but they fundamentally require a tabula rasa model of development from scratch. If contemporary urban utopian thinking can gain traction, the historical lessons suggest that it will take root in existing cities, as a fragment rather than a holistic model. This fragment can be spatial, temporal, or both—and it operates as an experimental model that can grow or spread to other areas.

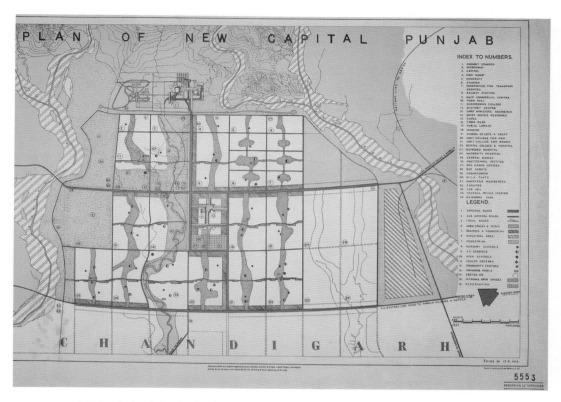

4.2 Le Corbusier's plan for Chandigarh, India, 1951. Image credit: © F.L.C./ADAGP, Paris/Artists Rights Society (ARS), New York 2019

4.3 The Woodlands, a planned community in Texas designed by McHarg.
Credit: Rick Kimpel, 2007. Sourced from Flickr

The architect and urban designer Roger Sherman has proposed an "if, then" logic for practices of engaging the future, one that is often used within architecture and urban design, albeit implicitly. Drawing on theories of complex adaptive systems and game theory, he notes the increment of a "change-inducing factor," which can be tracked through myriad interconnections, causes, and effects to play out a series of futures that this factor can engender. And, in reverse, we might imagine a future and work backward toward a change-inducing factor that can be designed and deployed—as Sherman says, "it is doubtful that design can ever 'express' future change . . . therefore, all the architect can do is 'set (design) the trap' to capture potential change."[11] Imagine, for example, that the emergence of autonomous vehicles may result in any number of possible futures: the elimination of private cars, the eradication of parking that is no longer necessary for continuously moving vehicles, the control of transportation by a handful of companies that only lease rather than sell cars, or the exacerbation of global warming because these companies are jointly owned by the fossil fuel extraction industry. But, then, imagine in reverse a landscape with no traffic, no pollution, and universal access to affordable transportation on the basis of autonomous vehicles. How, then, must the increment of the autonomous vehicle be designed, with all its materiality, urban, and socio-political embeddedness, to work toward that better future? If we can imagine it, we would want to "set a trap" for the future of pollution-free universal access and blockade the corporate-controlled scenario. This might entail focusing on solar-powered vehicles, vehicles designed for mass transit, and streets that accommodate cyclists, pedestrians, and autonomous public transit.

When imagining an if-then scenario set in motion by a change—say, for instance, a new building that is being planned—the designer is at some level narrating a fictional future. The narrative is a risk-free testbed, where material changes in the world are imagined but not effected. When architects design buildings, for example, they project into their drawings "doors swinging, drawers being pulled, corridors full of racing feet, people falling down unexpected steps, or jamming on landings."[12] And if such fictions are particularly thoughtful and intensive, the architects hope to avoid unforeseen consequences.

Deyan Sudjic, in *The Language of Cities*, states that "cities are formed as much by ideas as they are by things; in either case more often than not they are the product of unintended consequences."[13] The task for the urban humanist is to ground such ideas in rigorous, extensive study and to engage this work in propositional activity that grapples with these "unintended consequences." This territory is fraught with danger because the very underpinnings of academic credibility are called into question, threatening values of objectivity, the use of unbiased methods, and the ability to weigh contrasting views. The danger stems from adding a new register to our interpretive structures, so that we are looking not only at what has transpired and is currently occurring, but also into the future.

Another genre of narratives that engages the future is science fiction. Leaving aside the recent, vast, and exciting literature around world building, two tactics that stand out were explored by literary critic Darko Suvin.[14] The first tactic is estrangement: What are the realities that we face in our own contemporary world that are so daunting, or taken for granted, that the only way in which we can engage them is to take them out of our world, and put them into another? This same presumption is at the base of social theorist Karl Mannheim's deployment of utopia as a means to step outside all-encompassing ideological frameworks.[15] Indeed, science fiction has been used time and again to deal with the most intractable problems of difference, othering, and identity found in American society. In popular media, *Star Trek* and *X-Men* deal with "aliens" and "gifted youngsters," respectively, to engage readers (and watchers) with the notion of a future where questions of tribalism and learning to live with people unlike ourselves are pressing issues. Within the literature of Afrofuturism, the science fiction stories of Octavia Butler, such as the *Xenogenesis* trilogy, present characters who resist binary gender categories and have hybrid characteristics that are not only multiracial but also multispecies. Drawing on the deep histories of racial and economic violence, Butler's speculative fiction imagines alternative futures that both confront and resist the violence of the past by imagining possibilities for social and kinship structures out of the ruins of human-wrought catastrophes.

The second of Suvin's tactics is the novum: the framing of a hypothesis on the basis of a single new thing, which then has a dizzying array of consequences played out to their logical extreme. The most famous novum, perhaps, is that of time travel as explored in many works, from H. G. Wells's *The Time Machine* to the 2012 film *Looper*. But any number of other novums have been explored, from the ability to use the entirety of the brain (found in movies like *Limitless* or *Lucy*) to the presence of human-like AI (found in several of Isaac Asimov's books, or in the classic *Blade Runner*). The novum is similar to Sherman's change-inducing factor but here the focus is on exploring the logical implications of such a factor, rather than reverse-engineering the factor itself. This practice is especially useful for exploring the moral, ethical, and philosophical implications of a new technology, which are so often presented as value-neutral benefits to society rather than factors that have the potential to ameliorate or (more often) exacerbate the worst qualities of human nature and, in turn, society.

The tactics of science fiction engage with the future through narrative, fantasy, and play, but other fields hold their own models for thinking forward, and some of these may be useful to urban humanists. The most rigorously applied practice of the scientific method and inductive research, according to Karl Popper, also requires a leap into the future. As he describes in *Conjectures and Refutations*, the primary distinguishing factor that sets science apart from other human endeavors is, paradoxically, its limits: the best scientific theories are "prohibitions" from particular outcomes (e.g., the theory of relativity means we cannot travel faster than the speed of light); a scientific proposition is one that is limited in its capacity to explain the world (unlike, for example, the totalizing capacity of Freudian and Marxist theories that can explain the entirety of the world and therefore cannot be refuted); and science is distinguished not by its ability to confirm and explain but, rather, its ability to falsify and to test.[16] But at the inception of any scientific project or finding of "refutation" is first a "conjecture." That is, all scientific theories, laws, findings, and wisdom are tentative conjectures, guesses about the way the world operates, which await a future in which they may be falsified. According to Popper, the point is not to develop theories to *explain* the world and its future through scientific prediction. In fact, he specifically cautions that large-scale planning (as witnessed by authoritarian regimes in China and the Soviet Union) is both practically and theoretically unwise, since we cannot plan for the unexpected advances in our knowledge in the future. Instead, he teaches the importance of imaginative proposals and conjectures that may conflict with other proposals and that can evolve and change as they move forward in time.

Finally, moral philosophy and the study of ethics offer guidance to thinking through imaginative or projective scholarship. Kant to some extent distrusted the imagination, and the juxtaposition of imagination against reason persists in philosophical argument. For Kant, the imagination, because of its potential to be dominated by feelings, threatens moral judgment.[17] But according to Jane Collier, philosophers have more recently recognized the importance of imagination, particularly in literature, poetry, and the arts, and in moral deliberation, as long as rationality remains a "safeguard."[18] As she notes, imagination is still characterized as a fundamentally corrupting influence over thought, which reason can protect against.

An alternative formulation of imagination's role in moral judgment, reflected in Eshel's notion of futurity described previously, stems from pragmatism and the work of John Dewey and John Rawls. Dewey reshaped the concept of moral imagination, a phrase coined by Edmund Burke in his *Reflections on the Revolution in France*, as the comprehension of the *actual* in light of the *possible*.[19] In other words, imagination does not mean inventing entirely new objects but supplementing observation through "insight into the remote, the absent, the obscure."[20] To propose the possible, that is, what is absent but potential, is inherently a moral deliberation. Thus, moral imagination enacts both empathy, that is understanding otherness, and what Dewey called "dramatic rehearsal," meaning that moral deliberation is the imaginative process of depicting what is possible. Here, the relevance of architectural design is clear. But rather than dramatic rehearsals, design scenarios can be formulated as dramatic predictions or experiments, in so far as they portray future possibilities so that both their intended and unintended consequences might be foreseen.

The important and defining question that remains is how to adjudicate among pluralistic views, power differentials, contested positions, and contradictory values. That is, if we are to imagine urban futures, how can spatial justice be ensured? Here important precedents stem from the discipline of planning with its deliberative and participatory imaginative practices. From Rawls's theory of deliberative democracy to Chantal Mouffe's agonistic democracy, participatory planning strategies seek to structure discussion of future change in a just manner.[21] Mouffe extends the deliberative model to consider the impossibility of rational consensus in light of the crucial role of impassioned political beliefs. Even what might seem to be the most innocuous community meeting can quickly become a site where strongly held opposing views are voiced. "Mobiliz[ing] passions toward democratic designs" is a goal of agonistic pluralism.[22] Such deliberations are often a mandated part of urban planning processes in order to give representation to affected constituents, but there are no established rules about how the aggregation or accommodation of different views should occur. The political and practical complications of participatory planning are apparent in dominant Not In My Back Yard (NIMBY) planning narratives. NIMBY positions reflect, and ensure, the perseverance of status quo power relationships, which in turn reify racial privilege in a neoliberal economy. White upper middle-class residents, homeowners, long-term community residents, and economically stable residents are all privileged in the participatory process.

Thus, from practices as distinct as science fiction and participatory planning, we can see some of the outlines of how to think about the future. The broad contours of architecture, design, urban planning, literature, film, the social sciences, and positive sciences are full of gestures toward the future. Yet the work of research and intellectual thought often leaves "the practice of the future" as something unsaid, something implicit in our cultures, ways of knowing, and values. The urban humanities recognize the fundamental value and importance of the drive to engage with the future, and call for it to be made explicit and, moreover, prioritized in our all-too-often presentist or rear-facing engagements with the world of "what is."

Practicing the Future

For urban humanists, then, the task is to imagine future possibilities. But what does it mean for scholars to think their work forward? Can we study a place and its everyday life rigorously enough, equitably enough, and compassionately enough to say something about what might be done to improve it, and for whom? Even if there are insufficient grounds to issue proclamations about what ought to change, are the perils of getting it wrong offset by those

of inaction? If we learn about a contentious urban situation—
say, where residents are being evicted along a new transit line—
under what conditions can we venture into the debate with
recommendations? If residents promote some future scenario,
is the engaged scholar required to support it? The questions of
agency, ethics, positionality, power, and spatial justice, prominent
in other chapters of this book, echo loudly and clearly when we
speculate about the future. To this chorus, it is the generative
imperative of the urban humanities that brings a responsible,
engaged, creative, and hopeful imaginary of new possibilities. To
think forward toward a better world without creative direction is
to condemn the future both to trivial adjustments to the status quo
and to competent mediocrity.

We call this grounded imaginative thinking *immanent speculation*. It takes the possibility hidden in plain sight as its starting point.
Paradoxically embedded in our inability to see anything beyond the
present or the past, immanent speculation locates the spark of the
future, the unknown, and the possible within these spaces.

If we are to posit immanent speculation as a fundamental
practice of urban humanities, we must first grapple with the promise
and peril embedded within the term "speculation." And, again, we
can start in our own backyard. Los Angeles is a city made from
an assemblage of speculative practices. Spain colonized the region,
surmising it was unsettled territory to be conquered, and decimated
the Tongva, who had lived here for thousands of years. Later on, as
part of the United States, the region went through a stuttering period
of growth. Boosters proclaimed the magic of Southern California
throughout the Midwest and elsewhere, fueling land speculation,
as gullible investors would repeatedly and blindly bid up land
prices only to discover, more often than not upon a first visit, that
the real estate was essentially worthless. And, of course, people
imagine they know Los Angeles thanks to Hollywood projecting
moving images of fantasy plotlines onto screens around the world.
Each of these moments in history is a variation of speculation—
assumption, financial speculation, and fantasy—that demonstrates
its danger when untethered from reality.[23]

Across from La Placita, the mythical origin point of Los Angeles, is Union Station (figure 4.4). The last of the grand train stations built in the United States, it was approved in 1926 and completed thirteen years later during the throes of the Great Depression and with the world on the brink of war. A large portion of what was then Chinatown was demolished in the process, whitewashing the memory of the largest mass lynching in U.S. history with gleaming Spanish Colonial construction. It is the terminus of a city upon which it seemed almost anyone could project their own minor utopia. Sure enough, in 1938, a bigger, better Chinatown was built about a mile away under the

4.4 Union Station under construction during the summer of 1938. Credit: Dick Whittington, Security Pacific National Bank Collection. Los Angeles Public Library

4.5 New Chinatown in 1939. Credit: Harry Quillen, Harry Quillen Collection, Los Angeles Photographers Collection, Los Angeles Public Library

guidance of community leader Peter Soo Hoo, and with the help of Hollywood set designers in designing its core, Central Plaza (figure 4.5).

To speculate might mean to assume rather than to know based on facts (as in Spain's imposition of a tabula rasa on California), or it might mean to envision historical or fictional realities (as in the imaginative work of Hollywood). There are, of course, endless varieties of financial speculation, such as land speculation or the mining speculation in the goldfields of Northern California and the oilfields around Los Angeles. We might read into Chinatown's destruction an element of racial speculation: that the sullied, foreign, Chinese landscape was envisioned by city boosters as bleached clean, transformed into a gleaming beacon of Anglo LA. But we might also see the inverse of that in a work of speculative fiction such as Karen Tei Yamashita's *Tropic of Orange*, a stunning kaleidoscope of new ethnic formations situated in Los Angeles.[24] Decades of Anglo hegemony in the literature about Los Angeles have given us both Chandler's hard-boiled noir and Didion's upper-middle-class neuroses.[25] Yamashita gives us Bobby: "Chinese from Singapore with a Vietnam name speaking like a Mexican living in Koreatown. That's it." The book spans seven days, with seven narratives moving between Mexico and Los Angeles, just like its eponymous orange, which a character named Arcangel brings across the border. The book straddles magical realism and speculative fiction, suspending our disbelief about any number of perfectly plausible alternative realities for Los Angeles: palm trees as flags for the poor instead of street ornamentation for Beverly Hills, a traffic jam on the Cahuenga Pass as a meticulously conducted symphony, NAFTA as a *luchador* being defeated by *el gran mojado*.[26] Yamashita pulls from her wealth of experience living in Los Angeles to produce a literary form of immanent speculation.

In the university, speculative work most often involves theoretical development, from physics to philosophy. But there are some scholars today who, similar to Yamashita, eschew conventionally understood "academic speculation." This new form of speculation is rooted in race and place insofar as it aims to decolonize. Immanent speculation is the practice of engaging with an inherently unknowable future in order to create the conditions for that future to unfold. It aims to decolonize the future from the forward march of time, from the imperfect conditions of the present, freeing it to become something just beyond what we imagine to be possible. Such speculations are immanent because they are not pulled from thin air, but rather from the sites and places in which we live: the seeds for unimaginable futures can be found in our messy, layered, and imperfect present.

It seems appropriate for immanent speculation, this act long practiced by a subset of artists and storytellers, to find its way into the academy in California's public university. The city of Los Angeles and, indeed, the state at large were shaped by a network of actors who were imagining the future so that it would become their reality. Judged on the empirical and positivist terms common to education, immanent speculation might be seen as a trifling distraction. Yet such speculative trifles, appearing ungrounded while actually dwelling utterly immanent to the spaces and places from which they rise, have the capability to construct not only what we imagine to be our future but, moreover, what we might even conceive of as possible in the future. It is this speculative practice that Percy Bysshe Shelley saw in poetry when he proclaimed, "Poets are the unacknowledged legislators of the world."[27]

At the same time, thinking forward is inherently risky, and there is much at stake both for the future imagined and the one doing the imagining. What are the perils for engaging the future in scholarly work? How might we think through the ethical questions that attend such work, and can we construct a new ethics for such scholarly imagination? The generative imperative abandons conventions (or fantasies) of neutrality by arguing that it is the scholars' ethical responsibility to seriously consider what to "make" of their work. The real and problematic ethical quandary about potential negative impacts of propositional work has led to increasingly attenuated scholarship with a scope so narrowed and emaciated as to ensure its irrelevance. But here we offer the alternative ethical quandary: What damages are wrought by inaction? In urban humanities, the privilege of academic work is checked by deploying scholarly practices in pursuit of spatial justice.

Eric Cazdyn has explored what he calls a "non-moralizing materiality." In the aftermath of the Fukushima nuclear disaster in 2011, Cazdyn reflected on the immense and incomprehensible destruction through a proxy: the banal and weird emergence of the cicadas, their unmistakable and urgent buzz surfacing as usual, coming in and out of audibility, their songs lining their silence and vice versa. To anthropomorphize their behavior, their emergence, their desire to mate, their screaming calls, and their silence, is to set up a moral frame yet it is also to fundamentally not understand them at all. This is a common desire: to frame a situation by our preexisting understanding, rather than its lived materiality. Cazdyn links this parable to the aftermath of the disaster: "To moralize the Japanese disaster, for example, is to focus on the bad leaders, or the failed technology, or the well-mannered victims waiting patiently in food lines, or even on the inevitability of the disaster itself. To materialize the disaster, in contrast, requires not only resisting such a moralizing critique, but also reframing the event in order to mobilize it toward a radically different future."[28]

Here is the possibility of immanent speculation: in scholarly work, so often skewed toward the critical rather than the generative, we actually preclude the possibility of impact by focusing on the moral rather than the material. Rather than moral critiques that find affirmation among those who already agree and are ignored by those who do not, non-moralizing materialism pulls apart the threads of how something is actually existing, working, or acting, and points toward how it might radically change. Attention to banal material things and ordinary spaces of everyday life helps the urban humanist focus on opening a space for alternative futures. Finally, by opening possibilities and making them public, our scholarly engagement is itself available for the kind of critique that furthers the necessary (if not sufficient) collective discussion to advance spatial justice.

In one project conducted by urban humanities students, in LA's sister city of Mexico City, the metro system upon which millions of people take their daily commute is reimagined not as an alienating space to pass through, but as a site of human connection, a destination for performance of the self (see Project F: The Gentegrama Project). This immanent speculation pulls from Mexico City's metro system's prominent station iconography to develop "Gentegrama," a project of reflection upon urbanism, infrastructure, gentrification, and the increasing speed of our socially mediated world.

The Practical Future

Who is the future for? In a set of interrelated essays written at the end of his life, the philosopher of history Hayden White reflected on the ethical stakes of various narrative forms of engagement with the past, suggesting an answer to these questions. He argued that the "historical past"—a dubious narrative construct created by professional historians to organize events into meaningful units—is a product of the nineteenth-century drive to make the discipline of history into a science. Rooted in an objectivist, empiricist logic, these historians believed that past events could be resuscitated by following science-like rules for constructing it as "it really was." In contrast, White argues that the historical past exists "only in books and articles published by professional historians; it is constructed as an end in itself, possesses little or no value for understanding or explaining the present, and provides no guidelines for acting in the present or foreseeing the future."[29] This is because it is an abstracted, distant construct, divorced from contemporary social realities and political exigencies. No one, he goes on to argue, ever "lived or experienced the historical past" since it is constructed ex post facto, from a perspective and with knowledge that historical agents could never have had, let alone ways of organizing or explaining events that draw on later knowledge. Yet this was not always the case: in ancient, medieval, and even modern times, history was a pedagogical, rhetorical, and practical discipline that offered guidance, counsel, and lessons to help answer ethical questions. While there are certainly a great many scholars who continue to practice history in a public and practical fashion, White's provocation coincides with larger arguments and concerns regarding the "professionalization of the academy."[30]

In *The Practical Past*, White probes the origins of the discipline of history's professionalization to critique its inward-focused scientism and to champion, instead, historical writings that come from outside the professional field—in other words, the engagements with history that we might find in art, literature, and folklore—which serve as guideposts for action in everyday life. White's concept of the "practical past"—in contrast to the "historical past"—is borrowed from philosopher Michael Oakeshott and explicitly echoes Kant's notion of practical reason, that is, moral and ethical judgment about what we should and should not do. The practical past, White writes, "refers to those notions of 'the past' which all of us carry around with us in our daily lives and which we draw upon, willy-nilly and as best we can . . . [it] is also the past of repressed memory, dream, and desire as much as it is of problem-solving, strategy, and tactics of living, both personal and communal."[31] In this sense, the practical past is applied, strategic, emotive, and ethical, helping us play out scenarios and providing guidance for thought and action.

We might ask: How might we conceive of a mirror complement, so to speak, to White's defense of the practical past as a way to think about speculation and the future? If we take some imaginative liberties with his text and replace instances of the term "historical" with "speculative" and "history" with "the future," we read something like the following:

> Recent discussion on the periphery of mainstream [speculative] studies has revealed the extent to which "belonging to [the future]" (rather than being "outside of it") or "having a [future]" (rather than lacking one) have become values attached to certain modern quests for group identity. From the perspective of groups claiming to have been excluded from [the future], [the future] itself is seen as a possession of dominant groups who claim the authority to decide who or what is to be admitted to [the future] and thereby determine who or what will be considered to be fully human. Even among those groups which pride themselves on belonging to [the future] (here understood as being civilized) or in having a [future] (here understood as having a real as against a mythical genealogy), it has long been thought that [the future] is written by the victors and to their advantage and that [speculative] writing, consequently, is an ideological weapon with which to double the oppression of already vanquished groups by depriving them of their [speculative possibilities] and consequently of their identities as well.[32]

White's trenchant writing on the historical past might equally be applied to consider the ways in which imaginations of the future have, similarly, been co-opted, colonized, and controlled by particular powers and groups. Any group, and especially scholars and students who purport to desire radical and decolonizing action, must consider the need to rethink *who* can possess the future, and *how* such speculation ought to happen. We argue that White's concept of the practical past is equally informative in constructing a notion of the practical future. We all have a sense of "the future"—what we expect to happen, what we think lies within the realm of possibility, what we hope will come true—and we draw on these conceptions intentionally, and at times subconsciously, when we go about our lives. We use them to guide our decision-making or to help us solve problems as much as they are at times repressed dreams and desires. Where White sought to incorporate writers of historical fiction into the canon of the practical past—Sebald, Hugo, and Flaubert, for example— we might incorporate speculators of the future: Philip K. Dick, Ursula Le Guin, Octavia Butler, and others to enable us to create imaginative frameworks, possibilities, and values that help us construct a more equitable, more accessible, and more democratic future. In other words, the practical future considers ethical questions centrally within speculative thought.

In our preceding "translated" text, we might imagine that professional and expert predictors of the future are in danger of evacuating the future of its possibility by reducing it to abstracted statistics and scientific rules. The future—like the past—is a domain able to be staked out, fought after, and controlled, and as such, it is deeply enmeshed with power dynamics. Ultimately, the practical past and the practical future cannot fully be separated since our human capacities for speculation will always derive from the contingency of our knowledge, the positionality of our ways of seeing and knowing, and our imaginative wells steeped in the logics, epistemologies, and sediments of our times, places, and languages.

Rather than reifying or echoing such power dynamics, White instead draws our attention to the "practical"—that is, ethical— possibilities of fashioning historical narratives, which we might add are always speculative narratives. The practical past, like the practical future, is an approach to storytelling and narrative more generally that foregrounds the ethical question of what we should or ought to do. How, then, are we to use and interpret those speculations of the future that can both open up new possibilities and provide ethical guidance for how to act? Certainly, science fiction, or other speculative forms such as architectural plans, visionary films, and conceptual art are not meant to be read literally as an instruction manual for how to move into the future. They function as modes of emplotment for creating possible futures and in this sense are about the ethics of imagining and making. Perhaps for this reason White concludes with the idea that the practical past is "shifting the burden of constituting a useable past from the guild of professional historians to the members of the community as a whole."[33] Again, we can imagine a version of this statement about the guild of professional scholars responsible for predicting the future, called to open up agency from a preordained future toward a practical future, opening up the possibilities that the future has to offer to those who might have otherwise been excluded from the realm of the speculative "sciences." The practical future, like the practical past, is porous, publicly oriented, ethically engaged, and imaginatively poetic.

Project F: The Gentegrama Project
Mexico City

4.6 Proposal for interactive signage at La Raza Station in Mexico City. Credit: Authors

Alexander Abugov, Thomson Dryjansky, Carlos Guerrero Millán, Ryan Kurtzman, Paloma Olea Cohen, and Danmei (Melanie) Xu

Have you ever been underground with thousands of others? You cram into the same train compartment, while attempting to keep perfect emotional distance from one another. Finally, you step onto the escalator that will resurface you back to the reality above. The station you are about to enter, La Raza, is a transfer station in Mexico City that combines the underground transport for Line 3 and surface rail for Line 5. In envisioning La Raza in future tense, we invite you to reconsider the corridors that you rush through daily instead as a terminal destination where social interaction, interpersonal communication, or even collective disruptions take place.

Gentegrama is an interactive display technology and wayfinding system for the stations of Metro CDMX (Mexico City's metro system). "Thickening" the station pictogram's original design—a design that was conceptualized by American graphic designer Lance Wyman in 1968, the year of the Olympics and of the Tlatelolco massacre—the *Gentegrama* will offer a polyvocal, community-informed representation, while simultaneously retaining its original wayfinding function. *Gentegrama* changes its purpose from "passive" display to the dynamic and ever-shifting representation of the constituent users.

Geolocated and hashtagged social media posts are displayed as a changing image feed on the station signpost (figures 4.6 and 4.7). These social media posts have a lifespan of thirty-six hours, allowing for communication across days and work schedules. Posts are also uploaded from interactive panels located in the stations. Using this device, users can "like" images from the feed, extending their display time. To focus on the input from the actual users of the station, "liking" can only occur from the in-station device. There is also a station feedback component that would collectively create a mood temperature map of the entire metro system.

While users may add to and browse the image feed from their cellphones, the heart of the installation is the interactive panel. The in-station *Gentegrama* installation offers accessibility to those without smartphone technology. Users may browse the feed, like and upvote images and take pictures of themselves, others, and the station.

Another unique feature of the *Gentegrama* design is the station feedback feature. Passersby can weigh in with their feelings and opinions about the station and its condition with the single push of a button. This is visualized as a colored stripe on the display. It functions as a collective barometer to users within the station and is exported to the administration as a map of the entire system. Finally, crowdsourcing, as a strategy heavily employed in *Gentegrama*, can be employed in creative and open-ended ways by the public.

As the *Gentegrama* project evolves through user interaction, we imagine that *Gentegrama* will grow out of its physical confines of navigation stations and into the digital world. *Gentegrama* will replace all existing pictograms, whether online, in information stations, or on the screen of other transportation systems like the bus or suburban rail. We envision an app for your phone, allowing new connectivities between stations and mapping your transit journey.

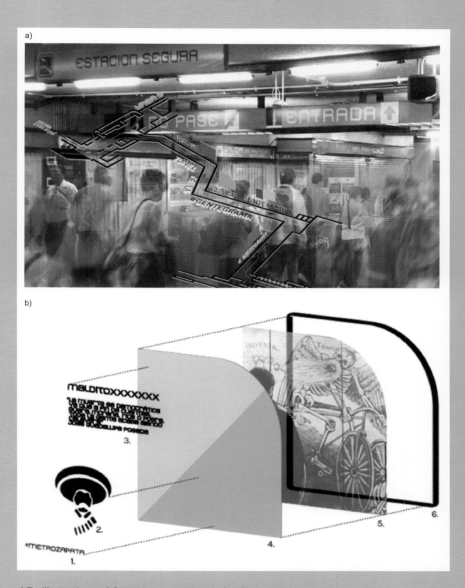

4.7 Illustrations of Gentegrama proposal. Credit: Authors

Interlude 4:

Shanghai

The House on
Xinhua Road

Jonathan Banfill (杨宁远)

4.8 The family is present in the contemporary city, *The House on Xinhua Road*. Credit: Authors

I created two linked digital video projects as part of the Urban Humanities Initiative's Shanghai year (2014–2015) to offer a portrait of a house that once belonged to my family, and is located on what was the city's western fringes during the 1930s. The first film was created from afar in Los Angeles out of archival materials, drawing from both primary sources and my family, including photos and Super 8 film footage of the house, and secondary materials on Shanghai. The second film was built out of live footage captured during the experience of returning to the house. The videos utilize two different film-media strategies developed in the Urban Humanities Initiative: the archival essay film and filmic sensing. The weaving of my own subjective experience in both films adds another dimension, used to shape the narrative of the first film, which comes into tension with the real-time unfolding experience of the second.

My family's former home has changed its function during its existence spanning more than eight decades of Shanghai's turbulent history. It sits off Xinhua Road, down a small lane, with other old houses on either side, remnants from a different era. In the present, you walk down the lane and come to a gatehouse and a newly built fence. Behind, apartment blocks of contemporary Shanghai rise up into the sky, creating the sort of visual intersection of past and present that is so common in the city. Noise from the surrounding streets can be heard in the distance, but it seems strangely far away, as if the weight of the past eighty years is heavier here, giving the house a certain silence that speaks of its role as a witness to a changing city.

In March 2015, I stood in the lane pressing my face against the cold metal of the fence and gazing at the house through a small opening between panels. Here is where my grandmother grew up as part of the city's Chinese elite. After the house was confiscated by the government in the 1950s, it took on different functions during the socialist period. Since China opened up in the late 1970s, it has continued to change functions, and my family has regularly returned to the house, bearing witness to the ways that it has changed along with the city around it. We do not own it any longer, yet it serves as my family's central reference point

The house is a central reference point of the city. . .

4.9 Film still from *The House on Xinhua Road*. Credit: Authors

to the city, a way to understand Shanghai and our connection to it (figure 4.9).

Since I was last in Shanghai, a few years before my filming project, the function of the house has again changed. Through researching for the film and combining this research with knowledge of family members, I constructed its history. The house was built in 1935 by Zhao Chen and Chen Zhi of The Allied Architects, members of the first generation of Chinese architects in Shanghai. It was built as a two-story Spanish-style mansion with green glazed roof tiles, steel doors and windows, and cement outer walls.

In the 1930s, Xinhua road was called Amherst Avenue. In 1947, it was renamed Fahua Road. In 1965, it gained its current name: Xinhua Road, *Xinhua* meaning "New China." Each house in the development was built in a different western style. As British sci-fi author J. G. Ballard, who grew up here, describes, "the French built Provencal villas and art deco mansions, the Germans Bauhaus white boxes, the English their half-timbered fantasies of golf-club elegance."

My great-grandfather, a prominent lawyer of the Republican Era (1912–1949), moved his family into the house, and they were its first residents. My grandmother grew up in the house, coming of age in a city occupied by the Japanese after 1937. After the war, she would marry in the yard of the house before leaving for America in 1946, never to return. The rest of the family would follow, settling in the United States, Hong Kong, and Taiwan.

After 1949 the house was left empty, taken over by the new communist government. In 1959 it was given to the Changning District Military Sports Commission and made into a gymnasium, with its green lawn concreted over into a basketball court. By the 1980s, it had become a government office and later a Japanese restaurant. During the 2000s, it became the WTO conference center, which led to its restoration and historical protection, and now it has evolved into something less discernible. This is part of the larger reappropriation of Shanghai's old houses and other historic buildings happening in the process of reglobalization.

On the screen, a grainy image of a house appears: it looks old and used. Previously, the viewer has been oriented with images and sounds of Shanghai, in order to open a portal to the past: a shot of the city skyline, a map of the pre-1949 city, sound tracked by an old Chinese jazz song. In the film, my family are almost like ghosts, and their images bleed into those of the Super 8 footage, which moves through an emptied-out version of the house (figure 4.8). The time contrast is some thirty years, an ocean of time and trouble in Shanghai's history, with the footage taken after China's awakening from the Cultural Revolution. The film highlights visually this sense of temporal loss, and the narrative voice shifts slightly, no longer recounting history but taking an investigatory tone, "I seek memories in empty rooms, to reconstruct what may have been . . . looking for connections." In the film's dénouement, the images of the family and the house reappear collaged into the contemporary and future depictions of the city (figure 4.10), concluding that the city is "a refuge of memories" that leads to the future.

The second film starts with the camera following me walking down the lane to the house. It does not show the scene of a man coming out, refusing to let me visit the house, and slamming the door on my face, but focuses instead on the emotional aftereffects, as the camera locks onto my face, and the image of the house

4.10 Time layers of the house on Xinhua Road. Credit: Andre Comandon

4.11 The house in June 2018. Photo credit: James Banfill

comes in and out of focus. The film ends with shots that contrast my view of the house with the reactions on my face: anger, grief, reflection, ambivalence, acceptance.

The two films represent an attempt to express the complexities and layers of history, time, and memory that can manifest in a single place within a city, while at the same time universalizing the experience in order to communicate something larger about Shanghai. What will become of the house (figure 4.11)? That I cannot say, but I do know that I will return to it again and again as a reference point and continue to read Shanghai's changes through its windows and walls, perhaps finding new ways to film and present it.

5
Engaged Scholarship and Pedagogy

Engaged research starts in the classroom. Indeed, engaged research and engaged pedagogy are very difficult to set apart in the context of urban humanities. While the pedagogy of urban humanities may be situated in the university, it also becomes an extramural endeavor that leaves the campus, involves the city (or at least some of its neighborhoods), interacts and learns from communities, and becomes engaged scholarship (figures 5.1 and 5.2). Symmetrically, research findings through community engagement come back to the campus to shape pedagogy. For example, research on spatial justice (or lack thereof) takes urban humanists beyond the confines of the university and even beyond national borders and helps them better understand the social and spatial inequalities that exist within cities but also within the academic fabric and the classroom. However, this reciprocal relationship between university and city must be complicated. Much in the same way that the nature-city dichotomy is a useful analytic—yet it breaks

5.1 Urban humanities students building an exhibition for final projects, 2013. Photo credit: Authors

5.2 Urban humanities students taking measurements in the central plaza of the Tokyo Metropolitan Government Building. Photo credit: Authors

down as we increasingly understand that nature is not separate from but, in fact, *part* of the city—so too for urban humanities the university exists as *part* of the city.

This chapter untangles some of these relationships. It starts with a discussion of the evolution of the university as an institution of privilege, power, and knowledge to set the stage for the emergence of the "porous pedagogies" of urban humanities that welcome knowledge and tools that come not only from within but also from beyond and outside the university. The chapter proceeds to offer a detailed account of the research and pedagogical principles of urban humanities (positionality, empathy, inclusiveness), and their active dialogue with, and contribution to, the changing landscape of graduate education. To gather a detailed portrait of urban humanities in action, this chapter's Coda (see page 235) describes the activities of one year of urban humanities students and instructors and discusses their projects to illustrate how engaged pedagogy intersects with engaged scholarship.

Toppling the Ivory Tower

In its conventional, historical sense, "pedagogy" seems to command obedience. We see this quite clearly in the etymology of the term: A *pedagogue*, from the Middle French, is a schoolmaster, someone "charged with overseeing a child or youth"; the Latin word *paedagogus* refers to a "slave who took children from school" and generally supervised them; in Greek, the word *paidagogos* was built from *pais* or "child," and *agogos*, meaning "leader," from *agein* "to lead."[1] A pedagogue, then, was an adult (teacher, instructor, supervisor, or slave) who watched over and attended to children, someone who could lead them in a certain direction, and depending on social and political standing, could supervise or teach them. In every case, the pedagogue stands watch over those who are immature, and who are required to be obedient, tractable subjects.

In the eighteenth century, the multivalent German term for education—*Bildung*—begins to reimagine this history by foregrounding the cultivation of the individual as a process of self-formation. A new *Bildungsideal* was born out of the optimistic, Enlightenment notions of progress, rationality, refinement, and moral education. It was marked by the belief that all individuals can improve themselves through aesthetic, moral, and physical education. Its originators—Lessing, Mendelssohn, Herder, Kant, Humboldt, Schiller, and especially Goethe—believed that Bildung was the crucible for human potentiality and freedom. Far from a focus on obedient, docile subjects, Bildung became a testament to the expression of growth, courage, and self-determination in the Enlightenment. As Kant famously declared: "*Sapere aude*! 'Have courage to use your own reason!' That is the motto of the Enlightenment."[2]

As a deliberate break from political and religious authorities and calcified dogma, the University of Berlin, founded in 1810, was built on the principles of free inquiry and enlightened reason. With its faculty linked across the natural sciences and humanities, the goal was to bring together multidisciplinary knowledge and critical methods from all domains of research. Established under the vision of Wilhelm von Humboldt, the *Universitas litterarum* sought to unify teaching and research by providing students with a holistic, open-ended humanist education. As Humboldt remarked about the vision for the University of Berlin, its task was to be "national upbringing and *Bildung*. Everyone in Germany who is interested in *Bildung* and Enlightenment shall find a sanctuary here."[3] As an ideal, Bildung was, ostensibly, open to everyone, and the university was the site for its realization. The main buildings of the campus were located in the heart of old Berlin, linking the city and its citizens to the academy and its students.

More literally translated as "formation," *Bildung* also referred to the processual cultivation and maturation of the subject-citizen to enter into civil society.[4] The term has resonances that come from creation theology, sculpture, and educational practice, perhaps most famously articulated in Goethe's *Bildungsroman*,[5] *Wilhelm Meister* (1796).[6] In the novel, the young Wilhelm embarks on a journey of self-discovery and education in order to become *gebildet* (educated). In the process, he not only discovers himself but also becomes integrated into the social, economic, and political fabric of civil society. Because educated individuals were to be part of a greater community, Bildung quickly became associated with citizenship, civic society, and the emancipatory hopes of the Enlightenment, although never quite in a truly universal way.[7]

Despite its admirable intentions and ideals, Bildung also solidified a normative process in which good, respectable citizens were cultivated, while deviations were variously excluded, mollified, and sometimes even killed off. The underbelly of Bildung, like the dialectic of Enlightenment, reveals how the concept also checked, defused, and ultimately eliminated transgressions to the social order. This is even represented in Goethe's Bildungsroman. Along his pathway to education and self-formation, Wilhelm encounters other people, such as the androgynous singer Mignon, who occupies a liminal zone outside of civil society and the protective affordances of Bildung. While Wilhelm's educational journey is secretly guided and supported by the omniscient "Tower Society," Mignon, "the silly androgynous creature"[8] with irregular features and arrested development[9] is not allowed to survive, is revealed to be the product of incest, and, at the end of the story, is "embalmed" in "The Hall of the Past" as part of the massive, protofascist architecture of the Tower Society, before being entirely forgotten.

In the novel, the Tower Society—as the certification and institutionalization of Bildung itself—represents a hierarchical system of socialization that reinforces a set of broader social values rooted in the strictures of patriarchy, the heterosexual family, inheritance rights, and economic stratification. The metaphor of the Tower Society captures not just a top-down hierarchy, but also an internal set of isolated social relations separated from the everyday world. At the same time that the Tower Society guides, educates, cultivates, and directs, it also corrects, renders docile, and overpowers transgressions. Mignon, the "half-developed,"[10] free-spirited wanderer, who cannot sublimate her pleasure and be properly socialized, is killed off in the novel, while Wilhelm is admitted into the upper echelons of bourgeois society by becoming a respectable, cultivated father and acquiring "the virtues of a solid citizen."[11]

The goal, then, is not just the Bildung of the individual but also the production of a broader social ideal. As Jarno, one of the highest-ranking members of the Tower Society enthusiastically declares at the end of *Wilhelm Meister*, the pedagogy of the Tower Society should be "[extended] to every corner of the globe, and people from all over the world will be allowed to join it." His reason, however, is not world-wide altruism and genuine openness but rather strategic self-preservation and land holding: "We will cooperate in safeguarding our means of existence, in case some political revolution should displace one of our members from the land he owns."[12] Only Friedrich, the society's sole critic, disparages its self-preserving pedagogy, panoptic control, and even colonial goals, referring to its members as a bevy of "young colonists."[13] The Tower Society, however, is already preparing to send its missionaries off "to Russia and the United States" to secure its future and spread Bildung and Enlightenment. Perhaps it was not until Adorno and Horkheimer that this dubious achievement would be most trenchantly assessed: The "fully enlightened earth radiates disaster triumphant."[14]

As the idea of the university evolved and developed throughout the nineteenth century, the Tower Society, we would argue, has variously persisted as a dubious model of college education marked by elitism, socio-economic stratification, and hierarchical privilege and power, even while the venerable goals of Bildung spread more widely in society. It is no coincidence, of course, that the university is often called an ivory tower—something that celebrates its pure white color and luxurious isolation from, if not above, the rest of the world. To be sure, we are not suggesting that quiet spaces of contemplation and thoughtful reflection are unnecessary. But we also recognize, like Goethe's secret Tower Society, that our contemporary ivory towers are places of privilege and power, sometimes operating in ways that are quite consonant with secret societies.

In many ways, this is a tension that has remained behind the admirable goals of the university as a site of open-ended research, unfettered thought, and free inquiry. For all its grand ambitions of reckoning with the world, the university remains a relatively

5.3 Royce Hall, on enrollment day in 1930, the first academic year on the UCLA campus. Photo credit: Thelner Barton Hoover, from the Thelner and Louise Hoover Collection, UCLA

isolated institution, all too often its campus walled in, as well as walled off from surrounding communities, accessible to a chosen few, stratified by economic, social, and racial differences, and perhaps too invested in the security of its storied past. Many of the physical buildings of the university themselves evoke this space of exception, a grand past of privilege and prestige.

At UCLA, Royce Hall, the university's architectural and cultural landmark, was built in the early twentieth century in Romanesque style (figure 5.3). Its towers reference Milan's ancient Basilica of Sant'Ambrogio, which acquired its Romanesque style in the twelfth century—800 years after it was originally founded.

Carved into stone above the stage in Royce Hall is an unattributed quote: "Education is learning to use the tools which the race has found indispensable." It comes from Ernest Carroll Moore, a philosophy professor who served until 1936 as UCLA's first provost. One may wonder: What tools has "the race" found to be "indispensable"? Pen and paper, paintbrush, camera, clay, word processing programs, Photoshop? Is learning to use such tools enough, or might we need to interpret the objects created, assess their significance, and probe their conditions of possibility? And *who*, after all, can learn to use these tools found to be indispensable by the race? We know from Moore's other writings on education, for example, that not every human being counted as part of the human race, and we know all too well that racial thinking, eugenic paradigms, and social Darwinism were not just part and parcel of late nineteenth- and early twentieth-century thought but were also framing assumptions in his published writings.[15]

How do we confront these profound histories of exclusion and hierarchy that are literally inscribed in the edifices of the university? Clearly it involves opening the university to other stories and histories, particularly those from the outside. At UCLA, that begins with acknowledging that the grand campus of the land grant university was built on grounds that were originally occupied by the Native American tribes of Gabrielino-Tongva, whose thousand-year histories are all but erased. How does knowledge of the deeply layered histories of place inform—or fail to inform—our positions, our ways of knowing, and our actions in the present? These are urgent and vital questions that come from historical, cultural-critical, and ethical perspectives influenced by the humanities.

A critical objective of urban humanities pedagogy is to break from the ivory tower model of the university, where knowledge tends to be produced, preserved, guarded, and stratified in ways that reinforce, rather than transform, broader social and political norms. Here, the counterarguments penned by education reformer Paulo Freire in 1970 remain quite relevant: "Authentic thinking, thinking that is concerned about *reality*, does not take place in ivory tower isolation, but only in communication. . . . [It] has meaning only when generated by action upon the world."[16] Many educational situations, however, tacitly reinscribe social, economic, and racial hierarchies of inclusion and exclusion, of permitted speech and permissible discourse, where students are judged by their facility in reflecting predigested knowledge formed with "the tools which the race has found indispensable." Following the feminist poet Audre Lorde, we might ask: Can the master's tools dismantle the master's house?[17] Is it possible to use "the tools" to transform the ivory tower model and even the brick walls themselves? If not, new tools may need to be invented, ones that imagine and bring about new possibilities, create spaces for other voices, and build futures that are distinct and different from the stratifications of the past inscribed into the educational edifices themselves.

The university's built environment can also contribute in myriad ways in opening up the ivory tower, constructing places that acknowledge and promote transformation. In an essay entitled "Campus Design and Critical Pedagogy," architectural educators Thomas Dutton and Bradford Grant discuss how campus architecture can challenge the social hierarchies that universities have historically embedded, by foregrounding "concepts of diversity" and "transformative politics of difference," since architecture intrinsically manifests the institution's values.[18] Campus buildings can resist complicity with the established relations of power to reinforce the wider goal of critical pedagogy in the university. Along with a series of "National Heritage Rooms" built between the 1930s and 1990s at the University of Pittsburgh, they describe architect Lucien Kroll's participatory design process and unconventional architectural solution for the Catholic University of Louvain in Belgium (1969) (figure 5.4). All who participated in making the building were urged to creatively contribute, from engineers and carpenters to students, so that the final project embodies a sense of flexibility, changeability, and involvement. Charles Moore had a similar idea for Kresge College at the University of California, Santa Cruz, where students were

5.4 Lucien Kroll's mixed-use Medical Faculty Housing, with hospital in the background.
Photo credit: Bastin & Evrard

5.5 Interior social space within the McMurtry Building at the Department of Art and Art History, Stanford University. Architects: Diller Scofidio + Renfro, 2015. Photo credit: Iwan Baan

encouraged to build out the interiors of relatively open dormitory rooms. Participatory challenges to academic hierarchies can come in less radical forms as well, when students' active engagement is foregrounded in the architecture. At Stanford University, Diller Scofidio + Renfro's McMurtry Building for the Department of Art and Art History (2015) creates a range of open communal spaces for collaboration (figure 5.5). At the University of Utah, student residences are combined with "garage space" for innovative tech learning and living. And at UCLA, the Center for the Art of Performance is partnering with a downtown hotel to bring the campus into the city with creative programming in the hotel's historic theater.

Porous Pedagogies

To elaborate the idea of opening up the ivory tower through engaged pedagogy, we begin by reflecting locally, starting with the very bricks of UCLA's Royce Hall, home to many departments in the humanities.[19] As it happens, UCLA still acquires its bricks from the Alberhill Coal and Clay Company, now renamed Pacific Clay (see figure 5.6), the same factory that produced the first bricks that set the foundation of the University of California's southern branch in Westwood in the late 1920s. When modernist architect Louis Kahn spoke to his students, he famously suggested they ask the brick what it wants to be. He was speaking of the brick's capacity for making form and structure (the brick says, "I like an arch"),[20] but there is another important characteristic of the brick: namely, its porosity.

5.6 Pacific Clay (formerly Alberhill Coal and Clay Company) where bricks for Royce Hall at UCLA were produced. Credit: Pacific Clay Company

This chapter argues that porosity is also a defining trait of urban humanities pedagogy and research: "In contrast to other molded or pre-cast building materials, the porosity of brick is attributed to its fine capillaries. By virtue of the capillary effect, the rate of moisture transport in the brick is ten times faster than in other building materials."[21] Porosity—that is, the ability to breath, in and out, and to open up to what lies outside—and the "capillary effect"—in other words, to rapidly and evenly transport and expand moisture (life) and knowledge—is the modus operandi, or even the modus vivendi of a new, "fluid" university model based on permeability, openness, interdisciplinarity, collaboration, and community involvement, at the local, national, and transnational levels.

The digital era and the (relatively new) reality of knowledge production and consumption patterns based on digital networking and widespread "horizontal" virtual learning have heavily contributed to the "softening" and increasing porousness of "real" universities, with a noticeable effect on the uses of their physical and institutional spaces as well. But it is not only the digital that has enabled this softening; it is also an ethic based on diversity and difference that reimagines the university as a part of multiple networks—past, present, and future—and sites of engagement that are multidirectional, public, and nonhierarchical.

In contrast to so-called apocalyptic thinkers who only perceive a crisis of higher education and mourn the downfall of the humanities,[22] "integrated" and "generative" approaches optimistically speak of a radically "new ecology of teaching and learning" that not only acknowledges but also openly embraces the opportunities of a paradigm shift. "What is different at this historical moment," Sidonie Smith contends, "is the intensification of cross-institutional collaborative activity in the humanities and opportunities for modeling collaborative graduate education."[23] Her assertion can be extended to cross-departmental activity and undergraduate education. Thus in fitting response to the zeitgeist and as part of a new ecology of teaching and learning, Smith's "Manifesto for a Sustainable Humanities" proclaims the need of "preserving the intimacy of the small and [stewarding] the distinctiveness of the local while recognizing the attraction [and potential] of global networks," and of "relishing the commitment to teaching through innovations in the classroom, among them explorations of participatory and project-based humanities inquiry."[24] More importantly, she urges the humanities to "reconceptualize the scholarly ecology as a flexible collaboratory, one that positions the scholar as singular producer of knowledge, but also as a member of a collaborative assemblage involving students, colleagues, computer engineers and graphic designers, project designers, and strangers of the crowd."[25]

"Strangers of the crowd" may be read to stand for diverse communities not always sufficiently integrated into the knowledge networks or institutional formations that focus singularly on teaching the "correct" use of tools (and the correct production of artifacts) considered to be indispensable "for the race." Instead, there are valuable tools that stem from beyond or outside the university. And there are ways of knowing, thinking, seeing, speaking, and creating that come from communities not traditionally selected to partake in the knowledge formations and credentialing programs prized by the university. How might a pedagogy of porosity expose students to possibilities and potentialities from the outside? And what does this mean for the mission of the university embedded in multiple critical networks that extend far beyond its walls to ways of creating and thinking that are "foreign" to it? Critically inflected forms of community engagement are certainly one of the imperatives of a new ecology of teaching and learning that shares with bricks the fundamental quality of porousness and permeability.

This push for more creative, relevant, and diverse scholarship arises not only from humanists but also social scientists within the academy. In his 2011 article "Towards a Public Social Science," urban sociologist Herbert J. Gans highlights the distinction between "academic and public social scientists" and enthusiastically advocates for the latter.[26] According to him, the social sciences deal with humanity's most pressing problems, but there are barriers between practitioners and the public. We must restructure these disciplines from the ground up. In times of economic and political distress, the social sciences must become more relevant and useful by devoting their attention to society's major problems. Such calls to reform are already surfacing, accompanied by mini social movements inside the disciplines: Sociologists have called for public sociology, anthropologists for public ethnography, political scientists for "perestroika," and economists for a heterodox economics.

Gans further adds that "in the past, these movements have eventually disappeared or been marginalized by the academic social scientists who rule the disciplinary roosts," and cautions that "since distressing times could continue for a while, . . . publicly minded social scientists should come together and transcend their disciplinary differences to pursue the interests they have in common," including "intellectual and infrastructural changes needed to establish public social science disciplines."[27]

Gans's plea for "public sociology," "public anthropology," and "perestroika" or public political science is now widely accepted, and the idea that academic research in the social sciences could take place without directly addressing and engaging with key social issues appears outlandish and even ethically inexcusable. In fact, as a new, publicly oriented mission takes root in the university writ large, new models of engaged scholarship and pedagogy have flourished under the rubrics of "service learning" and "community engagement," although not always unproblematically.[28]

The phrase "scholarship of engagement" was coined by education reformer Ernest Boyer in 1996. His broad commitment to elevating teaching alongside research instigated his thinking about scholarly engagement, as well as his investigation into studio formats and architectural education.[29] The New England Resource for Higher Education (NERCHE) has helped to catalyze and disseminate what is now considered the standard definition of "engaged scholarship" as an increasingly meaningful, and even urgent academic practice:

> Engaged scholarship is defined by the collaboration between academics and individuals outside the academy—knowledge professionals and the lay public (local, regional/state, national, global)—for the mutually beneficial exchange of knowledge and resources in a context of partnership and reciprocity. The scholarship of engagement

includes explicitly democratic dimensions of encouraging the participation of non-academics in ways that enhance and broaden engagement and deliberation about major social issues inside and outside the university. It seeks to facilitate a more active and engaged democracy by bringing affected publics into problem-solving work in ways that advance the public good *with* and not merely *for* the public.[30]

NERCHE's description is peppered with terms and concepts to which the engaged scholar and urban humanist enthusiastically adhere, such as interdisciplinarity, democratic participation, the direct engagement with social issues, and the conviction that problem-solving work should always "advance the public good *with* and not merely *for* the public." However, the definition does not emphasize what the truly invested engaged scholar and urban humanist unavoidably encounters: partnerships are uneven and privilege is not equally distributed. Gans's article eloquently defends the need for and importance of engaged scholarship in the social sciences, but like NERCHE's definition, it neglects to point out that when an affluent university or academic initiative partners with a disadvantaged community, chances are that the partnership will not escape, but rather replicate, the dynamics of power and social inequality. Even the term "lay public" obscures the significant knowledge held by its members that complements that of the markedly more esteemed "knowledge professional." One can be "open" to what lies outside (the era of Western expansion and colonization was certainly open—too open and eager, we would argue—to all things foreign), but such openness is no guarantee that the engagement with the other will benefit the latter. To be relentlessly aware of such potentials for unevenness and to embark on engaged scholarship in order to begin to counter such injustices is precisely the urban humanist's most difficult and urgent task. And we must begin at home, in the spaces we know and inhabit most intimately. As our colleague Ananya Roy pointed out in an urban humanities seminar at UCLA, the problematics of so-called engaged scholarship ought to be reframed as "research justice."[31]

Let us return, then, to our own ivory towers to shed light beyond the masters of the house, the grand rooms with sweeping vistas, the carefully appointed offices where tenured faculty and well-paid administrators reign. The very concept of the ivory tower renders invisible and thus silences those who make the inner workings of ivory towers possible, namely, a veritable army of low-salaried staff, a rapidly growing teaching cadre of lecturers and adjuncts lacking security of employment, an increasing number of students deep in debt, some of whom are undocumented immigrants, come from foster homes or are homeless, and, last but not least, the literally thousands of maintenance workers on low wages who keep the campus clean, green, and trash-free. Ivory towers build one floor on top of the next, the upper one oblivious to what lies beneath it and to which it owes its lofty height.

This comes poignantly across in Maite Zubiaurre's (2013) illustrated short piece "Diosa Cochambre: UUCLA at Night" (*Diosa Cochambre* means "Goddess Filth")—an homage to Unionized-UCLA (hence "UUCLA," with two Us) and to the janitors (almost all Hispanic or African American), who clean the floors of the buildings when the sun falls.[32] Suddenly, dimly lit floors come alive with the sounds of Mexican, Salvadorian, and Guatemalan Spanish, while Bible wisdom erupts out of boom boxes traveling on carts holding a trash can and cleaning supplies. The smell of burritos, the sounds of salsa and cumbia, the sweeping of brooms resurface punctually every night, and then punctually disappear at dawn. Indeed, so much disappears on campus and becomes invisible, so much happens in parallel universes that never touch—that is, until they do, and the chance for change appears.

Every year, the UCLA Center for Labor Research and Education (Labor Center) organizes a campus counter-tour—a kind of field trip that mimics and "counters" the official campus tours taken by prospective students and their parents. The counter-tour includes a picnic and sports activities, such as the traditional Oaxacan ball game for the janitors, gardeners, and domestic workers (many of them part of LA's immigrant indigenous community originally from Oaxaca, Mexico) who are parents of high school students.

And every year, the tour ends at Special Collections in the Charles Young Research Library, because in 2012 UCLA acquired the historical records of Justice for Janitors—a social movement organization that fights for the rights of janitors in Los Angeles (figures 5.7 and 5.8).[33]

5.7 Flyer announcing the 2018 tour organized by UCLA Labor Center that brought the families of prospective undocumented migrant students to campus. Credit: UCLA Labor Center

a)

b)

5.8 Traditional Oaxacan ball game during the UCLA Labor Center event in 2018. Credit: UCLA Labor Center

According to Gaspar Rivera Salgado, one of our urban humanities partners and the project director of the UCLA Labor Center, the library visit is always fraught with tension. Special Collections—with its rarified museum air, a Picasso painting hanging from its walls, and security surveillance—is not a space of easy welcome. Janitors may "fit" at night, when they hold a broom or wheel around a cleaning supply cart, but a new and distinct fit must be formulated during the day, when their hands are free to hold books, free to explore the archives that record the history of their struggles for social and economic justice. The counter-tour makes visible the Oaxacan maintenance workers as patrons and readers (of their own history, in this case), and challenges the faculty and librarians who often may only welcome them in Special Collections (and elsewhere on campus) when their labor makes them automatically and conveniently invisible. Such projects are emblematic of a locally engaged, porous pedagogy that not only calls into question the ivory tower model of the university, but also unveils the ways this model—a myth in its own right—reinforces social and economic blindness in its sheer cultural redundancy.

Let us now broaden our gaze beyond UCLA to the city of Los Angeles to think through this myth-making further. Deliberately countering the modernist image of Los Angeles where leisure and sun reside in private suburban landscapes (perhaps most emblematically represented in paintings created in the 1960s by David Hockney), the queer Chicano visual artist Ramiro Gomez asks us to see and recognize the janitors, domestic workers, caregivers, and gardeners who essentially make the scene possible. Reworking one of Hockney's most famous paintings, *A Bigger Splash* (1967) (figure 5.9), Gomez adds the bodies and labor of the domestic workers into the scene to reveal the hidden economic, social, and cultural conditions of possibility for the image itself (figure 5.10).

Gomez's painting, *No Splash*, has neither splash nor willful modernist ignorance: the brown bodies of the workers keep this pool clean and, in turn, help us interrogate urban myth-making. Building on this intervention, Gomez also created life-size

5.9 *A Bigger Splash*, 1967, David Hockney (1937–). Photo credit: ©Tate, London 2019

5.10 *No Splash*, Ramiro Gomez, 2013. Credit: Ramiro Gomez

cardboard portraits of workers and installed them strategically throughout the city of Los Angeles. The portraits publicly dignify their subjects and simultaneously bring attention to the laborers who are unseen until their presence is indisputably marked on swimming pool decks, in front yards, on sidewalks, and in domestic interiors (figures 5.11 and 5.12). Gomez, who was a nanny himself and whose relatives serve as models for his artwork, creates installations that pull back the curtain to expose the myth-making of urban purity, making us confront the spatial manifestations of social and economic injustices.[34]

Clearly, the conventional representation of academia as an ivory tower is yet another "myth of purity"[35] for it portrays universities as a compact and uniform block, a condensed and well-delimited form of elitism surrounded by—and all too often insensitive to— social inequality. But if we care to look, the interior of the ivory tower is far more uneven and messy, and much closer to a mirror that reflects "outside" injustice and social inequality, than to a self-enclosed tower exclusively inhabited by the powerful. Fortunately, porosity goes both ways: academic knowledge trickles out and social reality trickles in, each potentially transforming the other.

To be sure, power dynamics lie at the heart of any teaching or research practice, even the most democratic ones. Inclusive, porous, and activist pedagogies embrace the fact that the contestation of the status quo often comes from those least invested in and least protected by it (hence students tend to be more inclined than faculty to identify and counter social injustice on campus, for example). As a consequence, when students become activists, it is the faculty who learn from them. As a porous pedagogical and research enterprise, urban humanities not only seek to radically reconfigure the boundaries within the university between disciplines, but also the boundaries of the university between the activities of the ivory tower and the reality of daily life both inside and outside its walls. This porosity is produced by the confluence of bricks and the positions of the inhabitants: staff, students, and teachers rethinking their roles, forging partnerships of commitment across and beyond the university, and speaking in languages other than those of neoliberalism.

5.11 *Gardener on North Beverly Drive*, by Ramiro Gomez. Credit: David Feldman

5.12 *Nannies*, by Ramiro Gomez. Credit: David Feldman

In one such "porous" project, urban humanities students from UCLA partnered with Libros Schmibros, a community organization that provides a free lending library, books, and literature-related programming in the Los Angeles neighborhood of Boyle Heights. In their project La Caja Mágica (The Magic Box), design skills were put to work in producing a magical box that was both eye catching and mobile, filled with materials for pop-up storytelling sessions in the community (see Project G: La Caja Mágica: Seeking Literary Justice).

Certain architectural practices have also functioned as models of engaged scholarship and pedagogy, pushing the boundaries of conventions in the field. For example, Rural Studio at Auburn University under the guidance of architect Samuel Mockbee led students to design and build structures in poor communities of Alabama. Working closely with the inhabitants, Mockbee and his students sought to "help create the opportunity for people to realize their innate nobility." Rural Studio wanted to turn from good intentions to creating good, actual results so that architecture made a difference in the lives of the residents and demonstrated the power of architecture to students.[36] Even after Mockbee's passing in 2001, the Rural Studio has remained active. Students raise funds to help build the projects, which most often take the form of a home built for a client. In addition to performing a service and engaging students in new communities, Rural Studio continues to act as a research laboratory investigating extremely low-cost housing approaches. Their ongoing "20K Initiative" (with Fannie Mae and other partners) shares findings from their research on comfortable, dignified, sustainable—and very inexpensive—housing to ensure it impacts the wider shortage of affordable rural housing (figure 5.13).[37]

In Chile, the Pritzker Prize winner Alejandro Aravena of Elemental designed social housing at Quinta Monroy (2003) for one hundred families who had been living on the site for three decades (figure 5.14). In order to avoid displacement and keep costs low while providing as much space as possible, Aravena built half of each house, leaving space for the residents to complete the rest when they could. It is also significant that this design openness

5.13 Photograph of the Harris family Butterfly House designed and built by Mockbee and Rural Studio students (1997). Photo credit: Timothy Hursley

gave residents an opportunity to customize their homes, in contrast to reformist social housing that imposed a moral and social order on its inhabitants. In both the Chilean and the Alabama examples, the inhabitant was transformed into a client with meaningful involvement in the creative process, such that design served as a form of engagement with the occupants. This reconfiguration of relationships between professional and client, or between university affiliate and community member, is not unlike Herbert Gans's call for a "public architecture." Indeed, the language of Rural Studio articulates the goal of educating "citizen architects," and echoes Ernest Boyer's "scholarship of engagement." While these are housing projects, they are also much more, in the form of symbolic representation and the dialogic process of democratic engagement for students and community members alike.

5.14 Quinta Monroy Housing in Iquique, Chile, by Elemental, 2004.
Photo credit: Tadeuz Jalocha, Cristobal Palma

Bodies That Matter

One obvious challenge to the academy raised by engagement is that bodies matter as well as minds. In the case of Rural Studio, students and teachers build structures with their own hands for inhabitants whose lives are highly different from theirs. If the city is the place where face-to-face, embodied interaction is concentrated, then the university, where difference is sometimes abstracted to the detriment of its own relevance, could learn from its urban context. The centrality and critical attunement of the humanities to difference—be it determined by gender (feminism and gender studies), sexual orientation (LGBTQ studies), race (critical race studies and postcolonial studies), varied ability (disability studies), and class (sociology, labor studies)—have greatly contributed to transforming scholarship from the distanced and abstracted immateriality of the mind to the tangible reality of the body. Bodies marked by difference bear and make visible the effects of injustice, and when a particular mode of intellectual and ethical inquiry informed by the humanities focuses long enough on "different" bodies as sites of multifarious engagement and exploitation, a fundamental shift occurs in pedagogy and scholarship. The implications of movement (of bodies immigrating and emigrating, of bodies crossing or being prohibited from crossing borders), the materiality of suffering (of bodies policed and rendered docile, of bodies shunned, of bodies raped and exploited, of bodies enslaved and abused, of bodies that matter and bodies rendered superfluous) coupled with deliberate acts of witnessing, teaching, and researching body politics have the potential to trigger empathy and pivot epistemological inquiry from intellect to affect. They can also shift attention from the body that suffers or is made to suffer, to the body as the site of agency and empowerment endowed with richly nuanced abilities. As Seigworth and Gregg put it, attention to affect turns the body into "an ever more worldly sensitive interface," and pushes it toward "being present to the struggles of our time."[38]

Empathy, a powerful epistemological orientation located in and developed through the body, is fundamental to affect theory, a burgeoning area of recent humanistic inquiry. It also informs the ethical thought of a wide range of contemporary thinkers and humanists, among them Susan Sontag, Zygmunt Bauman, Sara Ahmed, Judith Butler, and Giorgio Agamben.[39] All of these authors connect ethos and empathy with questions of justice, and, more concretely, with the powers of political sovereignty, the reality of outcasts, and mass migrations throughout the urbanized world.

As Butler argues in *Precarious Life: The Powers of Mourning and Violence*, a book written in the aftermath of 9/11 and the "war on terror," not every human life counts or is grievable as human in the wake of the dehumanizing forces of displacement, indefinite detention, internment, border policing, and the politics of exceptionality.[40] An urban humanities lens on this literature would focus on a systematic assessment of bodies and spatial justice, bringing camps for refugees and displaced persons into the fundamental analysis of urbanism. A closer look at displacement and the space of camps provides a powerful example of spatial justice's reliance on embodied empathy.

Richard Ek calls Giorgio Agamben's "conclusion that the camp has replaced the city as the biopolitical paradigm of the West" a "radical notion . . . that is difficult to digest,"[41] and yet, digestible or not, more and more bodies migrate, and more and more migrants have harrowing testimonies of massive, forceful displacement and of provisional and makeshift encampments that solidify into permanent sites. These camps grow at a pace the urban world has never witnessed, with 65.6 million people pushed from their homes.[42] The massive refugee camps that are located in Jordan, Lebanon, and Kenya, among other places, house hundreds of thousands of refugees, and can hardly be considered temporary.[43] Successive generations live without the ability to work outside the camps, with great uncertainty about returning to their homes, and with severe overcrowding, inadequate services, and little opportunity for education. From this perspective, the city is becoming the camp, and the camp is turning into the city.

Agamben's biopolitical camp has a precursor in one of Italo Calvino's "invisible cities." The writer tells us:

The city of Sophronia is made up of two half-cities. In one there is a great roller coaster with its steep humps, the carousel with its chain spokes, the ferris wheel of spinning cages, the death-ride with the crouching motorcyclists, the big top with the clump of trapezes hanging in the middle. The other half-city is of stone and marble and cement, with the bank, the factories, the palaces, the slaughterhouse, the school, and all the rest. One of the half-cities is permanent, the other is temporary, and when the period of its sojourn is over, they uproot it, dismantle it, and take it off, transplanting it to the vacant lots of another half-city. And so every year the day comes when the workmen remove the marble pediments, lower the stone walls, the cement pylons, take down the Ministry, the monument, the docks, the petroleum refinery, the hospital, load them on trailers, to follow from stand to stand their annual itinerary. Here remains the half-Sophronia of the shooting-galleries and the carousels, the shout suspended from the cart of the headlong roller coaster, and it begins to count the months, the days it must wait before the caravan returns and a complete life can begin once again.[44]

Sophronia, "built" in 1972 by Calvino, has proven to be tragically prophetic, as marbled pediments, stone walls, ministries, monuments, and docks—characteristic landmarks of the traditional city—deteriorate with reduced public investment, are destroyed by war and disaster, and are replaced by the rapidly increasing social frailty and precariousness of the contemporary megalopolis. What remains, and becomes more and more permanent (more than marble, cement, and steel) is not stony solidity, but the pliable and strangely resilient materials such as the wood and laminate of trailers, the fabric of tents, the trash of human waste, and the flesh of human bodies. Ironically, we call these frail materials resilient because the informal city is undying, massively present, able to spring back to life, and unsettling to sensibilities in the privileged parts of the formal city. But the informal city is here to stay, as Calvino's circus city attests. It overpowers and makes disappear what looks solid and permanent (the status quo built on cement and stone), but which ultimately is not.

Positionality and Inclusiveness

Urban humanists are keenly aware that they inhabit and study a contemporary urban reality that enables spaces like Calvino's Sophronia, ones marked by world-wide mass migration, displacement, homelessness, rapidly expanding job and housing informality, and rampant social inequality. Thus, the approach of urban humanities focuses not only on the buildings that make a city (a cliché that regains meaning when biopolitical megacamps shape new urban formations), but also on the people whose spatial existence and materiality of bodies also construct the city. For this reason, we argue that the drive toward spatial justice must be yoked with an ethos of embodiment and empathy.

The ability to feel *for* and *with* the other is the pillar on which positionality, a concomitant research tool and prerequisite for ethically informed, engaged scholarship and pedagogy firmly stands. Positionality, by definition, is fundamentally spatial:

> Personal values, views, and location in time and space influence how one understands the world. In this context, gender, race, class, and other aspects of identities are indicators of social and spatial positions and are not fixed, given qualities. Positions act on the knowledge a person has about things, both material and abstract. Consequently, knowledge is the product of a specific position that reflects particular places and spaces. Issues of positionality challenge the notions of value-free research that have dismissed human subjectivity from the processes that generate knowledge and identities.[45]

Within the humanities and social sciences, especially in fields such as Chicana/o studies, African American studies, gender studies, and queer studies, positionality articulates our knowledge perspectives, historical circumstances, epistemological frameworks, and embodied realities. Positionality informs the ways reality and its representations are shaped and continuously reshaped. There is no value-neutral or objective position from which we all strive to see the world; instead, we are always already, in different and intersecting ways, embedded in embodied networks of social, economic, cultural, and linguistic relations that give rise to multiple ways of knowing and ways of seeing (or not knowing and not seeing). Positionality establishes our bodies as the sites from which knowledge and engagement emanate.

When urban humanists teach, learn, and embark in engaged scholarship, they are openly conscious of their positions as academics and often (though not always) of social and economic privilege. Positionality also informs the pedagogical practices of urban humanities (filmic sensing, thick mapping, artistic interventions, among others). Ultimately, positionality's main virtue is the fundamental fact that it *slows us down*, not only because the reality in front of us requires careful contemplation and sustained collaboration, but also because every step demands ethical scrutiny. It also demands complex, time-intensive modes of engagement with each other: dialogic processing is required to work through this thicket for scholars engaging with "participants" and "the community" but also with the diverse positionalities that are embodied by other collaborating scholars and students.

Naturally, this has a direct influence on the research practices employed. Rather than parachute into communities, engagement requires extensive research preceding fieldwork activity, taking time to get to know the community and to gain its members' trust, and teaming with local researchers and activists already familiar with the community. Engaged scholarship cannot be rushed, because precipitous actions may lead to mistakes and destroy trust. Moreover, a critical humanistic attentiveness to who and what comprises "the community" must be considered at the onset. This casually used term problematically "others" urban denizens who jointly bear both ownership of and responsibility for producing a collectively shared urban environment with university affiliates. As far back as 1955, sociologist George Hillery noted the multiplicity of competing definitions for "the community,"[46] and more recently critical theorists have noted the way in which facile use of the term "community" can erase difference and lump purported "community members" with those to whom they may have little or no relation.[47]

Positionality is a relentless reminder of ethical responsibility, and thus, diametrically opposed to what Paulo Freire defines as "the banking concept of education,"[48] where the latter becomes an act of depositing, with students being the depositories and teachers the depositors. In such an educational paradigm, the teacher issues communiqués and makes deposits, which the student (or the community) patiently receives, memorizes, and repeats. The scope of action allowed to students is delimited by the predigested and preconceived knowledge they obediently receive.[49] What the Brazilian educator and activist suggests instead, and what bell hooks later endorses in *Teaching to Transgress,* is the conviction that the student (and the community member) is an "active participant, not passive consumer," and that "education can only be liberating when everyone claims knowledge as a field in which we all labor."[50] True engagement demands working *with*, and not *for* a community, because knowledge is not something provided but rather a shared terrain where all participate, aware of differential positionality, privilege, and power.

Positionality is thus the backbone of inclusive pedagogy, engaged teaching, and ethically oriented research. What sets it apart from more conventional approaches is its readiness to acknowledge and encourage students, driven by pressing ethical imperatives, to change their immediate reality and surroundings. Educators in such settings are inclined to shun the "sage on stage" model of pedagogy, replacing it with the more inclusive "guide on the side" alternative. The urban humanities curriculum has proven to be a particularly fertile ground for the adoption and fostering of inclusive teaching practices, through the fruitful destabilizing triggered by interdisciplinary complexity, direct engagement with identity, affect, and body politics, as well as collaborative, project-based scholarship and the continuous quest for a noncolonizing engagement with society.

At the same time, urban humanities seek to unearth and bring back to life what lies buried, silenced, and erased. Not unlike Calvino, urban humanists know that "visible" cities stand and thrive on invisible (or rather made invisible) bodies, events, facts, and settings, whose plight is all too often conveniently forgotten. Seeking spatial justice starts by peeling back the layers and listening to the "voiceless"—who are typically quite vocal but merely ignored. In this way, urban humanities pursue futurity built on archaeology, opening possibilities for the future by shedding light upon histories ignored and places left to decay. So when urban humanists go to Tokyo, they write "ghost guides" of the sites and bodies that past and future Olympic Games erase from maps and memory. When they travel to Mexico City, they find not one "Calle Regina," but two "Calles Regina," one made hypervisible by a government-endorsed hipster scene, the other an everyday space stubbornly resisting capitalist colonization (see Project H: Dos Méxicos a Través de Regina). And when they research Los Angeles's El Pueblo and the 101 Freeway, they search beneath the colorful stands of Mexican souvenirs and the massive transportation infrastructures to find the unmarked sites of the Chinese Massacre of October 1871.

Urban humanities' pedagogy of engagement also owes a great deal to Martha C. Nussbaum's *Not for Profit: Why Democracy Needs the Humanities* and to hooks' *Teaching to Transgress: Education as the Practice of Freedom*.[51] Both Nussbaum and hooks take a careful look at the constructs of intellectual distance and academic rigor as constitutive elements of conventional university teaching and research, and come up with a pedagogical alternative that builds upon vulnerability rather than self-assured, authoritative presence. In her chapter "Educating Citizens: The Moral (and Anti-Moral) Emotions," Nussbaum explains in detail how education more often than not is constructed upon the male myth of total control, a myth that is the source of much unhappiness and leads to the systemic humiliation and discrimination of those perceived as weak: "To some degree," Nussbaum contends, "all cultures portray manliness as involving control, but certainly American culture does, as it holds up to the young the image of the lone cowboy that can provide for himself without any help."[52] Another such image is the lone, towering (male) professor standing on the podium who masters and imparts knowledge without external aid, a powerful brain devoid of bodily materiality and emotive life.

Nussbaum introduces an alternative pedagogy, namely the importance of acknowledging human vulnerability and weakness from the start:

We can see how crucial it is for children not to aspire to control or invulnerability, defining their prospects and possibilities as above the common lot of human life, but, instead, to learn to appreciate vividly the ways in which common human weaknesses are experienced in a wide range of social circumstances, understanding how social and political arrangements of different kinds affect the vulnerabilities that all human beings share.[53]

Nussbaum's chapter concludes by identifying the abilities that she considers fundamental for promoting a "humane, people-sensitive democracy." Such abilities are not based on intellectual skills but on affect and emotions: empathy ("the capacity to see the world from the view-point of other people, particularly the ones whom their society tends to portray as lesser, as 'mere' objects"); compassion ("the capacity for genuine concern for others, both near and distant"), and a strong sense of solidarity.[54] Nussbaum stresses that "weakness is not shameful and the need for others not unmanly" because "need and incompleteness" are occasions "for cooperation and reciprocity."[55] In a similar vein, bell hooks writes: "Engaged pedagogy does not seek simply to empower students. Any classroom that employs a holistic model of learning will also be a place where teachers grow, and are empowered by the process. The empowerment cannot happen if we refuse to be vulnerable while encouraging students to take risks. . . . [Professors] must practice being vulnerable in the classroom, being wholly present in mind, body, and spirit."[56]

Empathy—the central emotion born out of a keen sense of one's own vulnerability and the vulnerability of others—is the glue that ultimately attaches engaged pedagogy to engaged research, not to mention the messy reality of the campus to that of the outside world. Individual and collective vulnerability is the source of an emotive epistemology, in which a continuum between engaged pedagogy and engaged scholarship becomes part of urban humanities practices. The classroom expands and shifts perspectives on the life of the mind. When dominated by the isolated brain—all too often conceived as a distinctively white, male, heterosexual imaginary—higher education partitions off so much, including its potential relevance. Instead, teaching and learning have become notably messy endeavors, where students show up in body and spirit. It is bodies who enter the classroom, all of them outfitted with complex memories, histories, experiences, and heterogeneous ways of knowing and being. Bodies remember, and they certainly do not simplify and impoverish reality, for their mnemotechnics and epistemology are firmly anchored in complex emotions and inscribed on and through flesh.

Inversions

While the banking concept of pedagogy is deeply problematic, it remains the dominant pedagogical mode in all levels of education. It also exists in myriad forms outside the classroom: passively consumed media, conventional strategies of international development, and management-employee structures are but a few of these. Echoing Freire's arguments, Jacques Rancière argues in *The Ignorant Schoolmaster* that the conventional power relationship between the teacher and student must be questioned.[57] His book explores the implications of a true story: that of the teacher Joseph Jacotot, who in the early nineteenth century moved from his native France to teach in Brussels where he was presented with numerous students who only spoke Flemish, a language with which he had no familiarity. After doing nothing more than providing a dual-language copy of Fénelon's *Télémaque* and asking that they learn the French text, he was amazed to discover that the students did so without any help from him, the lauded teacher. As Rancière conveys, "until then, he had believed what all conscientious professors believe: that the important business of the master is to transmit his knowledge to his students so as to bring them, by degrees, to his own level of expertise."[58] Yet this discovery forced Jacotot—and us, in turn—to question the role of the teacher, in Rancière's words, as "explicator." This role, performed in Freire's banking system, relies on a power imbalance between the positions of student and teacher. Specifically, it implies more than a differential in knowledge, but on a more fundamental level, a differential between, to use Rancière's words, an "inferior intelligence and a superior one."

For Rancière, there are two outcomes: First, far from just teaching substance, the pedagogical process of explication also teaches students that they cannot learn without the teacher. He calls this phenomenon *abrutir*, to render stupid and brutish. And, curiously, this phenomenon only becomes stronger, the "better" a teacher may be. And second, Rancière describes the logical inverse of our typical assumptions regarding education: rather than students requiring a teacher, it is the teacher who requires students. By rupturing this extractive relationship, it liberates not only the students to exercise their intelligence freely, but enables teachers to become students. In other words, it can be emancipatory for the formerly disempowered *and* the empowered.

Rancière goes so far as to suggest that ignorant teachers are better than knowledgeable ones because they "will do *less* and *more* at the same time. [They] will not verify what the student has found; [they] will verify that the student has searched."[59] So this suggests that in an emancipated pedagogy, our very evaluative criteria will shift away from ascertaining that a particular set of facts was memorized or that a substantial structure of knowledge was learned, but instead focus on the practice that has occurred and continues to occur. This breaking of the "circle of powerlessness," far from being unique to student-teacher relations in the university, can be found in all "workings of the social world," as Rancière describes, providing an emancipatory method for beginning to address many systems of structural power differentials.

Yet this remains no easy task. In discussing such "universal teaching," where we learn by interacting with our surroundings without teachers, Rancière notes that "no one wants to cope with the intellectual revolution it signifies . . . one must dare to recognize it and pursue the *open* verification of its power."[60] Such openness is required not only for the public nature of this emancipation, but also for the fundamental attitude by which such learning occurs.

Alongside Freire and Rancière, we can also place American philosopher John Dewey whose writings in *How We Think* celebrate the openness of play and the attitude of playfulness that, from childhood, are the source for learning, art, and experience.[61] His pragmatist philosophy emphasizes the fundamental importance of experience in the process of learning, and that teachers—whose vocation he describes as an art, and teachers in turn as artists themselves—like Rancière's ignorant schoolmaster, are most effective when they set up opportunities for students to learn by doing, rather than any form of explication. For Dewey as well, the diametrical power structures of student and teacher are problematic—and to these he adds a third pole, the curriculum itself. In some ways, it is easier to think of an open position for curriculum, one that might morph over the course of the term. The questions raised in class, particularities of students' needs, and current events are part of the dynamic, evolving course content. To extend this openness to the positionality of the teacher and the student, we must acknowledge they are not generic figures, but our own actual bodies, minds, and experiences in the room.

For this reason, we are attuned to the dangers of the parachute model of urban research in which outsiders drop in, spend a short period of time in a given locale, and then leave enriched by their finite experiences. Against this model, we propose "thick collaborations" in which students and faculty establish long-term research bonds with local institutions, students, and faculty leading to collective knowledge creation (see figure 5.15). These bonds are aimed at "authentic thinking" (to use Freire's term), which at its core is a form of dialogue grounded in the human possibilities of transformation and emancipation, of actions that struggle to create a more just city that recognizes and values the humanity of everyone.

Thus, urban humanists must be vigilant about their position-alities, perspectives, histories, epistemologies, and backgrounds when they do research and must also be prepared to constantly subject them to critical scrutiny. They know that their knowledge systems may be partially or even radically incommensurate with the knowledge systems, experiences, and perspectives of others. As such, knowledge is not one-directional but rather multidirectional, hybrid, and oriented to action. It is created in collaboration with partners through dialogue and mutual investigation. As Freire argues, true dialogue—composed of reflection and action—forms the foundation of human liberation:

5.15 Collaborative studio in Tokyo with UCLA and Waseda University students, 2017.
Photo credit: Authors

> True dialogue cannot exist unless the dialoguers engage in critical thinking—thinking which discerns an indivisible solidarity between the world and the people and admits of no dichotomy between them— thinking which perceives reality as process, as transformation, rather than as a static entity—thinking which does not separate itself from action, but constantly immerses itself in temporality without fear of the risks involved.[62]

For Freire as in urban humanities, thinking and action go hand in hand. We thereby create new solidarities aimed at humanizing one another and transforming reality, rather than recognizing the latter as simply given or immutable. Such a transformation is always grounded in humanization and liberation, in the same way as our engagement with the city is rooted in the transformative possibilities of spatial justice. It is a temporal process precisely because "problem-posing education is revolutionary futurity . . . it affirms men and women as beings who transcend themselves, who move forward and look ahead . . . so that they can more wisely build the future."[63] In this regard, futurity is not merely an abstract hope for a better future but a praxis of engaged thinking and collaborative building to create a more just city.

The Studio as Engaged Pedagogy

Thinking concretely about the future is a central part of architectural education, and the setting for this projective pedagogy is the design studio. Urban humanities reinvents the studio to undertake urban research that will undergird speculation about spatial justice. While the conventional object of interest in design studios is the building and its site, courses about the city are a common part of architecture's and urban planning's curricula, and these have often involved research coupled with design. In the postwar period, architects Robert Venturi and Denise Scott Brown famously studied Las Vegas, and their project was influenced by Alison and Peter Smithson's earlier studies of everyday life in London's East End. Renewed attention was focused on the city when Rem Koolhaas undertook a series of research studios at Harvard called Project on the City from 1996–2000.[64] While the Project's studies of Lagos, the Pearl River Delta, and Rome can be legitimately criticized for their detachment from everyday life (Koolhaas observed Lagos at a safe distance from a helicopter, for instance), the work legitimated global urban studies as a subject for the architectural studio. The field of urban humanities situates its work in global megacities through its unique collaboration with the humanities, to bring into the studio setting the voices, positionalities, and narratives of everyday life in order to think about opening possibilities for the future.

The studio, which is the heart of architectural education, is a particular pedagogical platform.[65] It involves a relatively small group of students, usually about a dozen, who work individually or in teams under the guidance of a design practitioner-instructor. They work in physical proximity to one another, around computers and desks, in the fabrication laboratory and on sites, for many hours several days each week. The project orientation brings bodies to labor together around a shared undertaking, and this "making-in-common" distinguishes the studio from other forms of pedagogy in the university. The instructor generates a brief or program in which a design project is outlined, with levels of complexity and focus determined by the level of the students. The projects are speculative, that is, they spark the imagination about future conditions—such as a new library solely for electronic materials or a housing complex in a converted parking structure.

The studio format emerged out of a master-apprentice relationship common to tradecraft of the medieval era—precisely the sort of power relationship that urban humanities seek to disrupt. As Joan Ockman describes in her introduction to *Architecture School*, studio education in the United States was a mixture of this practice of apprenticeship codified in sixteenth-century guilds, with the loose regulations of a "new world," leading to the opening of a ragtag collection of associations, schools, and practicing firms that would take on upwardly mobile trainees, harking back to the figure of the gentleman scholar who could afford the travel and reading required to be adequately self-taught. It was only in the mid-nineteenth century that architectural schools emerged as we would recognize them today, modeled on the German polytechnic and the French École des Beaux-Arts, combining technical skills with "good taste."[66] Around this time, the American Institute of Architects held its first convening, further professionalizing the discipline. Yet despite this standardization of education— or, perhaps, because of it—the master-apprentice relationship remained the norm not only in architecture but in other professions as well. As in the Beaux-Arts *ateliers*, studios typically have a respected "master" instructor who assigns exercises and works closely with individual students as they produce drawings, culminating in a project that is judged in a public setting by a jury of architects. Despite many transformations in education since this time, from the diversification of students to the introduction of digital technologies, the fundamental format of the studio remains mostly unchanged, in spite of articulate calls for transformative pedagogies that resist reproducing asymmetrical power relations.[67]

By disrupting the master-apprentice relationship (which mirrors the teacher-student power dynamics described earlier), important elements of studio education can come to the foreground and serve as a model for engaged pedagogies. First, the instrument of learning is not the lecture or the reading but, instead, the project. A project-oriented pedagogy sets aside the typical curricular goals and expectations on a course organized by disciplinary topics as conventionally understood in favor, instead, of a project. A project is, at its simplest, a kind of assignment wherein students are given a set of open-ended instructions designed to lead them down an open-ended course of discovery. Moreover, a project-orientation considers the meta-level outcomes embedded in all actions undertaken in the classroom. Social philosopher Donald Schön has described the studio experience as follows:

> The architectural design studio is a practicum, a virtual world that represents the real world of practice but is relatively free of its pressures, distractions, and risks. Here students learn, by doing, to recognize competent practice, appreciate where they stand in relation to it, and map a path to it. They learn the "practice" of the practicum, its tools, methods, and media. They do these things under the guidance of a studio master who functions less as a teacher than as a coach who demonstrates, advises, questions, and criticizes. They work with other students, who sometimes play the coach's role. As they immerse themselves in the shared world of the practicum, they unconsciously acquire a kind of background learning of which they will become aware as they move to other settings later on.[68]

Schön recasts the studio master into a more informal and familiar role of the coach—a kind of coach for the hands and mind. He goes on to suggest that students learn from one another such that students themselves become coaches.

A second fundamental piece of studio education is that the speculative nature of making implicates the future. In architecture and urban planning, designs are future-oriented in the sense that they render worlds that do not (yet) exist, apart from their reality as representations. Studio pedagogy has been described as "reflective practice," in which a designer works on a particular project, with particular materials and media, in a complex, context-responsive making process.[69] The process of making recursively cycles through different elements: a discovery on the site might lead to a proposed intervention, which then might unexpectedly demonstrate an undesirable side effect, leading to further modification, such that projects themselves seem to "talk back" and become a form of discourse. Adaptive learning in response to a specific situation, in order to think about as-yet-nonexistent conditions, is a model for urban humanities pedagogy, which is likewise taught in a studio setting around specific projects.

Third and finally, projects undertaken in the studio often simulate projects on specific sites in the world, so that we might consider the *city as collaborative studio*, whether it is our home city of Los Angeles or a partner city across the world. In urban humanities, after returning from two weeks in another city where the issues of short-term fieldwork—the parachute studio—are consistently interrogated, we expect our home city to appear uncannily unfamiliar when we return. Accepting one's ignorance allows for two things: first, we can see our everyday surroundings anew with the defamiliarized eyes of a stranger visiting a new land, attuned to making observations that might slip past a local. And, second, we feel the imperative to set out into the city, giving it the greatest amount of attention and time that we possibly can. In a sense, the city itself becomes the "coach" that frames our reflection-in-action as we engage with it. Far from the tired incantations of professional schools having practical knowledge and an ability to provide academic departments with "real-world" questions to theorize, the city as studio provides a model for turning these distinctions on their head.

Particularly in the second half of the twentieth century, a time characterized by socio-political upheaval, radical pedagogies in architectural education emerged to destabilize both the profession and the academy.[70] The primary intent behind architectural activism around the world, from Santiago to New Haven and Paris, was to remake architecture's relationship to culture in a more relevant, politically responsive manner, and to promote ethical involvement. Compared to the 1960s and 1970s, today's architectural studio lacks such radical energy in spite of a similar upheaval in the social world around the university. The urban humanities approach is an experimental pedagogy that sits within this activist trajectory, not inside of architecture but at its margins, to construct a provocative bridge linking design, urban studies, and the humanities.

Urban Humanities in Action

Classrooms are becoming increasingly diverse, but what makes the urban humanities pedagogical experience notable is that it turns diversity into an essential ingredient of its modus operandi. From the first session on, urban humanities acknowledge difference, and the sense of vulnerability and challenge that comes with it. Moreover, diversity and difference are intensified by the fact that students and faculty come from three different disciplines, namely, architecture, urban planning, and the humanities at large. These three student/faculty cohorts with very different ways of looking at the world share the limited space of a classroom for a year, work together toward a common goal, and, more important, do so with intense self-reflection (figure 5.16). Confronted by architects, for example, urban planners not only learn from them, but also take a closer look at their own ways of operating—and vice versa. The same applies to humanists, who may admire the hands-on attitude of architects and planners, and marvel at how fast and adroitly work gets done when in their hands. To the process, humanists not only add historical, cultural, and linguistic depth but also the all-important "why," creating a back and forth with the "how," between the doing and the undoing of reflective inquiry—a process that creatively shakes the

5.16 Final project review for the Summer Institute, UCLA 2013. Photo credit: Authors

pedagogical ground on which urban humanities stand. Incessantly confronted with the "other" and compelled to collaborate with widely divergent perspectives and ways of being in the world, urban humanists deal with and acknowledge difference and the acute sense of vulnerability that comes with it. They learn about power dynamics and positionality before they leave the classroom. In fact, it is the radical and self-reflective interdisciplinarity of the classroom that makes urban humanists particularly receptive to difference beyond the campus and that teaches them how to accept and even capitalize on the creative powers of vulnerability and empathy. It teaches urban humanists to be fearlessly open to the other and thus to productively and democratically engage with subjects, realities, and practices often diametrically different from their own. Throughout this book, specific examples of urban humanities projects born out of these pedagogical principles are described in the interludes and projects between chapters. (For a comprehensive walk through one year in the life of urban humanities at UCLA, turn to the Coda of this chapter).

The projects that this diverse cohort of students, faculty, and community partners create are neither grand statements nor utopian solutions. Instead, they tend to be more modest, small-scale interventions, speculative collaborations that are inserted into the fabric of the city in order to expose and begin to address a spatial injustice. They open up the public university to the outside and bring the outside in. They are porous in every sense of the word. As such, urban humanities bring a productive response to the oft-heard cries of crisis in the humanities and at the same time create avenues for political and cultural engagement in architecture and planning. Student projects are experimental, engaged, and speculative forms of knowledge-making rooted in the city, charged with creating new knowledge, new kinds of tools, and new possibilities for opening up the walls of the university and addressing spatial injustices through transnational creativity and networks. This is a prototype for the "fluid" university based on permeability, openness, interdisciplinarity, collaboration, and community engagement. Indeed, the decolonization of knowledge is never complete, but must also start somewhere. We see urban humanities as one possible start.

Coda: A Year in the Life of Urban Humanities at UCLA

Each summer from 2013 to the present, a diverse group of twenty-four graduate students and four or five faculty members come together for a three-week Summer Institute that uses Los Angeles as a research laboratory to put the urban humanities concepts of engaged scholarship and pedagogy into practice. Urban humanities students come from both PhD and professional master's programs in the humanities (literary studies, history, Chicana/o studies, the arts), architecture, and urban planning, and bring together a wide range of positionalities, life experiences, and perspectives.

The intensive summer program precedes a full academic year during which the students take additional courses and studios in urban humanities, and sets the tone for the entire year: thick, hierarchically flattened collaborations between students and faculty; exploratory engagement in unfamiliar urban settings; exposure to self-initiated studio projects; working with unlikely combinations of practices (thick mapping, filmic sensing) toward objectives like empathy, embodiment, data richness, activism, and creativity on projects that can have real-world impacts. Such objectives are brought to bear in a productive mix of ideas, and each team must collectively build its approach to attain a degree of confidence. Students and faculty therefore coproduce hands-on working knowledge of the city, its communities, and their agency therein.

During the 2015–2016 academic year, the Urban Humanities Initiative focused on Los Angles and Mexico City. In the Summer Institute of 2015 some students had grown up in Tijuana or Mexico City; others had never set foot in Mexico; more than half of the group spoke Spanish. Through historical investigations, multimedia mapping projects, and spatial ethnographies, the Summer Institute was framed around the investigation of contested urban histories, erasures, and spatial injustices in Los Angeles (figure 5.17). Students worked in collaborative, interdisciplinary teams to make films, produce thick maps, and propose digital activist interventions, all with the goal of creating a foundation for a cross-disciplinary learning community whose members prepared to work together for the remainder of the year. Projects were short and intense and the city laid bare students' quandaries about how to ethically open possibilities for better futures.

In comparing Los Angeles and Mexico City, places that spatially overlap in palimpsests of colonial history, the pedagogical and research practices of urban humanities were motivated by the bold question of whether it is possible to decolonize knowledge. Can knowledge ever be "decolonized"? The answers were far from clear-cut. We began with a relatively simple proposition: Rather than bring our knowledge and tools to Mexico City to "solve a problem" there, how might we engage with Mexico City in order to explore the knowledge and tools that could be brought back to Los Angeles, so that we see our "home city" differently? To ask this question demands collaboration with Mexican counterparts who could ask, reciprocally, how they might study Los Angeles to illuminate their own circumstances in Mexico City? And how might we identify, address, and challenge the spatial injustices in Los Angeles with toolsets, perspectives, and knowledge from another city and set of experiences? What

5.17 Project in Boyle Heights neighborhood of Los Angeles, where students collaborated with a local nonprofit and Latino bike activists to make streets safer for people who bike to work out of necessity rather than for recreation (see also Project B). Credit: Authors

kind of intellectual groundwork would have to be put in place to begin to orchestrate such a transformation? To do so, we would have to imagine new kinds of transnational knowledge, new kinds of collaborations beyond the walls of the university, the limits of the city or the country, and utilize a range of tools to develop new kinds of speculative knowledge and historical awareness. The cities themselves provide a geographically distinct space from the university for such iterative, unconventional undertakings. Their common ground, both material and historical, of streets, markets, neighborhoods, contested spaces, public spheres, and so on, offers the starting point for comparative reflection.

The Summer Institute acted as the foundational platform upon which the rest of the year was constructed, creating a new collective conception of what the classroom can be and how knowledge is generated. While Los Angeles and its many neighborhoods provide a living laboratory, the university offers a different set of learning opportunities. The Summer Institute resides far from a typical lecture hall; its classroom is more like a studio with materials for creation close at hand. The chairs and tables are mobile, while the walls and floor are used for work spaces and to pin up project work for collective review. One session focused on mapping the events of the 1871 Chinese massacre. Tables were pushed aside, as one map was projected on the wall, while another map was unfurled on the floor, where students spent hours annotating it with a multiplicity of narratives, temporal inquiries, data, and comparative analyses—both historical and synchronic—culminating in contemporary examples of racial injustice and urban erasure.

During other sessions, the cohort left the classroom behind entirely. Outside the classroom itself, we moved from Westwood (where UCLA is located) to other key sites in Los Angeles, such as El Pueblo and Chinatown. By experiencing the city together, the hierarchical order of traditional classroom space was overcome. The urban humanities approach proposes something closer to a collaborative workshop, a messy garage or busy laboratory, where knowledge can be co-created with a spirit of porosity across visible and invisible borders: disciplinary, national, spatial, linguistic, social, and cultural.

Throughout the academic year, Los Angeles and Mexico City were put into productive conversation. The two subsequent ten-week seminars built a flexible, open knowledge of the thematic confluences between the two cities—dependence on water, resilience from earthquakes, challenges of traffic and mobility, precarious housing, political and social violence, urban displacement—creating a dialogic circuit for deeper understanding. In the fall seminar, the focus was specifically on Mexico City: watching films and documentaries, reading novels and histories, considering artistic production, studying architecture as material culture, and learning about events such as the 1968 Tlatelolco massacre and the 1985 earthquake in Mexico City. In the destructive aftermath of a catastrophe, the idea was to apprehend the creativity of life in Mexico City as a way of rethinking, rebuilding, reimagining, and surviving after disasters, whether human-made or natural, contemporary or historical. How could such knowledge, creativity, and imagination be brought back to Los Angeles? Could the gift that Mexico offered be returned by California?

In the winter, we focused on the theme of borders and transgressions, where the U.S.-Mexico border was not just understood in its embodied, physical, and geographic manifestation, but also as a symbolic, economic, and cultural formation. This included a study trip to Tijuana and San Diego, where the theoretical and abstract knowledge of the classroom encountered the material reality of the border. The Tijuana experience was encapsulated by an evening visit to *Playas de Tijuana*, where a visually porous, politically hardened border fence extends across a sandy beach and disappears into the Pacific. Here, shrouded in an eerie ocean fog, we walked the border, touched it, stuck our hands through the vertical openings, read the messages scrawled on the fence and the pieces of political art, bodily grasping the immensity of the divide, as we peered across into the United States. We were forced to materially confront our relationship with the border—including, for most of us, our privilege of being able to freely cross it back and forth—and to think through where our knowledge might better open up spaces for circulation and justice through such a seemingly insurmountable edifice.

The rest of the year followed such practices, continuously creating a growing bank of reflexive knowledge built across Los Angeles, Mexico City, and the geographic, cultural, linguistic, and social borderlands in between. By the time we arrived in Mexico City in the spring, a shared conceptual toolset existed for engaging in situated community projects. Each of three partner organizations—an arts organization (inSite/Casa Gallina), an architecture firm (PRODUCTORA and LIGA, their public program space), and a city government urban think tank (Laboratorio para la Ciudad)—provided a different lens for interpreting the city. Representatives of each first came to Los Angeles to work with us, and then we went to Mexico City to work with them on site, and later still, our students returned during the summer to deepen their interventions. The idea was not to package and ship "expert" knowledge in either direction, but rather to forge partnerships, grow collaborations, recognize the unfamiliar even in our home cities, and open critical perspectives for networks of engagement.

In this two-way process, knowledge was "forged and produced," to quote Freire, "in the tension between practice and theory."[71]

The result was a series of projects of engaged, speculative scholarship that were realized in specific urban sites characterized by spatial inequities and contestations. The goal was never to "master" Mexico City, but rather to engage with local community organizations around specific issues within specific locales in the city—street vending, children's safety, gentrification—in order to bring back knowledge, insights, and perspectives that might inform analogous issues in Los Angeles. As Peter Chesney, a PhD student in history at UCLA, reflected: "The most important experience in Mexico City was learning about the limitations of our own systems of knowledge, so that we could come back to Los Angeles and speculate about a place we think we know." And this is what we did upon returning to California by extending, at least conceptually, the work done in Mexico City in a series of collaborative, humanistic, spatial interventions with community groups in LA's Boyle Heights neighborhood.

In the spring studio, the urban humanities students worked with five Los Angeles-based community organizations—Libros Schmibros, The East Los Angeles Community Corporation, From Lot to Spot, Multicultural Communities for Mobility, and Self Help Graphics—grappling with critical issues currently unfolding in Boyle Heights, a neighborhood rife with spatial contestations and tensions between the residents and the ambitions of developers, city planners, business leaders, transit authorities, and government policies. These community organizations work on literacy, housing, green space, transportation, and activist visual arts, respectively, trying to find ethical, ground-up ways to enact change, struggling with questions such as: How do you develop a neighborhood that protects its residents, rather than enabling gentrifying forces? How does gentrification differentially affect residents of a neighborhood and what are the significant conflicts? How do you intervene in ways that are ethical and attuned to the needs of greater LA? As outsiders to the neighborhood, our students occupied a liminal zone inflected with perspectives, knowledge, and activist practices stemming from Mexico City.

The projects that emerged were attempts, however provisional, to fuse these experiences and imagine scenarios that were ethically grounded, truly collaborative, and imaginatively engaged with the possibilities of translational, humanistic knowledge: A magic storytelling box for children's literacy, a manual for community greening, a *fotonovella* imagining a just future for the neighborhood, a successful city arts activation grant for making a series of installations advocating for safer streets for bike commuters. And now there is also transnational circulation of these projects, with ideas spreading back from Los Angeles to Mexico City: creating safer streets for vulnerable cyclists, families, and children, which has influenced policy in Mexico City through the work of our partners at Laboratorio para la Ciudad, a collaboration that continues as one of our Mexican collaborators joins UCLA as a graduate student.

Project G:

La Caja Mágica:
Seeking Literary Justice
Los Angeles

5.18 Demonstration of La Caja Mágica. Photo credit: Authors

Maricela Becerra, Cat Callaghan, Will Davis, Grace Ko, Benjamin Kolder, and Alejandro Ramirez Mendez

La Caja Mágica is the symbolic and material center of an urban humanities project: a chrome-coated plywood box that unfolds to reveal an interior of grass (figure 5.18). The box stores grass mats, creating audience seating. The strange, mirrored, rolling box shifts to a storytelling space containing all the necessary tools: it is a box, but also a storyteller's seat, an object but also a location.

The mobile box/library reflects its surroundings to dazzling effect, emulating its environment. When children approach, they see themselves playing in its surface as the box blends into its surroundings. Once open, the mirrored box's interior is covered in artificial turf providing the storyteller a place to sit. La Caja Mágica transports the audience from an anonymous sidewalk into a place where fiction emanates; a box unfolds to become a little public library enlivened by magical stories. It plays, in a minimalistic way, with the basic conditions needed to transform any space into a public library, to share the pleasures of reading and storytelling.

La Caja Mágica was created in collaboration with Libros Schmibros, an independent lending library and the local elementary school in Boyle Heights, as a way to enhance what the team came to call "literary justice." Literary justice describes equal access for all to books and stories. It is premised on the idea of a culture that embraces stories as a part of life and as a part of a community-building effort. Some challenges that literary justice faces are the availability of resources (books, magazines, novellas, etc.); limited scheduling times or hard-to-reach public library locations; and the knowledge of where distribution points such as libraries are located. By shifting the time, place, and publicness to meet unexpected conditions, La Caja Mágica creatively

weds literacy and community engagement to the advantage of both. Literary justice promotes the importance of reading aloud in the public realm as a means to enhance and empower community participation in public space.

La Hora Mágica was a planned storytelling event that took place in the kiosk at the center of Mariachi Plaza (figure 5.19). In Spanish and English, children's librarians read aloud tales to enchant a young audience and their parents who had come to the gazebo (figure 5.20). Crowns, books in both languages, and puppets spilled from La Caja Mágica, adding to the dancing and stories. Spectacle and performance represent key components of this literary intervention. The event, not only a symbolic transformation of public space into library, also brought unity, peace, and pleasure to the participants. The project proposed, on the one hand, a change in the spatial practices of the neighborhood by making accessible the art of storytelling, but on the other hand, the whole experience allowed a reconfiguration of the reading and storytelling expectations of the people. And every child was encouraged to take home a book.

5.19 Bringing La Caja Mágica to the storytellers' gazebo
in Boyle Heights, East LA. Photo credit: Authors

5.20 Stills showing children at storytelling event with La Caja Mágica. Photo credit: Authors

Project H:

Dos Méxicos a Través de Regina
Mexico City

5.21 Views of Calle Regina in Mexico City. Credit: Authors

Neta Nakash, Gabriela Barrios, Kim Zacarias, Ale Guerrero,
Dulce González, and Max Greenberg

Calle Regina, situated in Mexico City's historic downtown—its Centro Histórico—offers a glimpse of the gentrifying process here that reflects both displacement and adaptation (figure 5.21). The process of nation building in twenty-first-century Mexico is represented here through visible and invisible elements of the street and its social dynamics. This nation-building process and its role in (re)imagining Mexico intersects with the gentrification process that has swept through the west side of Calle Regina. We see this intersection most prominently in the following elements: the commissioned street art on the western side of the street, representing Mexican identity through pre-Hispanic symbols as well as popular culture icons; and the ease with which significant historic locations on the eastern side of Regina are overlooked by popular imaginaries of the street—such as Aguilita Plaza, the supposed site on which Tenochtitlán was founded, and Futura CDMX, a museum about the city's urban transformation.

Centro Histórico has been home to different ethnic minority groups, including immigrants from central, southern, and eastern Europe, and the Middle East, who settled in Mexico City at the turn of the twentieth century. In the past several decades, Calle Regina has undergone a transformation, spearheaded in part by descendants of the ethnic minority communities that settled here a century earlier. Calle Regina retains its highly specialized nature, which calls customers from all over the city for the *papelerías* (stationery and school supply stores), bars, and *jarcherías* (stores selling rope, sponges, brooms, etc.).

As scholars who are new to the street, we take this historical background as a tool to inform our ideas of the change on the street. Our process takes its lead from one of our respondents, a street artist who has painted two murals on Regina. His approach to gentrifying neighborhoods is comprised of three steps: *Listen, Evaluate, Intervene*. This process acknowledges the existing conditions of a space while also attempting a collaborative intervention that seeks to include rather than displace or exclude. In our own project, we first created a video that allowed us to listen and move toward constructing a thick map to show the temporal differences, thresholds, flow, and movement across the street (figure 5.22). Through binaries such as "Fresa (posh, nouveau riche neighborhood)/Barrio" and "Visible/Invisible," we begin to see more clearly the ambiguities and communication between the two sides of the street. As a next step, we created *monografía*-style images that allow users to imagine an intervention that brings the invisible into the urban imaginary. The method of our "intervention" was inspired by one of the primary commercial markets along Calle Regina: papelerías. Since the 1920s, monografías have served as a pedagogical tool in Mexican public education that takes a visual and interactive approach to teach culture and identity. Students are prompted to cut out and interpret images of famous historical/contemporary figures and monuments. Our monografía features human subjects and material objects not mentioned in history books and sometimes not visible on the street yet still influential along Calle Regina and the surrounding streets of Mexico City's Centro Histórico.

We recognize that our nonspatial intervention alone does not offer the possibility of substantial change. As the aforementioned street artist told us, art, as well as speculative intervention, needs the collaboration of the municipal government, as well as the community, to really bring about change.

5.22 Interactive mapping of Calle Regina, Mexico City. Credit: Authors

Interlude 5:

Los Angeles
Million Dollar Hoods

Kelly Lytle Hernandez

Los Angeles County operates the largest jail system in the United States, which imprisons more people than any other nation on Earth. At a cost approaching $1 billion annually, more than 20,000 people are caged every night in county jails and city lockups. But not every neighborhood is equally impacted by Los Angeles's massive jail system. In fact, LA's prison budget is largely committed to incarcerating many people from just a few neighborhoods. In some communities, more than $1 million is spent annually on incarcerations. These are LA's Million Dollar Hoods.

Million Dollar Hoods (MDH) is a digital mapping project (www.milliondollarhoods.org) that uses police data to monitor how much local authorities spend on locking up residents in different Los Angeles neighborhoods (figure 5.23). MDH also documents that the majority of LA's jailed population is black, brown, and poor. Moreover, MDH provides the only full and public account of the leading causes of arrest in Los Angeles County, revealing that drug possession and DUIs are the top booking charges in LA's Million Dollar Hoods. Finally, MDH produces rapid-response research that documents current policing trends in the city. To date, our reports have revealed that 43 percent of all arrests in Los Angeles are of unemployed persons. We have documented that arrests of homeless persons are skyrocketing and have unmasked the scale of the money bail system. Collectively, this public-facing research counters the popular misunderstanding that incarceration advances public safety by removing violent and serious offenders from the streets. In fact, local authorities are investing millions in locking up the county's most economically vulnerable, geographically isolated, and racially marginalized populations for drug- and alcohol-related crimes.

An ongoing collaboration between UCLA researchers and community organizations, MDH is a university-based but community-driven research project. Across Los Angeles our community partners include Youth Justice Coalition, Los Angeles Community Action Network, Dignity and Power Now!, and JusticeLA. At UCLA, our team is comprised of an interdisciplinary group of students, staff, and faculty. Together, we conceptualized the project, acquired the data, and mapped it. To date, our maps and reports have been marshaled by advocates to advance a variety of justice reinvestment campaigns, while the UN Special Rapporteur on Extreme Poverty cited our research in his report on the criminalization of homelessness in America. But our report on the money bail system is probably the most widely cited of our works.

In California, all persons facing criminal charges are guaranteed the right to freedom before trial, except in a few cases. But there is a price for that freedom. The money bail system requires many people to pay for pretrial release. When a person, or their representative, pays money bail up front and in full, the money is refunded so long as the person charged with a crime shows up for all of their court proceedings. But most people eligible for money bail cannot afford to pay the total sum up front. Instead, most people eligible for money bail are left with one of two options. The first is to stay in jail until the conclusion of their court proceedings, which can take weeks, months, or even years. The second is to contract with a bail bond agent who provides a surety bond to the court on their behalf. The surety bond operates like a promissory note: the bail bond company does not pay up front but, rather, promises to pay the full money bail amount if the accused fails to appear in court. For this service, a bail bond agent requires the arrested person, or their representative, to pay a nonrefundable deposit, typically amounting to 10 percent of the total bail amount. A bail bond agent will also charge a series of service fees and often requires some form of collateral, such as a home or car. In California, an estimated 97 percent of the people who pay money bail use a bail bond agent.

MDH research has provided an unprecedented glimpse at the scale of the money bail system in Los Angeles, documenting that more than $23 billion was levied in the city of Los Angeles between 2012 and 2017. Of that, most people could not pay for their freedom so they remained in custody. The reasons why people did not pay for release during the booking process are not recorded in Los Angeles Police Department (LAPD) records but poverty was likely a major factor. Mapping LAPD data shows that the greatest sums of money bail were levied in the City Council districts with the highest rates of unemployment. Moreover, more than $4 billion in money bail was levied on houseless persons. But, of those who used a bail bond agent to pay for their constitutional right to pretrial release, African Americans paid more than $50 million and Latinos paid more than $100 million in nonrefundable bail bond deposits. In turn, the money bail system is a multibillion-dollar toll that strips tens of millions of dollars annually in cash and assets from some of LA's most economically vulnerable and racially marginalized persons, families, and communities.

In sum, the MDH project is using mapping, data analysis, and a community-based methodology to make a wealth of data broadly available to the public. In particular, our scholarship is used by advocates and activists who are pressing local authorities to divest from police and jails and invest in the community-based services needed to build a healthier, safer, and more equitable community for all.

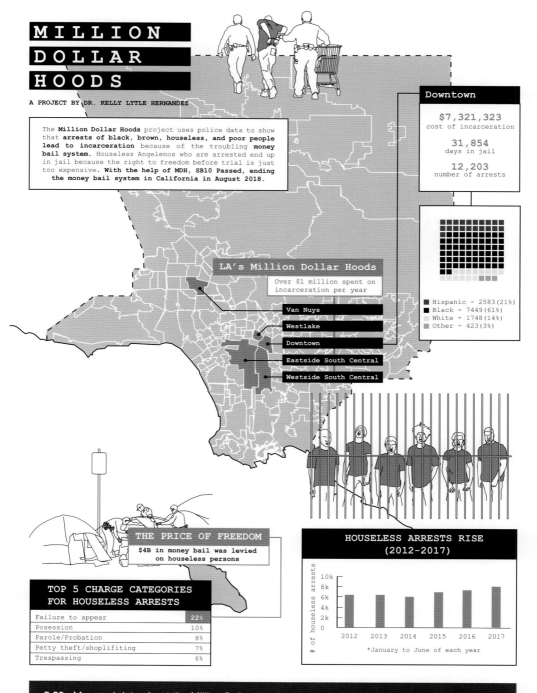

MILLION DOLLAR HOODS

A PROJECT BY DR. KELLY LYTLE HERNANDEZ

The **Million Dollar Hoods** project uses police data to show that **arrests of black, brown, houseless, and poor people lead to incarceration** because of the troubling **money bail system.** Houseless Angelenos who are arrested end up in jail because the right to freedom before trial is just too expensive. **With the help of MDH, SB10 Passed, ending the money bail system in California in August 2018.**

LA's Million Dollar Hoods

Over $1 million spent on incarceration per year

Van Nuys
Westlake
Downtown
Eastside South Central
Westside South Central

Downtown

$7,321,323
cost of incarceration

31,854
days in jail

12,203
number of arrests

■ Hispanic - 2583 (21%)
■ Black - 7449 (61%)
□ White - 1748 (14%)
■ Other - 423 (3%)

THE PRICE OF FREEDOM

$4B in money bail was levied on houseless persons

TOP 5 CHARGE CATEGORIES FOR HOUSELESS ARRESTS

Failure to appear	22%
Posession	10%
Parole/Probation	8%
Petty theft/shoplifting	7%
Trespassing	6%

HOUSELESS ARRESTS RISE (2012-2017)

of houseless arrests

10k
8k
6k
4k
2k
0

2012 2013 2014 2015 2016 2017

*January to June of each year

5.23 Map and data about the Million Dollar Hoods project. Credit: Joshua Nelson

6

Conclusion:

Assessing Urban Humanities

It would be impossible (if not counter-productive) to provide a neat and tidy conclusion that summarizes the field of urban humanities. Like their object of study—the city—urban humanities are a dynamic, ever-changing work in progress. At the same time, in the preceding chapters we have articulated some of the interdisciplinary and experimental practices and multimedia projects for studying the urban through forms of engaged scholarship and pedagogy. These are not prescriptive but rather descriptive of a state of knowledge in an emerging conjunction of disciplines. At the core of urban humanities is the pursuit of spatial justice through a carefully contextualized attention toward the future.

While a definition of urban humanities will always remain provisional, the strength of this shortcoming is that the boundaries of this field fluctuate to embrace new subjects, methods, and objects, thus leaving open a range of possibilities as cities change and demand ever-newer strategies and approaches to documenting, understanding, and intervening in them.

This openness is a key element of urban humanities, creating an alternative space where new ideas and propositions are explored and tested. We can jump into projects and activities that might not fly elsewhere; we can enact new models of community engagement; and we can develop experimental scholarly outputs and pedagogies. While grounded in the layered spaces of the past and the exigencies of the present, urban humanities have always been invested in speculative practices that imagine the possibility of a more just, more equitable future—and this openness ensures that futurity belongs not only to the city, our object of study, but also, self-reflexively, to the practice of urban humanities.

But there are shortcomings and tensions that remain. Foremost is the urban humanities' lack of a strong disciplinary profile and preferred fusion of methodologies and practices from different fields. Disciplines come with an armory of epistemologies and methods that legitimize them, as they have been based on often centuries-long canonical practices of research, scientific inquiry, and know-how. Urban humanities' insistence of selectively borrowing from other disciplines and "fusing" them into hybrid practices may appear as shallow and not rigorous enough to social science scholars, who might ask "where is the empirical evidence?" Similarly, humanities scholars may doubt the seriousness of an enterprise that speculates about an unknown future, and architects may find as constraining the type of justice-oriented criticality that urban humanities want to promote. As our formulation of urban humanities has thus far operated at the interstices of urban planning and social sciences, design and architecture, and the humanities, this is all to say nothing of the critiques that may be contributed by disciplines that have yet to (but may in the future) enter the fusion of urban humanities.

A second shortcoming or tension that may not be the fault of urban humanities per se but may certainly impact and put the future of this field at risk relates to the structure of the university. As we have already discussed, the university, as a centuries-old institution, has long established the operational rules of the academy. And while academic authorities have recently purported to value multidisciplinarity and collaboration, the structure of the university (from its intellectual and administrative divisions into distinct disciplinary and departmental units respectively, to its rewards system for faculty promotions and advancement) often counteracts or at least makes more difficult experimentation, disciplinary fusion, and the breaking of disciplinary and departmental silos. Collaborative, experimental scholarship and pedagogy are far from the norms at most universities. In addition, the university upholds the independence of disciplines, which in turn hinges upon boundaries that are definitive. Scholars in each field hold to their core constituent theories and objects, even as they may criticize their canon. Urban humanities seep across the boundaries, which at times appears as trespass. We have found this problem particularly challenging for our multidisciplined doctoral students, whose very task in graduate school is to come to terms with and situate their own work within their chosen fields. An unwritten academic convention is for novitiates to remain within a field's boundaries so that they may be trained and judged accordingly. Urban humanities respect these disciplines, but not the proprietary claims on which their projects for autonomy are based.

A third tension of the urban humanities relates to the privilege that accompanies each one of us as established faculty or doctoral students at first-tier research universities. We want to work with and for communities; we value community empowerment, participation, openness, and social and spatial justice. But our positionality puts us distinctively on the side of power. Why would less-privileged communities trust us? What do we have in common with them? How can they be assured that they are not yet another "academic inquiry," that their neighborhoods are not mere sites for hosting a new academic undertaking, which in the end will, at best, have no impact on them or, at worst, may even bring along negative dividends? Urban humanities have become increasingly self-reflective, in an effort to avoid the neo-colonialist "parachuting in" model to study a foreign city or an underserved community in our own city. With the goal of spatial justice, every practice—be it scholarly research or activist intervention—carries an ethical dimension. The field of urban humanities is in a state of constant negotiation with itself and its collaborators, the realities that surround it, and the communities with which it engages, as it seeks to counteract the hegemony of expertise. It is effectively and constantly revising its intellectual and ethical parameters based on new information, most importantly by the new perspectives contributed by the positionalities of collaborators that join along the way. In many ways, it embodies intellectual inquiry at its best, which is never static, never self-satisfied, in a constant state of productive disquiet and dynamic self-scrutiny. In other words, it is a force ultimately that shakes academic complacency, and by doing so stimulates engaged teaching and learning to inspire students across disciplines.

The future of urban humanities is dependent on how we respond to and benefit from these tensions. The presently rather murky criteria of what constitutes a "good" urban humanities project—both in its process and outcomes—need to be more clearly delineated. Good in what ways, and for whom? What does it mean to truly see spatial justice manifest? Our visibility within the university world and our alliances with university actors need to be strategic to allow us to go against the grain of disciplinarity and "departmentality." And, above all, our relationships with communities need to be profoundly and equitably bidirectional; we need to find a way to close the gap between scholarly expertise and expertise on the ground that is held by the various communities with whom we wish to collaborate. Further, this critical work must not come at the expense of abdicating our responsibility to use our privilege and scholarly expertise to see spatial justice manifest—an "easy way out" often deployed, even with the best of intentions, by those paralyzed by these important questions. Over the past years, engaged scholarship seems in greater danger of inaction than of misplaced spatial justice interventions. Prior to action, critical hesitation and mindful collaboration are absolutely necessary, but so is designing our scholarly practices to have real-world implications beyond the walls of the academy.

As such, it is important to think through two related pieces of the Urban Humanities Initiative: how can it redefine and shape the university, in an inward-focused sense, and how can it structure and sustain collaborative relationships and partnerships with nonprofit organizations and public entities, in an outward-focused sense. Urban humanities are a system of knowledge, relationships, values, and practices. The field challenges certain structures of higher education: it isn't a major, a course, a discipline, or a department. It temporarily brings people together (students, faculty, artists, community leaders, filmmakers, architects, planners, and more) to work on projects for which both the working relationships and the project outcomes are contingent, partial, and speculative. But despite good intentions, spatial justice cannot be achieved within an academic year, and projects almost always warrant more time. Urban humanities augment disciplinary perspectives but have not (yet) fully gained traction within the university or for that matter within communities; the urban humanist's work advances the more often it is practiced under a variety of conditions by a variety of actors (for example, through experiments in thick mapping, new configurations and conditions of engagement with community partners, and so forth). This alone is not sufficient, but also de-mands a setting for reflection and critique of urban humanist work.

To date, the contributions of the different fields and disciplines to urban humanities have been uneven. The city, for urban planners, is a multifaceted object and there is recent attention to diversity and environmental justice, but these concerns have not always warranted interpretation, polyvalent narratives, or artistic action. Urban planning has few connections to conventional humanist traditions. Unlike architecture, which has strong roots in the arts and cultural studies, planning in an academic context is tied to the social sciences, and has a presentist bias toward current problems that can be solved through its well-defined subdisciplines (transportation, housing, international development, urban economics, environmental planning, and so forth). It often privileges quantitative analyses and statistical evidence over qualitative research and ethnography, and urban humanities may have overcorrected this imbalance, instead overlooking the often valuable contributions of quantitative analysis. Such work in conjunction with explorations of big data and critical data studies represents an area where urban humanities can be pushed forward. On the other hand, notions of participatory planning represent a key contribution to urban humanities from urban planning.

In some ways, the humanistic fields have been most difficult to engage because they themselves are so diverse. The spaces between philosophy, art history, music, anthropology, and literature are already so vast—in terms of method, objects of study, and scholarly traditions—that there is no built-in coherence among the wide-ranging humanistic fields, in contrast to architecture and planning. But perhaps more urgently: The city is not a pre-given construct of study for any particular humanistic field (although any humanistic field may, of course, study the city). Perhaps this is because temporality—not spatiality—has historically been privileged in most humanistic fields. As the field of urban humanities takes shape in the coming decade within humanities divisions, where it is most likely to find an academic home, it is likely to be a magnet for individuals from many different fields. The disciplinary contribution from the humanities will thus be tied to the contribution of an array of humanists rather than to any established scholarly community.

Finally, contributions from the architectural discipline need re-inforcement. The city is certainly the site where architecture meets its intrinsic political nature, and urban humanities are capable of making architecture's social and cultural status explicit, which is a central interest of many architecture students. This is the "import" project for the architectural discipline (architecture imports urbanism and humanities). The "export" project, however, is also important for other disciplines. Studio methods, material culture practices (that is, building design and architecture itself), as well as aesthetic practices play two important roles: they construct a shared reality, and they offer critical and creative agency. The urban humanities project has incorporated a version of architecture's studio methods in its pedagogy, but less so its potential for a more substantive contribution. The damaging stereotypes within architecture (its collusion with capital, its privileging of aesthetics and form, its white maleness) must continue to be addressed, and more deeply. In the future, architecture's humanistic underpinnings (history, theory, art) should be made more explicit. At the same time, along with our colleagues within architecture, we can more fully explore potential means to address its problematic social history and contemporary position in order to raise questions about spatial justice, such as through recuperating positive architectural histories, or championing alternative forms of agency and political engagement in the built environment.

This may go hand in hand with the expansion of the geographic focus of the urban. While our approach to urban humanities has derived foremost from the study of the megacities of the Pacific Rim (Los Angeles, Tokyo, Shanghai, and Mexico City), there are certainly plenty of other cities and regions in the world that can be studied using an urban humanities approach. It would be interesting and useful to do a more macro-scale analysis of the flows that pass through Los Angeles (or other cities in comparison) in terms of capital, labor, goods, tourism, migration, and so forth in order to map out a more rigorous justification as to why we have focused on the megacities of the Pacific Rim beyond the obvious geographic logics. We have always had a sense of the particularity of Pacific Rim urbanism, but a theory as such has never been fully articulated.[1] At the same time, we might productively examine geographies that would be considered "nonurban," or at least not megacities, to characterize the intimacies that exist nearly everywhere in our globalized and urbanized world. Our work in the Tijuana–San Diego region and U.S.-Mexico borderlands at large, for example, has already begun to expand the practices of urban humanities to emphasize material culture, forensics, memory landscapes, migration, and fundamental questions of ethics and responsibility. How might urban humanities further shift and develop if we looked at regions in Central America, or Southeast Asia, which are part of the Pacific Rim but aren't necessarily urban cores? Or even the Global South in our own backyard, as found in the impoverished regions that are deeply interconnected with Los Angeles yet also astonishingly overlooked and marginalized, such as the Coachella Valley or the cities of California's Central Valley?

Finally, we might ask: Why are urban humanities situated at the university and not embedded, perhaps, within the city? While we may rightfully critique the history of exclusivity and elitism of the university, we believe that the university offers something exceptional that deserves to be defended and protected: namely, a commitment to knowledge and the pursuit of truth. To be sure, there isn't a singular truth out there but rather a multiplicity of truths, systems of knowing, and ways of creating knowledge—and the university gives us the space to pursue them. In every case, this knowledge serves to stave off falsehood, ideology, dogma, and prejudice. We believe that knowledge can—and must—be in the service of democratic ends, promoting justice and equity, especially in times when the distinction between true and false, and right and wrong has become utterly blurred and upended in certain sectors of society and political life. The university is a privileged site, to be sure, but one in which truths can—and must—still speak back to power. Such truths come from the accumulation of data, knowledge, history, culture, and language; they are found in the archives and libraries at the center of our institutions; they are disseminated in the pedagogical and communicative practices that encourage students and scholars to question, critique, interpret, convey, and extend the cultural record of our humanity; and they are debated but also credentialed in the disciplinary and departmental practices of faculty in research and teaching.

As the university has begun to change, it has become a more open, more public, and more engaged institution in which knowledge is created and flows in multiple directions. Knowledge can be dangerous to some because it exposes ideology, disabuses stereotypes, and unmoors conventional beliefs. Knowledge in the pursuit of justice not only hinges on ethics but propels social change and thus is inimical to the status quo. Even with all its faults and shortcomings, the university is a powerful generator of knowledge and ethical change. It is for this reason that urban humanities emerge from the confluence of disciplines and knowledge practices of the university, but will not remain in the university alone. Urban humanities have already begun to suffuse the city by bringing the city into the university and the university into the city. Indeed, we speculate about a future embedded in the present where these spaces that have long been set up in opposition overlap, eventually becoming one and the same. This is the transformative potential of urban humanities today.

Notes

Chapter 1

1. This definition is drawn from several sources that include P. V. Aureli, *The City as a Project* (Berlin: Ruby Press, 2016); M. Hajer and A. Reijndorp, *In Search of a New Public Domain: Analysis and Strategy* (Rotterdam: NAi Publishers, 2001); and U. Beck, "Risk Society's 'Cosmopolitan Moment,'" *New Geographies* 1 (2009): 24–35.

2. See for example, R. Sennett, "New Ways of Thinking about Space," *The Nation*, September 24, 2012; S. Sassen, *Expulsion: Brutality and Complexity in the Global Economy* (Cambridge, MA: Belknap Press of Harvard University, 2014); and D. Harvey, "The Crisis of Planetary Urbanization," in *Uneven Growth: Tactical Urbanisms for Expanding Megacities,* ed. P. Gadanho, 26–31 (New York: MoMA, 2014).

3. "Urban humanities" is a term coined at UCLA by the authors, through research and pedagogy sponsored by the Andrew W. Mellon Foundation's initiative entitled "Architecture, Urbanism, and the Humanities." Launched in 2011, this initiative has funded more than a dozen academic institutions to explore the intersection of these diverse fields.

4. See, for example: A. Burdick, J. Drucker, P. Lunenfeld, T. Presner, and J. Schnapp, *Digital_Humanities* (Cambridge, MA: MIT Press, 2012); R. Emmett and D. Nye, *The Environmental Humanities: A Critical Introduction* (Cambridge, MA: MIT Press, 2017); and T. R. Cole, R. A. Carson, and N. S. Carlin, *Medical Humanities: An Introduction* (Cambridge: Cambridge University Press, 2014).

5. T. Morton, *Hyperobjects: Philosophy and Ecology after the End of the World* (Minneapolis: University of Minnesota Press, 2013).

6. W. Benjamin, "Theses on the Philosophy of History," in *Illuminations*, trans. Harry Zohn (New York: Schocken, 1968), 254.

7. In 2012, Russell Berman called for a "new era" in graduate education in the humanities, proposing, among other things, a five-year PhD degree as well as curricular changes that included more "professionalization opportunities" to prepare students for the reality of multiple possible career tracks. He concluded by citing past Modern Language Association (MLA) president Sidonie Smith,

who herself had called for institutions to start supporting and legitimizing "alternatives" to the dissertation monograph to reflect the changing nature of scholarly communication and research in the digital information age. See R. Berman, "New Era for Ph.D. Education," *Insider Higher Ed* 9 (January 2012), http://www.insidehighered.com/views/2012/01/09/essay-urges-reforms-doctoral-education-humanities, accessed May 5, 2019; and S. Smith, "President's Column: Beyond the Dissertation Monograph," *MLA Newsletter* 42, no. 1 (Spring 2010): 2–3, Modern Language Association website, https://apps.mla.org/pdf/nl_421_web_no_links.pdf, accessed May 16, 2019.

8. Some of these ideas were first articulated in T. Presner, "Welcome to the 20-Year Dissertation," *The Chronicle of Higher Education*, November 25, 2013, https://www.chronicle.com/article/Welcome-to-the-20-Year/143223/, accessed May 1, 2019.

9. For an articulation of the program and function in Eisenman's House VI, see R. Gutman, "House VI," in *Architecture from the Outside In: Selected Essays by Robert Gutman*, ed. D. Cuff and J. Wreidt, 119–126 (New York: Princeton Architectural Press, [1977] 2010).

10. M. Desmond, *Evicted: Poverty and Profit in the American City* (New York: Crown Publishing Group, 2016).

11. See R. Koolhaas, "Bigness, or the Problem of the Large," in *S,M,L,XL* (New York: Monacelli Press, 1995), which explicitly sets "big architecture" up as a new form of urbanism that—with shocking rhetorical effect—has no need for the city.

12. See M. Castells, *The Rise of the Network Society*, vol. 1, *The Information Age: Economy, Society, and Culture* (Oxford, UK, and Cambridge, MA: Blackwell, 1996); S. Sassen, "Cities and Communities in the Global Economy," in *The Global City Reader*, ed. N. Brenner and R. Keil, 82–88 (New York: Routledge, 2006).

13. L. Lowe, *The Intimacies of Four Continents* (Durham, NC: Duke University Press, 2015), 20.

14. See J. Walton and L. Masotti, eds., *The City in Comparative Perspective: Cross-National Research and New Directions in Theory* (New York: Sage, 1976). See also: H. J. Dyos, "Editorial," in *The Urban History Yearbook* (Leicester: Leicester University, 1974).

15. In addition to Walton and Masotti, *The City in Comparative Perspective*, see S. Sassen, *The Global City: New York, London, Tokyo* (Princeton: Princeton University Press, 1991); and M. Dear, *From Chicago to Los Angeles: Making Sense of Urban Theory* (Thousand Oaks, CA: SAGE, 2001).

16. See R. Madgin, *Heritage, Culture, and Conservation: Managing the Urban Renaissance* (Saarbrucken: VDM Verlag, 2009).

17. D. Cohen and M. O'Connor, "Introduction: Comparative History, Cross-National History, Transnational History—Definitions," in *Comparison and History: Europe in Cross-National Perspective* (New York: Routledge, 2004), ix–xxiii.

18. See, for example, the work of H. Bhabha, *The Location of Culture* (New York: Routledge, 1994); G. Anzaldúa, *Borderlands/La Frontera: The New Mestiza*, 4th ed. (San Francisco: Aunt Lute Books, [1987] 2012); and S. Greenblatt, *Cultural Mobility: A Manifesto* (Cambridge: Cambridge University Press, 2009).

19. See G. Agamben, *Homo Sacer: Sovereign Power and Bare Life* (Redwood City: Stanford University Press, 1998).

20. See H. Ferriss, *The Metropolis of Tomorrow* (New York: Ives Washburn, 1929); L. Mumford, *The Story of Utopias* (New York: Boni and Liveright, Inc., 1922).

21. J. Rancière, *The Politics of Aesthetics: The Distribution of the Sensible* (London and New York: Continuum, 2004).

22. See, for example, H. Lefebvre, "The Right to the City," in *Writings on Cities* (Oxford: Blackwell Publishing, 2008); and D. Harvey, "The Right to the City," *New Left Review* 53 (September–October 2008): 23–40.

23. E. Soja, *Seeking Spatial Justice* (Minneapolis: University of Minnesota Press, 2010).

24. P. Bourdieu, *The Logic of Practice* (Redwood City: Stanford University Press, 1990).

25. D. Cuff and J. Wolch, "Urban Humanities and the Creative Practitioner," *Boom: A Journal of California* 6, no. 3 (Fall 2016): 12–17.

26. Soja, *Seeking Spatial Justice*.

27. S. Ortner, "Theory in Anthropology since the Sixties," *Comparative Studies in Society and History* 26, no. 1 (1984): 126–166.

28. T. Presner, D. Shepard, and Y. Kawano, *HyperCities: Thick Mapping in the Digital Humanities* (Cambridge, MA: Harvard University Press, 2014).

29. C. Geertz, "Thick Description: Toward an Interpretive Theory of Culture," in *The Interpretation of Cultures* (New York: Basic Books, 1973), 5–10.

30. J. Corner, "The Agency of Mapping: Speculation, Critique and Invention," in *Mappings*, ed. D. Cosgrove, 213–252 (London: Reaktion, 1991).

31. Geertz, *Interpretation of Cultures*.

32. See, for example, P. Rabinow, *Reflections on Fieldwork in Morocco* (Berkeley: University of California Press, 1977).

33. See W. H. Whyte, *The Social Life of Small Urban Spaces* (New York: The Project for Public Spaces, 1980); also Whyte's film of the same name, available on Kanopy Streaming.

34. See, for example, the following three texts: D. E. Cosgrove, *Apollo's Eye: A Cartographic Genealogy of the Earth in the Western Imagination* (Baltimore: Johns Hopkins University Press, 2003); J. B. Harley, *The New Nature of Maps: Essays in the History of Cartography* (Baltimore: Johns Hopkins University Press, 2002); and D. Wood, *The Power of Maps* (London: Routledge, 1993).

35. A. Kim, *Sidewalk City: Remapping Public Space in Ho Chi Minh City* (Chicago: University of Chicago Press, 2015), 10.

36. A. Spirn, *The Eye Is a Door* (Boston: Wolf Tree Press, 2014), 12.

37. This term comes from design theorist Horst Rittel. See H. Rittel and M. Webber, "Dilemmas in a General Theory of Planning," *Policy Sciences* 4 (1973): 155–169.

Chapter 2

1. T. Bunnell and A. Maringanti, "Practicing Urban and Regional Research beyond Monocentricity," *International Journal of Urban and Regional Research* 34, no. 2 (2010): 415–420; 418.

2. The title of this section references architect Rem Koolhaas's seminal book *Delirious New York*, first published in 1978, in which he advances a "delirious" understanding of New York City urbanism based on the endless possibility enabled by the combination of its gridiron street plan and its use of elevator and steel technology to build skyscrapers that effectively multiply available space. He calls this "culture of congestion" theory "Manhattanism," while the "delirious" term he borrows from Salvador Dali's "paranoid-critical method," which uses "delirious associations and interpretations." See R. Koolhaas, *Delirious New York* (New York: Monacelli Press, [1978] 1994), 237.

3. A. Rossi, *The Architecture of the City* (Cambridge, MA: MIT Press, 1982).

4. R. Venturi, D. Scott Brown, and S. Izenour, *Learning from Las Vegas* (Cambridge, MA: MIT Press, 1972).

5. Ibid.

6. See R. Banham, *Los Angeles: The Architecture of Four Ecologies* (Berkeley: University of California Press, [1971] 2009).

7. Koolhaas, *Delirious New York*.

8. *The Ten Books on Architecture*, trans. Morris Hicky Morgan (New York: Dover Publications, 1960), 5–6. (De Architectura, bk. 1, ch 1, sect. 3.)

9. D. Harvey, *The Condition of Postmodernity* (Oxford: Basil Blackwell, 1989).

10. D. Massey, "Power Geometry and a Progressive Sense of Place," in *Mapping the Futures: Local Cultures, Global Change*, ed. J. Bird, B. Curtis, T. Putnam, G. Robertson, and L. Tickner (London and New York: Routledge, 1993), 60–70.

11. E. Soja, *Postmodern Geographies: The Reassertion of Space in Critical Social Theory* (New York: Verso, 1989).

12. Ibid., 155.

13. In E. Mendieta, "The Production of Urban Space in the Age of Transnational Mega-urbes," *City* 12, no. 2 (2008): 148–152; 151.

14. H. Lefebvre, *Writings on Cities*, trans. E. Kofman and E. Lebas (New York: Wiley-Blackwell, 1996), 16–17.

15. The essay was written in 1937 but only published in 1975, the year of Bakhtin's death, and was not translated into English until 1981, as part of his book *The Dialogic Imagination*. See M. M. Bakhtin, *The Dialogic Imagination: Four Essays*, trans. Caryl Emerson and Michael Holquist (Austin: University of Texas Press, 1981).

16. Ibid., 248.

17. Bakhtin's 1930s essay on the chronotope in the novel is now identified as one of the foundational stones of the spatial turn in the humanities. But there are other salient names and examples, among them Gaston Bachelard's crucial phenomenological study *The Poetics of Space* (Boston: Beacon Press, 1969); Ernst Cassirer's neo-Kantian reflections on space, "Mythischer, aesthetischer, und theoretischer Raum," in *Aufsaetze und Kleine Schriften (1927–1931)* (Hamburg: Felix Meiner Verlag, 2004); Joseph Frank's highly influential essay "Spatial Form in Modern Literature: An Essay in Two Parts," *The Sewanee Review* l53, no. 2 (Spring 1945): 221–240; George Poulet's *Les Métamorphoses du Circle* (Paris: Flammarion, 1966), yet another homage to phenomenology; Elisabeth Frenzel's *Stoff und Motivgeschichte: Grundlagen der Germanistik* (Berlin: Erich Schmidt

Verlag, 1966); Gerard Genette's "concession" to space in "La Littérature et l'espace," in *Figures II* (Paris: Seuil, 1970), despite the clear preference of narratology for time over space; and Ricardo Gullón's *Espacio y Novela* (Madrid: Taurus, 1970).

18. D. Massey, *Space, Place, and Gender* (Minneapolis: University of Minnesota Press, 1994).

19. Ibid., 64.

20. F. Cunningham, "Triangulating Utopia: Benjamin, Lefebvre, Tafuri," *Cities*. 14, no. 3 (2010): 268–277.

21. Massey, *Space, Place, and Gender*.

22. Lefebvre, *Writings on Cities*.

23. S. Kostof, *The City Shaped: Urban Patterns and Meanings through History* (Boston: Little Brown and Co., 1991).

24. Cunningham, "Triangulating Utopia," 291.

25. In P. Rabinow (ed.), *The Foucault Reader* (New York: Pantheon Books, 1984), x.

26. Cf. Soja, *Postmodern Geographies*.

27. M. Foucault, "Of Other Spaces," trans. Jay Miskowiec, *Diacritics* 16 (1986): 22–27; 23.

28. M. de Certeau, *The Practice of Everyday Life* (Berkeley: University of California Press, 1984).

29. Ibid., 98.

30. N. Blomley, *Rights of Passage: Sidewalks and the Regulation of Public Flow* (New York: Routledge, 2011).

31. C. Jencks, *The Language of Postmodernism* (New York: Rizzoli, 1977).

32. E. Said, *Orientalism* (New York: Vintage Books, 1979).

33. See C. Barnett, "Reflections: The Cultural Turn: Fashion or Progress in Human Geography?" *Antipode* 30, no. 4 (1998): 379–394; and Bhabha, *The Location of Culture*.

34. A. Loukaitou-Sideris, "Regeneration of Urban Commercial Strips: Ethnicity and Space in Three Los Angeles Neighborhoods," *Journal of Architectural and Planning Research* 19, no. 4 (2002): 334–350.

35. S. Sassen, "Analytic Borderlands: Race, Gender and Representation in the New City," in *Re-Presenting the City*, ed. A. King, 183–202 (New York: University Press, 1996), 195.

36. M. Featherstone, "Localism, Globalism, and Cultural Identity," in *Global/ Local: Cultural Production and Transnational Imaginary*, ed. R. Wilson and W. Dissanayake, 46–77 (Durham, NC, and London: Duke University Press, 1996).

37. Bhabha, *The Location of Culture*.

38. A. Gupta and J. Ferguson, "Culture, Power, Place: Ethnography at the End of an Era," in *Culture, Power, Place: Explorations in Critical Anthropology*, ed. A. Gupta and J. Ferguson, 1–31 (Durham, NC, and London: Duke University Press, 1997), 3.

39. R. Rosaldo, "Ideology, Place, and People without Culture," in Gupta and Ferguson, *Culture, Power, and Place*, 77–87; 87.

40. N. Rodriguez, "U.S. Immigration and Intergroup Relations in the Late 20th Century: African Americans and Latinos," *Social Justice* 23, no. 3 (1996): 111–125.

41. S. Zukin, *The Culture of Cities* (Cambridge, MA: Blackwell Publishers Inc., 1995), 289.

42. R. Wilson and W. Dissanayake, "Introduction: Tracking the Global/Local," in *Global/Local: Cultural Production and Transnational Imaginary*, ed. R. Wilson and W. Dissanayake (Durham, NC, and London: Duke University Press, 1996): 1–18.

43. Walton and Masotti, *The City in Comparative Perspective*.

44. N. Kenny and R. Madgin, *Cities beyond Borders: Comparative and Transnational Approaches to Urban History* (Farnham, Surrey: Ashgate, 2015).

45. M. P. Smith, *Transnational Urbanism: Locating Globalization* (Malden, MA: Blackwell, 2001).

46. Madgin, *Heritage, Culture, and Conservation*.

47. J. Friedmann and G. Wolff, "World City Formation: An Agenda for Research and Action," *International Journal of Urban and Regional Research* 6, no. 3 (1982): 309–344.

48. J. Friedmann, "The World City Hypothesis," *Development and Change* 17, no. 1 (1986): 69–83; 69.

49. In his original article, Friedmann lists eleven "primary" world cities: London, Paris, Rotterdam, Frankfurt, Zurich, New York, Chicago, Los Angeles, and Tokyo from "core countries" and Sao Paolo and Singapore from "semi-peripheral countries."

50. S. Sassen, *Globalization and Its Discontents: Essays on the New Mobility of People and Money* (New York: New Press, 1998).

51. N. Brenner, "Thesis on Urbanization," *Public Culture* 25, no. 1 (2013): 85–114.

52. J. Robinson, "Introduction to a Virtual Issue on Comparative Urbanism," *International Journal of Urban and Regional Research* (2014), n.p., https://onlinelibrary.wiley.com/doi/full/10.1111/1468-2427.12171, accessed May 8, 2019.

53. Lowe, *The Intimacies of Four Continents*, 18.

54. Ibid., 21.

55. Cohen and O'Connor, "Introduction: Comparative History, Cross-National History, Transnational History—Definitions."

56. C. A. Bayly, S. Beckert, M. Connelly, I. Hofmeyr, W. Kozol, and P. Seed, "AHR Conversation on Transnational History," *American Historical Review* 111, no. 5 (2016): 1440–1464.

57. M. Castells, *The Informational City: Information Technology, Economic Restructuring and the Urban Regional Process* (Oxford and Cambridge, MA: Blackwell, 1989).

58. M. Castells, *The Rise of the Network Society*, vol. 1, *The Information Age: Economy, Society, and Culture* (Oxford, UK and Cambridge, MA: Blackwell, 1996).

59. S. Khagram and P. Levitt, "Constructing Transnational Studies," *The Transnational Studies Reader: Intersections and Innovations* (New York: Routledge, 2008).

60. Kenny and Madgin, *Cities beyond Borders*, 4.

61. Khagram and Levitt, "Constructing Transnational Studies."

62. A. D. King, "Colonialism, Urbanism, and the Capitalist World Economy," *International Journal of Urban and Regional Research* 13, no. 1 (1989): 1–18.

63. See J. Robinson, *Ordinary Cities: Between Modernity and Development* (London: Routledge, 2006); Bunnell and Maringanti, "Practicing Urban and Regional Research beyond Monocentricity"; Lowe, *The Intimacies of Four Continents*.

64. Said, *Orientalism*.

65. D. Cuff and A. Loukaitou-Sideris, "Neither Here nor There: Engaging Mexico City and Los Angeles," *Boom* 6, no. 3 (2016): 101–105.

66. J. Robinson, "Global and World Cities: A View from off the Map," *International Journal of Urban and Regional Research* 26 (2002): 531–554; J. Robinson, "Postcolonialising Geography: Tactics and Pitfalls," *Singapore Journal of Tropical Geography* 24 (2003): 273–289; J. Robinson, "In the Tracks of Comparative Urbanism: Difference, Urban Modernity and the Primitive," *Urban Geography* 25, no. 8 (2004): 709–723; Robinson, *Ordinary Cities*, and Robinson, "Introduction to a Virtual Issue."

67. Robinson, "In the Tracks of Comparative Urbanism," 710.

68. A. Roy, "The 21st Century Metropolis: New Geographies of Theory," *Regional Studies* 43 (2009): 819–830; A. Roy, "Conclusion: Postcolonial Urbanism: Speed, Hysteria, Mass Dreams," in *Worlding Cities: Asian Experiments and the Art of Being Global, ed. A.* Roy and A. Ong, 307–335 (West Sussex, UK: John Wiley & Sons Ltd, 2011).

69. Roy, "The 21st Century Metropolis," 821.

70. Anzaldúa, *Borderlands/La Frontera*, 25.

71. Ibid.

72. An earlier version of this section appeared in J. Crisman, "Urban Humanities in the Borderlands," introduction to *Urban Humanities in the Borderlands: Engaged Scholarship from Mexico City to Los Angeles* (Los Angeles: UCLA Urban Humanities Initiative, 2016).

73. U. Beck, *The Risk Society: Towards a New Modernity* (London: SAGE Publications, Ltd., 1992).

74. T. Cruz, "Foreword: Borderwalls as Public Space," in *Borderwall as Architecture: A Manifesto for the U.S.-Mexico Boundary*, ed. R. Rael (Berkeley: University of California Press, 2017), ix.

75. Ibid.

76. T. Cruz and C. Hooper, "Political Equator 3: Reimagining the Border," *Domus,* June 24, 2011, https://www.domusweb.it/en/architecture/2011/06/24/political-equator-3-reimagining-the-border.html, accessed May 12, 2019.

77. Cruz, "Foreword: Borderwalls as Public Space."

78. R. Rael, *Borderwall as Architecture* (Berkeley: University of California Press, 2017).

79. W. Benjamin, *The Arcades of Paris* (Cambridge, MA: Harvard University Press, [1928] 1999).

80. E. Leslie, trans., *Walter Benjamin Archives* (London and New York: Verso, 2007).

81. de Certeau, *The Practice of Everyday Life*, xiv.

82. J. Chase, M. Crawford, and J. Kaliski, eds., *Everyday Urbanism* (New York: Monacelli Press, 2008); V. Mukhija and A. Loukaitou-Sideris, *The Informal American City: Beyond Taco Trucks and Day Labor* (Cambridge, MA: MIT Press, 2014).

83. Roy, "The 21st Century Metropolis."

84. See D. Judd and S. Fainstein, eds., *The Tourist City* (New Haven: Yale University Press, 1999); A. Loukaitou-Sideris and V. Mukhija, "Responding to Informality through Urban Design Studio Pedagogy," *Journal of Urban Design* 21, no. 5 (2015): 577–595.

85. V. Mukhija, "Urban Design for a Planet of Informal Cities," in *Companion to Urban Design, ed.* T. Banerjee and A. Loukaitou-Sideris, 574–584 (London: Routledge, 2011).

86. M. Rios, "Learning from Informal Practices: Implications for Urban Design," in Mukhija, and Loukaitou-Sideris, *The Informal American City,* 173–192; 173.

87. Lefebvre, *Writings on Cities*, 158.

88. Ibid., 194–195.

89. D. Harvey, *Social Justice and the City* (Baltimore, MD: Johns Hopkins Press, 1973), 94.

90. D. Harvey, *Megacities Lecture 4* (Amersfort, The Netherlands: Twynstra Gudde Management Consultants, 2000), 81.

91. Soja, *Seeking Spatial Justice.*

92. Ibid.

93. E. Soja, "The City and Spatial Justice" ["La ville et la justice spatiale," trans. Sophie Didier, Frédéric Dufaux], *justice spatiale | spatial justice*, no. 1 (Septembre 2009), http://www.jssj.org, 3.

94. S. Fainstein, *The Just City* (Ithaca, NY: Cornell University Press, 2010).

95. Members of the Los Angeles School included Michael Dear, Mike Davis, Ed Soja, Michael Storper, and Alan Scott.

96. Banham, *Los Angeles: The Architecture of Four Ecologies.*

97. M. Davis, *City of Quartz: Excavating the Future in Los Angeles* (New York: Verso, 1990); and Cuff and Wolch "Urban Humanities and the Creative Practitioner."

98. Presner, Shepard, and Kawano, *HyperCities.*

99. Cuff and Wolch, "Urban Humanities and the Creative Practitioner."

100. K. Lynch, *The Image of the City* (Cambridge: MIT Press, 1960).

101. C. McWilliams, *Southern California: An Island on the Land* (Salt Lake City: Peregrine Smith Books, [1946] 1973).

102. Davis, *City of Quartz*.

103. W. Deverell, *Whitewashed Adobe* (Berkeley and Los Angeles: University of California Press, 2004).

104. D. Hayden, *The Power of Place* (Cambridge, MA: MIT Press, 1995).

105. D. Cuff, *The Provisional City: Los Angeles Stories of Architecture and Urbanism* (Cambridge, MA: MIT Press, 2000).

106. E. Avila, *Popular Culture in the Age of White Flight: Fear and Fantasy in Suburban Los Angeles* (Berkeley and Los Angeles: University of California Press, 2006).

107. L. Pulido, *Black, Brown, Yellow, and Left: Radical Activism in Los Angeles* (Berkeley and Los Angeles: University of California Press, 2006).

108. L. Pulido, L. Barraclough, and W. Cheng, *A People's Guide to Los Angeles* (Berkeley and Los Angeles: University of California Press, 2012).

Chapter 3

1. "Through Positive Eyes," (http://throughpositiveeyes.org/) is a fine example of putting cameras in people's hands so they can tell their own stories.

2. M. de Certeau, F. Jameson, and C. Lovitt, "On the Oppositional Practices of Everyday Life," *Social Text* 3 (Autumn 1980): 7. Also M. de Certeau, *The Practice of Everyday Life*, trans. Steven Rendall (Berkeley: University of California Press, 2011).

3. While he doesn't use the term "spatial ethnography," James Clifford introduced a broad set of concepts and approaches that emphasize border crossings, travel, and diaspora to underscore the importance of movement, mobility, and cultural translation in space. See, for example, J. Clifford, *Routes: Travel and Translation in the Late Twentieth Century* (Cambridge, MA: Harvard University Press, 1997). The specific term "spatial ethnography" appears as early as 1988 in Amr Ezzeldin Abdel-Kawi, *A World of Otherness: A Spatial Ethnography of the Oasis of Farafra (Egypt)* (Ann Arbor: University of Michigan, 1988), but references increase significantly from about 2005 onward.

4. G. Marcus, "Ethnography in/of the World System: The Emergence of Multi-Sited Ethnography," *Annual Review of Anthropology* 24 (1995): 95–117.

5. S. Chari and V. Gidwani, "Grounds for a Special Ethnography of Labor," *Ethnography* 6, no. 3 (2005): 267–281.

6. See H. Lefebvre, *The Production of Space* (Oxford: Oxford University Press, [1974] 1991); also Harvey, *Social Justice and the City*; Soja, *Postmodern Geographies*.

7. A. Sen and L. Silverman, eds., *Making Place: Space and Embodiment in the City* (Bloomington: Indiana University Press, 2014), 9.

8. Lynch, *The Image of the City*.

9. Ibid., 2.

10. The rich field of cognitive mapping has proliferated from architecture and planning through comparative literature in the conclusion to Fredric Jameson's *Postmodernism, or The Cultural Logic of Late Capitalism* (Durham, NC: Duke University Press, 1991).

11. See, for example, the following article that refines how we interpret the particular forms of markings on cognitive maps: J. W. Curtis, E. Shiau, B. Lowery, D. Sloane, K. Hennigan, and A. Curtis, "The Prospects and Problems of Integrating Sketch Maps with Geographic Information Systems to Understand Environmental Perception: A Case Study of Mapping Youth Fear in Los Angeles Gang Neighborhoods," *Environment and Planning B* 41, no. 2 (January 1, 2014): 251–271.

12. Whyte, *The Social Life of Small Urban Spaces*, 16.

13. Ibid., 102.

14. Ibid., 60, 98.

15. M. Castells, *The City and the Grassroots: A Cross-Cultural Theory of Urban Social Movements* (Berkeley: University of California Press, 1984); J. Hou, ed., *Insurgent Public Space: Guerilla Urbanism and the Remaking of Contemporary Cities* (London: Routledge, 2010).

16. Kim, *Sidewalk City*.

17. Sen and Silverman, *Making Place*.

18. D. Wood, *Rethinking the Power of Maps* (New York and London: Guilford Press, 2010).

19. E. Tufte, *Envisioning Information* (Cheshire, CT: Graphics Press, 1990), 12.

20. Wood, *Rethinking the Power of Maps*; D. Cosgrove, ed., *Mappings* (London: Reaktion Books, 1999); Harley, *The New Nature of Maps*; Massey, "Power-geometry and a Progressive Sense of Place."

21. J. B. Harley and D. Woodward, eds., *The History of Cartography* (Chicago: University of Chicago Press, 1987).

22. A book that assesses this history and also offers possibilities for postcolonial mapping is: J. Akerman, ed., *Decolonizing the Map: Cartography from Colony to Nation* (Chicago: University of Chicago Press, 2017).

23. See, for example, K. Harmon and G. Clemans, *The Map as Art: Contemporary Artists Explore Cartography* (New York: Princeton Architectural Press, 2009).

24. See her three city atlas projects: R. Solnit, *Infinite City: A San Francisco Atlas* (Berkeley: University of California Press, 2010); R. Solnit, *Unfathomable City: A New Orleans Atlas* (Berkeley: University of California Press, 2013); and R. Solnit, *Nonstop City: A New York Atlas* (Berkeley: University of California, 2016).

25. L. Parks, *Cultures in Orbit: Satellites and the Televisual* (Durham, NC: Duke University Press, 2005).

26. The Mercator projection is a cylindrical map projection used for nautical navigation that was developed in the sixteenth century by Flemish cartographer Gerardus Mercator.

27. R. Dominguez, "Transborder Immigrant Tool and Ricardo Dominguez, under Attack for Border Activism," 2010, *East Los Angeles Dirigible Air Transport Lines* blog, https://atomikaztex.wordpress.com/2010/05/15/transborder-immigrant-tool-and-ricardo-dominguez-under-attack-for-border-activism/, accessed December 1, 2017.

28. Ricardo Dominguez, conversation with authors (January 23, 2016).

29. Rael, *Borderwall as Architecture*.

30. Ibid., 167–168.

31. L. Kurgan, *Close Up at a Distance: Mapping, Technology and Politics* (New York: Zone Books, 2013), 14.

32. Laura Kurgan and Eric Cadora, "Million Dollar Blocks," n.d., http://spatialinformationdesignlab.org/projects/million-dollar-blocks, accessed May 1, 2019.

33. *Iconoclasistas*, "Manual of Collective Mapping," 2016, http://www.iconoclasistas.net/, accessed May 12, 2019.

34. Ibid., 14.

35. R. Koselleck, *Sediments of Time: On Possible Histories*, trans. Sean Franzel and Stefan-Ludwig Hoffmann (Stanford: Stanford University Press, 2018).

36. The concept of "thick mapping" was first articulated in the HyperCities digital mapping project and the subsequent book *HyperCities: Thick Mapping in the Digital Humanities* by Todd Presner, David Shepard, and Yoh Kawano. Through the urban humanities, it has gained significantly more dimensionality and application in varied contexts. In addition, Philip Ethington has developed an analogous approach to thick mapping in his study of the regional regimes that occupied the Los Angeles basin over some ten thousand years of varied rule, which will appear in his forthcoming work, *Ghost Metropolis*.

37. W. Benjamin, *Das Passagen-Werk*, 2 vols., ed. Rolf Tiedemann (Frankfurt: Suhrkamp, 1983), 596.

38. Ibid., 574.

39. Geertz, *The Interpretation of Cultures*.

40. David Bodenhamer developed the concept of the "deep map" in his essay "The Potential of Spatial Humanities," in *The Spatial Humanities: GIS and the Future of Humanities Scholarship*, ed. D. Bodenhamer, J. Corrigan, and T. Harris, 14–30 (Bloomington: Indiana University Press, 2010).

41. Wood, *Rethinking the Power of Maps*.

42. Geertz, *The Interpretation of Cultures*, ix.

43. Ibid., 15.

44. Ibid., 29.

45. Ibid., 30.

46. Ibid., 25.

47. K. A. Appiah, "Thick Translation," *Callaloo* 16, no. 4 (1993): 808–819.

48. Ibid., 808.

49. Ibid., 812.

50. Ibid., 817.

51. Ibid., 818.

52. Accounts of the 1871 massacre vary, including the number of men of Chinese descent who were killed, which ranges between 17 and 20.

53. A filmic sensing fifty years ago would have relied on easily portable and accessible film stock such as Super 8, a medium we have occasionally explored in urban humanities projects.

54. S. Alifragkis and F. Penz, "Dziga Vertov's Man with a Movie Camera: Thoughts on the Computation of Style and Narrative Structure," *Architecture and Culture* 3, no. 1 (2015): 33–55.

55. L. Manovich, *The Language of New Media* (Cambridge, MA: MIT Press, 2001).

56. Ibid., 239

57. M. Turvey, "Can the Camera See? Mimesis in 'Man with a Movie Camera,'" *October* 89 (1999): 25–50.

58. Ibid., 30

59. A. Tracy, "Deep Focus: The Essay Film," *Sight & Sound* 23, no. 8 (2013): 44–52.

60. E. Cazdyn, "Semi-ology of a Disaster or, Toward a Non-Moralizing Materialism," *Scapegoat Journal* 2 (2011): 32.

61. S. Pink, *Situating Everyday Life* (London: Sage, 2012), 34.

62. Ibid.

63. C. Jones, *Sensorium: Embodied Experience, Technology and Contemporary Art* (Cambridge, MA: MIT Press, 2006), 44.

64. G. H. Kester, *Conversation Pieces: Community and Communication in Modern Art* (Berkeley and Los Angeles: University of California Press, 2004).

65. C. Bishop, *Artificial Hells: Participatory Art and the Politics of Spectatorship* (London: Verso, 2012).

66. H. Becker, *Art Worlds* (Berkeley: University of California Press, 1982).

Chapter 4

1. A. Davis, *Are Prisons Obsolete?* (New York: Seven Stories Press, 2003).

2. M. Castells, ed., *Another Economy Is Possible* (Malden, MA: Polity Press, 2017).

3. O. Butler, *Bloodchild and Other Stories* (New York: Seven Stories Press, 2005).

4. Hannah Arendt wrote "With word and deed we insert ourselves into the human world, and this insertion is like a second birth, in which we confirm and take on ourselves the naked fact of our original appearance." She described this as "natality": the unpredictable novelty that comes with new birth as reflective of human capacity for agency, change, and a future is also present in the moment that we insert ourselves into the social world through our own volition and action. H. Arendt, *The Human Condition* (Chicago: University of Chicago Press, 1958), 176.

5. A. Eshel, *Futurity: Contemporary Literature and the Quest for the Past* (Chicago: University of Chicago Press, 2013), 17–19.

6. Ibid., 5.

7. The notion of a "generative humanities" has also informed other field-defining manifestos such as those of the digital humanities. For the authors of *Digital_Humanities*, the "generative humanities" speak to iterative, project-oriented, imaginative, and open-ended humanities focused on making and creative knowledge design. Cf. Burdick et al., *Digital_Humanities*, 23–26.

8. Mumford, *The Story of Utopias*.

9. M. Reinhold and J. Crisman, "Conjuring Utopia's Ghost," *Thresholds 40: Socio-,* ed. J. Crisman (Cambridge, MA: MIT Press, 2012), 11–20.

10. A. Griffiths, "Oma/Progress at the Barbic," *Dezeen,* October 5, 2011, https://www.dezeen.com/2011/10/05/omaprogress-at-the-barbican.

11. R. Sherman, "If, Then," *Log 5: Postcriticality* (Spring/Summer 2005): 58.

12. W. R. Ellis and D. Cuff, eds., "Introduction" (quoting Robert Maxwell). In *Architects' People, ed. W. R.* Ellis and D. Cuff (Oxford: Oxford University Press, 1989), 6.

13. D. Sudjic, *The Language of Cities* (London: Penguin Books UK, 2016), 27.

14. D. Suvin, *Metamorphoses of Science Fiction: Studies in the Poetics and History of a Literary Genre* (New Haven: Yale University Press, 1979).

15. K. Mannheim, *Ideology and Utopia* (Orlando, FL: Harcourt, Inc., [1936] 2015).

16. K. Popper, *Conjectures and Refutations* (New York: Routledge, [1962] 2002).

17. I. Kant, "Part One. Critique of Aesthetic Judgement," *Critique of Judgement,* trans. James Creed Meredith (New York: Oxford University Press, 2007), 35–164; 140.

18. J. Collier, "The Art of Moral Imagination: Ethics in the Practice of Architecture," *Journal of Business Ethics* 66 (2006): 307–317; 313.

19. E. Burke, *Reflections on the Revolution in France* (Oxford: Oxford University Press, [1970] 2009).

20. J. Dewey, *The Later Works of John Dewey,* vol. 8, ed. J-A. Boydston (Carbondale: Southern Illinois Press, 1974), 351. Cited in Collier, *The Art of Moral Imagination,* 313.

21. See, for example, John Rawls's discussion of "public reason" in *Political Liberalism* (New York: Columbia University Press, 1993); and Chantal Mouffe's discussion of "agonistic pluralism" in *The Return of the Political* (London: Verso, 1993).

22. C. Mouffe, "Deliberative Democracy or Agonistic Pluralism," *Social Research* 66, no. 3 (1999): 745–758; 746.

23. An earlier version of this section appeared in J. Crisman, "Practicing the Future: Exercises in Immanent Speculation," *Boom: A Journal of California* 6, no. 3 (Fall 2016): 25–31.

24. K. T. Yamashita, *Tropic of Orange* (Minneapolis: Coffee House Press, 1997).

25. See, for example, R. Chandler, *The Long Goodbye* (New York: Vintage Books, 1988); or J. Didion, *Play It as It Lays* (New York: Farrar, Straus and Giroux, 2005).

26. *El gran mojado* translates as "the big wet" and is a subversion of the offensive racial epithet "wetback" used in Yamashita's book as a metaphor for immigrants who persist in spite of globalization through tactics such as moving back and forth across national borders. Also, *luchador* translates as "wrestler," but refers more specifically to an athlete and performer who participates in Mexican *lucha libre* professional wrestling.

27. This quote is used in Eshel's *Futurity,* but originally comes from Shelley's essay titled "A Defense of Poetry" written in 1821.

28. Cazdyn, "Semi-ology of a Disaster," 32.

29. H. White, *The Practical Past* (Evanston, IL: Northwestern University Press, 2014), 9

30. See, for example, L. Menand, "The Ph.D. Problem," *Harvard Magazine* (November–December 2009): 27–31, https://harvardmagazine.com/2009/11/professionalization-in-academy, accessed May 10.

31. White, *The Practical Past*, 9.

32. Ibid., 41.

33. Ibid., 99.

Chapter 5

1. Oxford English Dictionary, entry for "pedagogue." Also, cf. the entry for "Pedagogue," *Online Etymology Dictionary*, http://www.etymonline.com/index.php?l=p&p=8.

2. I. Kant, "What Is Enlightenment?," in *Foundations of the Metaphysics of Morals*, trans. and ed. L. White Beck (Upper Saddle River, NJ: Prentice Hall, [1784] 1985), 83.

3. A. von Humboldt, *Gesammelte Werke*, vol. 4 (Berlin: De Gruyter, [1843] 2011), 113ff.

4. R. Koselleck, "On the Anthropological and Semantic Structure of *Bildung*," in *The Practice of Conceptual History: Timing History / Spacing Concepts*, trans. T. Presner (Redwood City: Stanford University Press, 2002), 170–207.

5. A *Bildungsroman* is a novel that deals with the formative, educational years of a main character.

6. J. W. Goethe, *Wilhelm Meister's Apprenticeship*, trans. and ed. Eric A. Blackall with Victor Lange (Princeton: Princeton University Press, [1796] 1989).

7. Enlightenment philosophies, while rooted in emancipatory goals, did not mean that women and men were truly on equal footing. Moreover, with the rise of racialized concepts of citizenship linked to blood in the nineteenth century, Jewish emancipation would suffer countless backlashes that essentially turned Jews into second-class citizens and eventually noncitizens in 1935.

8. Goethe, *Wilhelm Meister's Apprenticeship*, 113.

9. Ibid., 54.

10. Ibid., 321.

11. Ibid., 307.

12. Ibid., 345.

13. Ibid., 346.

14. T. Adorno and M. Horkheimer, *Dialectic of Enlightenment*, trans. John Cumming (New York: Continuum, 1993), 3.

15. The excellent discussion of Moore's works by our UCLA colleague Chon Noriega, "Director's Message," *Chicano Studies Research Center Newsletter* 12, no. 5 (January 2014), n.p. http://www.chicano.ucla.edu/about/news/csrc-newsletter-january-2014, accessed May 5, 2019.

16. P. Freire, *Pedagogy of the Oppressed*, trans. Myra Bergman Ramos (New York: Bloomsbury, [1970] 2015), 77.

17. A. Lorde, *Sister Outsider* (Toronto: Crossing Press, 2007).

18. T. A. Dutton and C. G. Bradford, "Campus Design and Critical Pedagogy," *Academe* 77, no. 4 (July–Aug. 1991): 36–43; 43.

19. Parts of this chapter were previously published as J. Banfill, T. Presner, and M. Zubiaurre, "Urban Humanities Pedagogy," *Boom: A Journal of California* 6, no. 3 (2017): 120–128.

20. See *My Architect*, the 2003 film produced by Nathaniel Kahn.

21. Claybricks.com, "The Basics of Bricks," *ClayBricks,* n.d., http://www.clay bricks.com/more_info/basic-of-bricks.html, accessed May 10, 2019.

22. While we don't disagree with the many struggles faced by the public university in an age of neoliberal corporatization, we don't see the university as being in ruins or the humanities in perpetual crisis. Cf. Bill Readings, *The University in Ruins* (Cambridge, MA: Harvard University Press, 1997).

23. S. Smith, *A Manifesto for the Humanities: Transforming Doctoral Education in Good Enough Times* (Ann Arbor: University of Michigan Press, 2016), 39.

24. Ibid., 108.

25. Ibid.

26. H. J. Gans, "Towards a Public Social Science," *Transformations of the Public Sphere*, Feb. 13, 2011, Institute for Public Knowledge, Social Science Research Council, http://publicsphere.ssrc.org/gans-toward-a-public-social-science/, accessed May 1, 2019.

27. Ibid.

28. While celebrated by some for getting students "outside" the walls of the university and into diverse communities, "service learning" has also been criticized as "a pedagogy of whiteness" for the ways it has reinforced, rather than undermined, social and economic divisions. As Mitchell, Donahue, and Young-Law argue in their influential article "Service Learning as a Pedagogy of Whiteness," service learning (like philanthropy more generally) is a "white invention" designed to further enrich the experience of the privileged, mainly geared towards instructing (white) students on how to "safely" venture into the "real world." Service learning is under the permanent suspicion of colonial violence, as is any endeavor that puts the privileged in contact with the disenfranchised in an era of radical social injustice. Cf. T. D. Mitchell, D. M. Donahue, and C. Young-Law, "Service Learning as a Pedagogy of Whiteness," *Equity & Excellence in Education* 45, no. 4 (2012): 612–629.

29. E. Boyer and L. Mitgang, *Building Community: A New Future for Architecture Education and Practice* (San Francisco: Jossey-Bass, 1996).

30. E. Boyer, "Scholarship of Engagement," New England Resource Center for Higher Education, University of Massachusetts Boston, 1996.

31. Presentation by Ananya Roy at Urban Humanities Faculty Seminar, UCLA, May 1, 2019.

32. M. Zubiaurre, "Diosa Cochambre: UUCLA at Night," *Pàrrafo, April 21, 2013,* http://blog.parrafomagazine.com/post/48578753894/diosa-cochambre-uucla-at -night/, accessed May 16, 2019.

33. M. Fraser, "UCLA Library Acquires Papers of Justice for Janitors, Historic L.A. Labor Organization," April 20, 2012, *Library Special Collections Blog*, UCLA Library, http://www.library.ucla.edu/blog/special/2012/04/20/ucla-library -acquires-papers-of-justice-for-janitors-historic-la-labor-organization-.

34. L. Weschler, *Domestic Scenes: The Art of Ramiro Gomez* (New York: Abrams, 2016).

35. M. C. Nussbaum, *Not for Profit: Why Democracy Needs the Humanities* (Princeton: Princeton University Press, 2010), 28–29.

36. D. A. Oppenheimer and T. Hursley, *Rural Studio: Samuel Mockbee and an Architecture of Decency* (New York: Princeton Architectural Press, 2002).

37. The "20K Initiative" is so named because, according to the Rural Studio's website, "When the 20K Project began in 2005, the Studio challenged the students to design a home that could be built by a contractor for $20,000" (http://www. ruralstudio.org/initiatives/20k-house, accessed June 14, 2019).

38. G. Seigworth and M. Gregg, "An Inventory of Shimmers," in *The Affect Theory Reader*, ed. M. Gregg and G. Seigworth, 1–28 (Durham, NC: Duke University Press, 2010), 12.

39. See for example: S. Sontag, *Regarding the Pain of Others* (New York: Picador, 2004); Z. Bauman, *Wasted Lives: Modernity and Its Outcasts (*Cambridge: Polity Press, 2004); S. Ahmed, *The Cultural Politics of Emotion* (London: Routledge, 2013); J. Butler, *Precarious Life: The Power of Mourning and Violence* (New York: Verso, 2006); Agamben, *Homo Sacer*.

40. Butler, *Precarious Life*.

41. R. Ek, "Giorgio Agamben and the Spatialities of the Camp," *Geografiska Annaler Series B Human Geography* 88, no. 4 (2006): 363–386; 363.

42. United Nations High Commission on Refugees, data (June 9, 2017), http:// www.unhcr.org/en-us/figures-at-a-glance.html, accessed June 1, 2018.

43. Palestinian refugee camps began after the war in 1948, while some camps in Africa have been in place for more than thirty years. Cf. A. Taylor, "The World's Largest Refugee Camp Turns 20," *The Atlantic*, April 14, 2011. https://www.theatlantic.com/photo/2011/04/the-worlds-largest-refugee-camp -turns-20/100046/, accessed June 1, 2018.

44. I. Calvino, *Invisible Cities* (Orlando, Fl: Harcourt Brace Jovanovich, [1972] 1978), 59.

45. B. Warf, ed., *Encyclopedia of Geography* (London: Sage, 2010).

46. G. A. Hillery, "Definitions of Community: Areas of Agreement," *Rural Sociology* 20, no. 1 (1955): 111.

47. L. Fisher, "'Community' as a Reference for American Minority Groups: A Theory of Unintended Negative Consequences," *Open Journal of Social Sciences* 5 (2017): 224–237.

48. Freire, *Pedagogy of the Oppressed*.

49. Ibid., 72.

50. bell hooks, *Teaching to Transgress: Education as the Practice of Freedom* (New York: Routledge, 1994), 14.

51. Nussbaum, *Not for Profit*.

52. Ibid., 39.

53. Ibid., 39–40.

54. Ibid., 45.

55. Ibid.

56. hooks, *Teaching to Transgress*, 21.

57. J. Rancière, *The Ignorant Schoolmaster: Five Lessons in Intellectual Emancipation* (Redwood City: Stanford University Press, 1991).

58. Ibid., 3.

59. Ibid., 31.

60. Ibid., 16.

61. J. Dewey, *How We Think* (New York: Cosimo, 2007).

62. Freire, *Pedagogy of the Oppressed*, 92.

63. Ibid., 84.

64. K. Varnelis, "Is There Research in the Studio?" *Journal of Architectural Education* 61, no. 1 (2007): 11–14.

65. For an ethnography of architectural practice and the education of novices, see D. Cuff, *Architecture: The Story of Practice* (Cambridge, MA: MIT Press, 1991).

66. J. Ockman, *Architecture School: Three Centuries of Educating Architects in North America*. (Cambridge, MA: The MIT Press, 2012).]

67. T. A. Dutton, "Design and Studio Pedagogy," *Journal of Architectural Education* 41, no. 1 (1987): 16–25.

68. D. A. Schön, "Toward a Marriage of Artistry & Applied Science in the Architectural Design Studio," *Journal of Architectural Education* 41, no. 4 (1988): 4–10; 5.

69. D. A. Schön, *The Reflective Practitioner: How Professionals Think in Action* (New York: Basic Books, 1982), n.p., from ch. 3, "Design as a Reflective Conversation . . ." on third page.

70. B. Colomina with E Choi, I. Gonzalez Galan, and A-M. Meister, "Radical Pedagogies in Architectural Education," *Architectural Review*, Sept 28, 2012, https://www.architectural-review.com/today/radical-pedagogies-in-architectural-education/8636066.article, accessed May 12, 2019.

Coda

71. P. Freire, *Letters to Cristina* (New York: Routledge, 1996), 85.

Chapter 6

1. Cuff and Wolch offer the clearest reasoning to date of urban humanities' study of Pacific Rim megacities and the field's origins in California, in "Urban Humanities and the Creative Practitioner."

References

Adorno, T. and Horkheimer, M. 1993. *Dialectic of Enlightenment*, trans. John Cumming. New York: Continuum.

Agamben, G. 1998. *Homo Sacer: Sovereign Power and Bare Life*. Redwood City: Stanford University Press.

Ahmed, S. 2013. *The Cultural Politics of Emotion*. London: Routledge.

Akerman, J., ed. 2017. *Decolonizing the Map: Cartography from Colony to Nation*. Chicago: University of Chicago Press.

Alifragkis, S., and F. Penz. 2015. "Dziga Vertov's Man with a Movie Camera: Thoughts on the Computation of Style and Narrative Structure." *Architecture and Culture* 3 (1): 33–55.

Amr Ezzeldin Abdel-Kawi. 1988. *A World of Otherness: A Spatial Ethnography of the Oasis of Farafra (Egypt)*. Ann Arbor: University of Michigan.

Anzaldúa, G. [1987] 2012. *Borderlands/La Frontera: The New Mestiza*, 4th ed. San Francisco: Aunt Lute Books.

Appiah, K. A. 1993. "Thick Translation." *Callaloo* 16 (4): 808–819.

Arendt, H. 1958. *The Human Condition*. Chicago: University of Chicago Press.

Aureli, P. V. 2016. *The City as a Project*. Berlin: Ruby Press.

Avila, E. 2006. *Popular Culture in the Age of White Flight: Fear and Fantasy in Suburban Los Angeles*. Berkeley and Los Angeles: University of California Press.

Bachelard, G. 1969. *The Poetics of Space*. Boston: Beacon Press.

Bakhtin, M. M. 1981. *The Dialogic Imagination: Four Essays*, trans. Caryl Emerson and Michael Holquist. Austin: University of Texas Press.

Banfill, J., T. Presner, and M. Zubiaurre. 2017. "Urban Humanities Pedagogy." *Boom: A Journal of California* 6 (3): 120–128.

Banham, R. [1971] 2009. *Los Angeles: The Architecture of Four Ecologies*. Berkeley: University of California Press.

Barnett, C. 1998. "Reflections: The Cultural Turn: Fashion or Progress in Human Geography?" *Antipode* 30 (4): 379–394.

Bauman, Z. 2004. *Wasted Lives: Modernity and its Outcasts*. Cambridge: Polity Press.

Bayly, C. A., S. Beckert, M. Connelly, I. Hofmeyr, W. Kozol, and P. Seed. 2016. "AHR Conversation on Transnational History." *American Historical Review* 111 (5): 1440–1464.

Beck, U. 1992. *The Risk Society: Towards a New Modernity*. London: SAGE Publications, Ltd.

Beck, U. 2009. "Risk Society's 'Cosmopolitan Moment.'" *New Geographies* 1: 24–35.

Becker, H. 1982. *Art Worlds*. Berkeley: University of California Press.

Benjamin, W. [1928] 1999. *The Arcades of Paris*. Cambridge, MA: Harvard University Press.

Benjamin, W. 1968. "Theses on the Philosophy of History." In *Illuminations*, trans. Harry Zohn. New York: Schocken.

Benjamin, W. 1983. *Das Passagen-Werk*, 2 vols., ed. Rolf Tiedemann. Frankfurt: Suhrkamp.

Berman, R. 2012. "New Era for Ph.D. Education." *Insider Higher Ed* 9 (January). http://www.insidehighered.com/views/2012/01/09/essay-urges-reforms-doctoral -education-humanities, accessed May 5, 2019.

Bhabha, H. 1994. *The Location of Culture*. New York: Routledge.

Bishop, C. 2012. *Artificial Hells: Participatory Art and the Politics of Spectatorship*. London: Verso.

Blomley, N. 2011. *Rights of Passage: Sidewalks and the Regulation of Public Flow*. New York: Routledge.

Bodenhamer, D., J. Corrigan, and T. Harris, eds. 2010. *The Spatial Humanities: GIS and the Future of Humanities Scholarship*. Bloomington: Indiana University Press.

Bourdieu, P. 1990. *The Logic of Practice*. Redwood City: Stanford University Press.

Boyer, E. 1996. "Scholarship of Engagement." *New England Resource Center for Higher Education*. Boston: UMass Boston.

Boyer, E., and L. Mitgang. 1996. *Building Community: A New Future for Architecture Education and Practice*. San Francisco: Jossey-Bass.

Brenner, N. 2013. "Thesis on Urbanization." *Public Culture* 25 (1): 85–114.

Bunnell, T., and A. Maringanti. 2010. "Practicing Urban and Regional Research beyond Monocentricity." *International Journal of Urban and Regional Research* 34 (2): 415–420.

Burdick, A., J. Drucker, P. Lunenfeld, T. Presner, and J. Schnapp. 2012. *Digital_ Humanities*. Cambridge, MA: MIT Press.

Burke, E. [1970] 2009. *Reflections on the Revolution in France*. Oxford: Oxford University Press.

Butler, J. 2006. *Precarious Life: The Power of Mourning and Violence*. New York: Verso.

Butler, O. 2005. *Bloodchild and Other Stories*. New York: Seven Stories Press.

Calvino, I. [1972] 1978. *Invisible Cities*. Orlando, Fl: Harcourt Brace Jovanovich.

Cassirer, E. 2004. "Mythischer, aesthetischer, und theoretischer Raum." In *Aufsaetze und Kleine Schriften (1927–1931)*. Hamburg: Felix Meiner Verlag.

Castells, M. 1984. *The City and the Grassroots: A Cross-Cultural Theory of Urban Social Movements*. Berkeley: University of California Press.

Castells, M. 1989. *The Informational City: Information Technology, Economic Restructuring and the Urban Regional Process*. Oxford, UK, and Cambridge, MA: Blackwell.

Castells, M. 1996. *The Rise of the Network Society*. Vol. 1 of *The Information Age: Economy, Society, and Culture*. Oxford, UK, and Cambridge, MA: Blackwell.

Castells, M., ed. 2017. *Another Economy Is Possible*. Malden, MA: Polity Press.

Cazdyn, E. 2011. "Semi-ology of a Disaster or, Toward a Non-Moralizing Materialism." *Scapegoat Journal* 2: 32–34.

Chandler, R. 1988. *The Long Goodbye*. New York: Vintage Books.

Chari, S., and V. Gidwani. 2005. "Grounds for a Special Ethnography of Labor." *Ethnography* 6 (3): 267–281.

Chase, J., M. Crawford, and J. Kaliski, eds. 2008. *Everyday Urbanism*. New York: Monacelli Press.

Claybricks.com. n.d. "The Basics of Bricks." *Clay Bricks*. http://www.claybricks.com/more_info/basic-of-bricks.html, accessed May 10, 2019.

Clifford, J. 1997. *Routes: Travel and Translation in the Late Twentieth Century*. Cambridge, MA: Harvard University Press.

Cohen, D., and M. O'Connor. 2004. "Introduction: Comparative History, Cross-National History, Transnational History—Definitions." In *Comparison and History: Europe in Cross-National Perspective*. New York: Routledge, ix–xxiii.

Cole, T. R., R. A. Carson, and N. S. Carlin. 2014. *Medical Humanities: An Introduction*. Cambridge: Cambridge University Press.

Collier, J. 2006. "The Art of Moral Imagination: Ethics in the Practice of Architecture." *Journal of Business Ethics* 66: 307–317.

Colomina, B., with E Choi, I. Gonzalez Galan, and A-M. Meister. 2012. "Radical Pedagogies in Architectural Education." *Architectural Review*, September 28, 2012. https://www.architectural-review.com/today/radical-pedagogies-in-architectural-education/8636066.article, accessed May 12, 2019.

Corner, J. 1991. "The Agency of Mapping: Speculation, Critique and Invention." In *Mappings*, ed. D. Cosgrove. London: Reaktion, 213–252.

Cosgrove, D., ed. 1999. *Mappings*. London: Reaktion Books.

Cosgrove, D. 2003. *Apollo's Eye: A Cartographic Genealogy of the Earth in the Western Imagination*. Baltimore: Johns Hopkins University Press.

Crisman, J. 2016. "Practicing the Future: Exercises in Immanent Speculation." *Boom: A Journal of California* 6 (3): 25–31.

Crisman, J. 2016. "Urban Humanities in the Borderlands." Introduction to *Urban Humanities in the Borderlands: Engaged Scholarship from Mexico City to Los Angeles*. Los Angeles: UCLA Urban Humanities Initiative.

Cruz, T. 2017. "Foreword: Borderwalls as Public Space." In *Borderwall as Architecture: A Manifesto for the U.S.-Mexico Boundary*, ed. R. Rael. Berkeley: University of California Press.

Cruz, T., and C. Hooper. 2011. "Political Equator 3: Reimagining the Border." *Domus*, June 24. https://www.domusweb.it/en/architecture/2011/06/24/political-equator-3-reimagining-the-border.html, accessed May 12, 2019.

Cuff, D. 1991. *Architecture: The Story of Practice*. Cambridge, MA: MIT Press.

Cuff, D. 2000. *The Provisional City: Los Angeles Stories of Architecture and Urbanism*. Cambridge, MA: MIT Press.

Cuff, D., and A. Loukaitou-Sideris. 2016. "Neither Here nor There: Engaging Mexico City and Los Angeles." *Boom* 6 (3): 101–105.

Cuff, D., and J. Wolch. 2016. "Urban Humanities and the Creative Practitioner." *Boom: A Journal of California* 6 (3): 12–17.

Cunningham, F. 2010. "Triangulating Utopia: Benjamin, Lefebvre, Tafuri." *Cities* 14 (3): 268–277.

Curtis, J. W., E. Shiau, B. Lowery, D. Sloane, K. Hennigan, and A. Curtis. 2014. "The Prospects and Problems of Integrating Sketch Maps with Geographic Information Systems to Understand Environmental Perception: A Case Study of Mapping Youth Fear in Los Angeles Gang Neighborhoods." *Environment and Planning B* 41 (2): 251–271.

Davis, A. 2003. *Are Prisons Obsolete?* New York: Seven Stories Press.

Davis, M. 1990. *City of Quartz: Excavating the Future in Los Angeles*. New York: Verso.

de Certeau, M. 1984. *The Practice of Everyday Life*. Berkeley: University of California Press.

de Certeau, M., F. Jameson, and C. Lovitt. 1980. "On the Oppositional Practices of Everyday Life." *Social Text* 3 (1980): 3–43.

Dear, M. 2001. *From Chicago to Los Angeles: Making Sense of Urban Theory*. Thousand Oaks: SAGE.

Desmond, M. 2016. *Evicted: Poverty and Profit in the American City*. New York: Crown Publishing Group.

Deverell, W. 2004. *Whitewashed Adobe*. Berkeley and Los Angeles: University of California Press.

Dewey, J. 1974. *The Later Works of John Dewey*, vol. 8, ed. J-A. Boydston. Carbondale: Southern Illinois Press.

Dewey, J. 2007. *How We Think*. New York: Cosimo.

Didion, J. 2005. *Play It as It Lays*. New York: Farrar, Straus and Giroux.

Dominguez, R. 2010. "Transborder Immigrant Tool and Ricardo Dominguez, under Attack for Border Activism." *East Los Angeles Dirigible Air Transport Lines* blog. https://atomikaztex.wordpress.com/2010/05/15/transborder-immigrant-tool-and-ricardo-dominguez-under-attack-for-border-activism/, accessed December 1, 2017.

Dutton, T. A. 1987. "Design and Studio Pedagogy." *Journal of Architectural Education* 41 (1): 16–25.

Dutton, T. A., and C. G. Bradford. 1991. "Campus Design and Critical Pedagogy." *Academe* 77 (4): 36–43.

Dyos, H. J. 1974. "Editorial." In *The Urban History Yearbook*. Leicester, UK: Leicester University.

Ek, R. 2006. "Giorgio Agamben and the Spatialities of the Camp." *Geografiska Annaler Series B Human Geography* 88 (4): 363–386.

Ellis, W. R., and D. Cuff, eds. 1989. "Introduction" (quoting Robert Maxwell). *Architects' People*. Oxford: Oxford University Press.

Emmett, R., and D. Nye. 2017. *The Environmental Humanities: A Critical Introduction*. Cambridge, MA: MIT Press.

Eshel, A. 2013. *Futurity: Contemporary Literature and the Quest for the Past*. Chicago: University of Chicago Press.

Fainstein, S. 2010. *The Just City*. Ithaca, NY: Cornell University Press.

Featherstone, M. 1996. "Localism, Globalism, and Cultural Identity." In *Global/ Local: Cultural Production and Transnational Imaginary*, ed. R. Wilson and W. Dissanayake. Durham, NC, and London: Duke University Press, 46–77.

Ferriss, H. 1929. *The Metropolis of Tomorrow*. New York: Ives Washburn.

Fisher, L. 2017. "'Community' as a Reference for American Minority Groups: A Theory of Unintended Negative Consequences." *Open Journal of Social Sciences* 5: 224–237.

Foucault, M. 1986. "Of Other Spaces," trans. Jay Miskowiec. *Diacritics* 16: 22–27.

Frank, J. 1945. "Spatial Form in Modern Literature: An Essay in Two Parts." *The Sewanee Review* l53 (2): 221–240.

Fraser, M. 2012. "UCLA Library Acquires Papers of Justice for Janitors, Historic L.A. Labor Organization." *Library Special Collections Blog*, April 20, UCLA Library. http://www.library.ucla.edu/blog/special/2012/04/20/ucla -library-acquires-papers-of-justice-for-janitors-historic-la-labor-organization-.

Freire, P. [1970] 2015. *Pedagogy of the Oppressed*, trans. Myra Bergman Ramos. New York: Bloomsbury.

Freire, P. 1996. *Letters to Cristina*. New York: Routledge.

Frenzel, E. 1966. *Stoff und Motivgeschichte: Grundlagen der Germanistik*. Berlin: Erich Schmidt Verlag.

Friedmann, J. 1986. "The World City Hypothesis," *Development and Change* 17 (1): 69–83.

Friedmann, J., and G. Wolff. (1982). "World City Formation: An Agenda for Research and Action." *International Journal of Urban and Regional Research* 6 (3): 309–344.

Gans, H. J. 2011. "Towards a Public Social Science." *Transformations of the Public Sphere*, Feb. 13. Institute for Public Knowledge, Social Science Research Council. http://publicsphere.ssrc.org/gans-toward-a-public-social-science/, accessed May 1, 2019.

Geertz, C. 1973. "Thick Description: Toward an Interpretive Theory of Culture." Chapter 1 in *The Interpretation of Cultures*. New York: Basic Books, 5–10.

Genette, G. 1970. "La Littérature et l'espace." In *Figures II*. Paris: Seuil.

Goethe, J. W. [1796] 1989. *Wilhelm Meister's Apprenticeship,* ed. and trans. Eric A. Blackall with Victor Lange. Princeton: Princeton University Press.

Greenblatt, S. 2009. *Cultural Mobility: A Manifesto*. Cambridge: Cambridge University Press.

Griffiths, A. 2011. "Oma/Progress at the Barbic." *Dezeen*, October 5. https://www.dezeen.com/2011/10/05/omaprogress-at-the-barbican.

Gullón, R. 1970. *Espacio y Novela*. Madrid: Taurus.

Gupta, A., and J. Ferguson. 1997. "Culture, Power, Place: Ethnography at the End of an Era." In *Culture, Power, Place: Explorations in Critical Anthropology*, ed. A. Gupta and J. Ferguson. Durham, NC, and London: Duke University Press, 1–31.

Gutman, R. [1977] 2010. "House VI." In *Architecture from the Outside In: Selected Essays by Robert Gutman*, ed. D. Cuff and J. Wreidt. New York: Princeton Architectural Press, 119–126.

Hajer, M., and A. Reijndorp. 2001. *In Search of a New Public Domain: Analysis and Strategy*. Rotterdam: NAi Publishers.

Harley, J. B. 2002. *The New Nature of Maps: Essays in the History of Cartography*. Baltimore: Johns Hopkins University Press.

Harley, J. B., and D. Woodward, eds. 1987. *The History of Cartography*. Chicago: University of Chicago Press.

Harmon, K., and G. Clemans. 2009. *The Map as Art: Contemporary Artists Explore Cartography*. New York: Princeton Architectural Press.

Harvey, D. 1973. *Social Justice and the City*. Baltimore, MD: Johns Hopkins Press.

Harvey, D. 1989. *The Condition of Postmodernity*. Oxford: Basil Blackwell.

Harvey, D. 2000. *Megacities Lecture 4*. Amersfort, The Netherlands: Twynstra Gudde Management Consultants.

Harvey, D. 2008. "The Right to the City." *New Left Review* 53 (September–October): 23–40.

Harvey, D. 2014. "The Crisis of Planetary Urbanization." In *Uneven Growth: Tactical Urbanisms for Expanding Megacities*, ed. P. Gadanho. New York: MoMA, 26–31.

Hayden, D. 1995. *The Power of Place*. Cambridge, MA: MIT Press.

Hillery, G. A. 1955. "Definitions of Community: Areas of Agreement." *Rural Sociology* 20 (1): 111–123.

hooks, b. 1994. *Teaching to Transgress: Education as the Practice of Freedom*. New York: Routledge.

Hou, J., ed. 2010. *Insurgent Public Space: Guerilla Urbanism and the Remaking of Contemporary Cities*. London: Routledge.

Humboldt, von A. [1843] 2011. *Gesammelte Werke*, vol. 4. Berlin: De Gruyter.

Iconoclasistas. 2016. "Manual of Collective Mapping." http://www.iconoclasistas.net/, accessed May 12, 2019.

Jameson, F. 1991. *Postmodernism, or The Cultural Logic of Late Capitalism*. Durham, NC: Duke University Press.

Jencks, C. 1977. *The Language of Postmodernism*. New York: Rizzoli.

Jones, C. 2006. *Sensorium: Embodied Experience, Technology and Contemporary Art*. Cambridge, MA: MIT Press.

Judd, D., and S. Fainstein, eds. 1999. *The Tourist City*. New Haven: Yale University Press.

Kant, I. [1784] 1985. "What Is Enlightenment?" In *Foundations of the Metaphysics of Morals*, trans. and ed. L. White Beck, Upper Saddle River, NJ: Prentice Hall.

Kant, I. 2007. "Part One. Critique of Aesthetic Judgement." *Critique of Judgement*, trans. James Creed Meredith. New York: Oxford University Press, 35–164.

Kenny, N., and Madgin, R. 2015. *Cities beyond Borders: Comparative and Transnational Approaches to Urban History*. Farnham, Surrey: Ashgate.

Kester, G. H. 2004. *Conversation Pieces: Community and Communication in Modern Art*. Berkeley and Los Angeles: University of California Press.

Khagram, S., and P. Levitt. 2008. "Constructing Transnational Studies." *The Transnational Studies Reader: Intersections and Innovations*. New York: Routledge.

Kim, A. 2015. *Sidewalk City: Remapping Public Space in Ho Chi Minh City*. Chicago: University of Chicago Press.

King, A. D. 1989. "Colonialism, Urbanism, and the Capitalist World Economy." *International Journal of Urban and Regional Research* 13 (1): 1–18.

Koolhaas, R. [1978] 1994. *Delirious New York*. New York: Monacelli Press.

Koolhaas, R. 1995. "Bigness, or the Problem of the Large." In *S,M,L,XL*. New York: Monacelli Press.

Koselleck, R. 2000. *Zeitschichten: Studien zur Historik*. Frankfurt: Suhrkamp.

Koselleck, R. 2002. "On the Anthropological and Semantic Structure of *Bildung*." In *The Practice of Conceptual History: Timing History / Spacing Concepts*, trans. T. Presner. Redwood City: Stanford University Press.

Koselleck, R. 2018. *Sediments of Time: On Possible Histories*, trans. Sean Franzel and Stefan-Ludwig Hoffmann. Stanford: Stanford University Press.

Kostof, S. 1991. *The City Shaped: Urban Patterns and Meanings through History*. Boston: Little Brown and Co.

Kurgan, L. 2013. *Close Up at a Distance: Mapping, Technology and Politics*. New York: Zone Books.

Kurgan, Laura, and Eric Cadora. n.d. "Million Dollar Blocks." http://spatial informationdesignlab.org/projects/million-dollar-blocks/, accessed May 1, 2019.

Lefebvre, H. [1974] 1991. *The Production of Space*. Oxford: Oxford University Press.

Lefebvre, H. 1996. *Writings on Cities*, trans. E. Kofman and E. Lebas. New York: Wiley-Blackwell.

Lefebvre, H. 2008. "The Right to the City." In *Writings on Cities*. Oxford: Blackwell Publishing.

Leslie, E., trans. 2007. *Walter Benjamin Archives*. London/New York: Verso.

Life Magazine. 1943. "Life Presents R. Buckminster Fuller's Dymaxion World." March 1, 41–55.

Lorde, A. 2007. *Sister Outsider*. Toronto: Crossing Press.

Loukaitou-Sideris, A. 2002. "Regeneration of Urban Commercial Strips: Ethnicity and Space in Three Los Angeles Neighborhoods." *Journal of Architectural and Planning Research* 19 (4): 334–350.

Loukaitou-Sideris, A., and V. Mukhija. 2015. "Responding to Informality through Urban Design Studio Pedagogy." *Journal of Urban Design* 21 (5): 577–595.

Lowe, L. 2015. *The Intimacies of Four Continents*. Durham, NC: Duke University Press.

Lynch, K. 1960. *The Image of the City*. Cambridge, MA: MIT Press.

Madgin, R. 2009. *Heritage, Culture, and Conservation: Managing the Urban Renaissance*. Saarbrucken: VDM Verlag.

Mannheim, K. [1936] 2015. *Ideology and Utopia*. Orlando, FL: Harcourt, Inc.

Manovich, L. 2001. *The Language of New Media*. Cambridge, MA: MIT Press.

Marcus, G. 1995. "Ethnography in/of the World System: The Emergence of Multi-Sited Ethnography." *Annual Review of Anthropology* 24: 95–117.

Massey, D. 1993. "Power Geometry and a Progressive Sense of Place." In *Mapping the Futures: Local Cultures, Global Change*, ed. J. Bird, B. Curtis, T. Putnam, G. Robertson, and L. Tickner, 60–70. London and New York: Routledge.

Massey, D. 1994. *Space, Place, and Gender*. Minneapolis: University of Minnesota Press.

McWilliams, C. 1946] 1973. *Southern California: An Island on the Land*. Salt Lake City: Peregrine Smith Books.

Menand, L. 2009. "The Ph.D. Problem." *Harvard Magazine* (November–December): 27–31. https://harvardmagazine.com/2009/11/professionalization-in-academy/, accessed May 10, 2019.

Mendieta, E. 2008. "The Production of Urban Space in the Age of Transnational Mega-urbes." *City* 12 (2): 148–152.

Mitchell, T. D., D. M. Donahue, and C. Young-Law. 2012. "Service Learning as a Pedagogy of Whiteness." *Equity & Excellence in Education* 45 (4): 612–629.

Morton, T. 2013. *Hyperobjects: Philosophy and Ecology after the End of the World*. Minneapolis: University of Minnesota Press.

Mouffe, C. 1993. *The Return of the Political*. London: Verso.

Mouffe, C. 1999. "Deliberative Democracy or Agonistic Pluralism." *Social Research* 66 (3): 745–758.

Mukhija, V. 2011. "Urban Design for a Planet of Informal Cities." In *Companion to Urban Design*, ed. T. Banerjee and A. Loukaitou-Sideris. London: Routledge, 574–584.

Mukhija, V., and A. Loukaitou-Sideris. 2014. *The Informal American City: Beyond Taco Trucks and Day Labor*. Cambridge, MA: MIT Press.

Mumford, L. 1922. *The Story of Utopias*. New York: Boni and Liveright, Inc.

Noriega, C. 2014. "Director's Message." *Chicano Studies Research Center Newsletter* 12 (5): n.p. http://www.chicano.ucla.edu/about/news/csrc-newsletter-january-2014/, accessed May 5, 2019.

Nussbaum, M. C. 2010. *Not for Profit: Why Democracy Needs the Humanities*. Princeton: Princeton University Press.

Ockman, J. 2012. *Architecture School: Three Centuries of Educating Architects in North America*. Cambridge, MA: The MIT Press.

Oppenheimer, D. A., and T. Hursley. 2002. *Rural Studio: Samuel Mockbee and an Architecture of Decency*. New York: Princeton Architectural Press.

Ortner, S. 1984. "Theory in Anthropology since the Sixties." *Comparative Studies in Society and History* 26 (1): 126–166.

Parks, L. 2005. *Cultures in Orbit: Satellites and the Televisual*. Durham, NC: Duke University Press.

Pink, S. 2012. *Situating Everyday Life*. London: Sage.

Popper, K. [1962] 2002. *Conjectures and Refutations*. New York: Routledge.

Poulet, G. 1966. *Les Métamorphoses du Circle*. Paris: Flammarion.

Presner, T. 2013. "Welcome to the Twenty-Year Dissertation." *The Chronicle of Higher Education*, Nov. 25. https://www.chronicle.com/article/Welcome-to-the-20-Year/143223/, accessed May 1, 2019.

Presner, T., D. Shepard, and Y. Kawano. 2014. *HyperCities: Thick Mapping in the Digital Humanities*. Cambridge, MA: Harvard University Press.

Pulido, L. 2006. *Black, Brown, Yellow, and Left: Radical Activism in Los Angeles*. Berkeley and Los Angeles: University of California Press.

Pulido, L., L. Barraclough, and W. Cheng. 2012. *A People's Guide to Los Angeles*. Berkeley and Los Angeles: University of California Press.

Rabinow, P. 1977. *Reflections on Fieldwork in Morocco*. Berkeley: University of California Press.

Rabinow, P., ed. 1984. *The Foucault Reader*. New York: Pantheon Books.

Rael, R. 2017. *Borderwall as Architecture*. Berkeley: University of California Press.

Rancière, J. 1991. *The Ignorant Schoolmaster: Five Lessons in Intellectual Emancipation*. Redwood City: Stanford University Press.

Rancière, J. 2004. *The Politics of Aesthetics: The Distribution of the Sensible*. London and New York: Continuum.

Rawls, J. 1993. *Political Liberalism*. New York: Columbia University Press.

Readings, B. 1997. *The University in Ruins*. Cambridge, MA: Harvard University Press.

Reinhold, M., and J. Crisman. 2012. "Conjuring Utopia's Ghost." In *Thresholds 40, Socio-*, ed. J. Crisman, 11–20. Cambridge, MA: MIT Press.

Rios, M. 2014. "Learning from Informal Practices: Implications for Urban Design." In *The Informal American City: Beyond Taco Trucks and Day Labor*, ed. V. Mukhija and A. Loukaitou-Sideris. Cambridge, MA: MIT Press, 173–192.

Rittel, H., and M. Webber. 1973. "Dilemmas in a General Theory of Planning." *Policy Sciences* 4: 155–169.

Robinson, J. 2002. "Global and World Cities: A View from off the Map." *International Journal of Urban and Regional Research* 26: 531–554.

Robinson, J. 2003. "Postcolonialising Geography: Tactics and Pitfalls." *Singapore Journal of Tropical Geography* 24: 273–289.

Robinson, J. 2004. "In the Tracks of Comparative Urbanism: Difference, Urban Modernity and the Primitive." *Urban Geography* 25 (8): 709–723.

Robinson, J. 2006. *Ordinary Cities: Between Modernity and Development*. London: Routledge.

Robinson, J. 2014. "Introduction to a Virtual Issue on Comparative Urbanism." *International Journal of Urban and Regional Research*, n.p. https://onlinelibrary .wiley.com/doi/full/10.1111/1468-2427.12171/, May 8, 2019.

Rodriguez, N. 1996. "U.S. Immigration and Intergroup Relations in the Late 20th Century: African Americans and Latinos." *Social Justice* 23 (3): 111–125.

Rosaldo, R. 1997. "Ideology, Place, and People without Culture." In *Culture, Power, and Place*, ed. A. Gupta and J. Ferguson. London: Duke University Press, 77–87.

Rossi, A. 1982. *The Architecture of the City*. Cambridge, MA: MIT Press.

Roy, A. 2009. "The 21st Century Metropolis: New Geographies of Theory." *Regional Studies* 43: 819–830.

Roy, A. 2011. "Conclusion: Postcolonial Urbanism: Speed, Hysteria, Mass Dreams." In *Worlding Cities: Asian Experiments and the Art of Being Global*, ed. A. Roy and A. Ong. West Sussex, UK: John Wiley & Sons Ltd, 307–335.

Said, E. 1979. *Orientalism*. New York: Vintage Books.

Sassen, S. 1991. *The Global City: New York, London, Tokyo*. Princeton: Princeton University Press.

Sassen, S. 1996. "Analytic Borderlands: Race, Gender and Representation in the New City." In *Re-Presenting the City*, ed. A. King. New York: University Press, 183–202.

Sassen, S. 1998. *Globalization and its Discontents: Essays on the New Mobility of People and Money*. New York: New Press.

Sassen, S. 2006. "Cities and Communities in the Global Economy." In *The Global City Reader*, ed. N. Brenner and R. Keil. New York: Routledge, 82–88.

Sassen, S. 2014. *Expulsion: Brutality and Complexity in the Global Economy*. Cambridge, MA: Belknap Press of Harvard University.

Schön, D. A. 1982. *The Reflective Practitioner: How Professionals Think in Action*. New York: Basic Books.

Schön, D. A. 1988. "Toward a Marriage of Artistry & Applied Science in the Architectural Design Studio." *Journal of Architectural Education* 41 (4): 4–10.

Seigworth, G., and M. Gregg. 2010. "An Inventory of Shimmers." In *The Affect Theory Reader*, ed. M. Gregg and G. Seigworth. Durham, NC: Duke University Press, 1–28.

Sen, A., and L. Silverman, eds. 2014. *Making Place: Space and Embodiment in the City*. Bloomington: Indiana University Press.

Sennett, R. 2012. "New Ways of Thinking about Space." *The Nation*, September 24.

Sherman, R. 2005. "If, Then." *Log 5: Postcriticality* (Spring/Summer): 58.

Smith, M. P. 2001. *Transnational Urbanism: Locating Globalization*. Malden, MA: Blackwell.

Smith, S. 2010. "President's Column: Beyond the Dissertation Monograph." *MLA Newsletter* 42 (1) (Spring): 2–3. Modern Language Association website, https:// apps.mla.org/pdf/nl_421_web_no_links.pdf, accessed May 16, 2019.

Smith, S. 2016. *A Manifesto for the Humanities: Transforming Doctoral Education in Good Enough Times*. Ann Arbor: University of Michigan Press.

Soja, E. 1989. *Postmodern Geographies: The Reassertion of Space in Critical Social Theory*. New York: Verso.

Soja, E. 2009. "The City and Spatial Justice." [<<La ville et la justice spatiale>>, trans. Sophie Didier, Frédéric Dufaux.] *justice spatiale | spatial justice* | no. 01 septembre. https://www.jssj.org/article/la-ville-et-la-justice-spatiale/, accessed May 7, 2019.

Soja, E. 2010. *Seeking Spatial Justice*. Minneapolis: University of Minnesota Press.

Solnit, R. 2010. *Infinite City: A San Francisco Atlas*. Berkeley: University of California Press.

Solnit, R. 2013. *Unfathomable City: A New Orleans Atlas*. Berkeley: University of California Press.

Solnit, R. 2016. *Nonstop City: A New York Atlas*. Berkeley: University of California.

Sontag, S. 2004. *Regarding the Pain of Others*. New York: Picador.

Spirn, A. 2014. *The Eye Is a Door*. Boston: Wolf Tree Press.

Sudjic, D. 2016. *The Language of Cities*. London: Penguin Books UK.

Suvin, D. 1979. *Metamorphoses of Science Fiction: Studies in the Poetics and History of a Literary Genre*. New Haven: Yale University Press.

Taylor, A. 2011. "The World's Largest Refugee Camp Turns 20." *The Atlantic*, April 14. https://www.theatlantic.com/photo/2011/04/the-worlds-largest-refugee-camp-turns-20/100046/, accessed June 1, 2018.

Tracy, A. 2013. "Deep Focus: The Essay Film." *Sight & Sound* 23 (8): 44–52.

Tufte, E. 1990. *Envisioning Information*. Cheshire, CT: Graphics Press.

Turvey, M. 1999. "Can the Camera See? Mimesis in 'Man with a Movie Camera.'" *October* 89: 25–50.

United Nations High Commission on Refugees. 2017. Data, June 9. http://www.unhcr.org/en-us/figures-at-a-glance.html, accessed June 1, 2018.

Varnelis, K. 2007. "Is There Research in the Studio?" *Journal of Architectural Education* 61 (1): 11–14.

Venturi, R., D. Scott Brown, and S. Izenour. 1972. *Learning from Las Vegas*. Cambridge, MA: MIT Press.

Vitruvius. 1960. *The Ten Books on Architecture*, trans. Morris Hickey Morgan. New York: Dover Publications.

Walton, J., and L. Masotti, eds. 1976. *The City in Comparative Perspective: Cross-National Research and New Directions in Theory*. New York: Sage.

Warf, B., ed. 2010. *Encyclopedia of Geography*. London: Sage.

Weschler, L. 2016. *Domestic Scenes: The Art of Ramiro Gomez*. New York: Abrams.

White, H. 2014. *The Practical Past*. Evanston, IL: Northwestern University Press.

Whyte, W. H. 1980. *The Social Life of Small Urban Spaces*. New York: The Project for Public Spaces.

Wilson, R., and W. Dissanayake. 1996. "Introduction: Tracking the Global/Local." In *Global/Local: Cultural Production and Transnational Imaginary*, ed. R.

Wilson and W. Dissanayake. Durham, NC, and London: Duke University Press, 1–18.

Wood, D. 1993. *The Power of Maps*. London: Routledge.

Wood, D. 2010. *Rethinking the Power of Maps*. New York and London: Guilford Press.

Yamashita, K. T. 1997. *Tropic of Orange*. Minneapolis: Coffee House Press.

Zubiaurre, M. 2013. "Diosa Cochambre: UUCLA at Night." *Pàrrafo*, April 21. http://blog.parrafomagazine.com/post/48578753894/diosa-cochambre-uucla-at -night/, accessed May 16, 2019.

Zukin, S. 1995. *The Culture of Cities*. Cambridge, MA: Blackwell Publishers Inc.

Index

Note: Figures and tables are indicated by "f" and "t" respectively, following page numbers.

Godzilla (film). See Gojira/Godzilla (film)

Goethe, Johann Wolfgang von, 194–196

Gojira/Godzilla (film), 146

Goldberg, Neil, 27, 125–126, 127f, 128

Golden Gai neighborhood, Tokyo, 96, 137f, 138–139, 138f, 139f

Gomez, Ramiro, 210, 211f, 212, 213f

Google Maps, 100

GPS. See Global Positioning System (GPS)

Graduate education, humanities, 5, 267n7

Grand Park, Los Angeles, 2

Grant, Bradford, 199

Graves, Michael, 46

Gregg, M., 217

Guggenheim museums, 48–49

Gupta, A., 48

Hallelujah Anyway (video series), 125–126

Harley, J. B., 97

Harvey, David, 88
 on city, right to, 17, 62
 on dialectical utopia, 62
 in spatial turn, 41

Hayden, Dolores, 66

Heidegger, Martin, 43

Heterotopia, 44–45

Hillary, George, 221

Histories, ignored, 222–223

History (Geschichte), 106–107

Ho Chi Minh City, Vietnam
 narrative map of, 94–95, 95f
 spatial ethnography of, 26, 87, 93–94, 94f, 95–96, 95f
 time-based study of, 94, 94f

Hockney, David, 210, 211f

Hollywood, 168, 170

Homelessness, 252–254, 255f

hooks, bell, 222–224

Horkheimer, Max, 196

Hou, Jeffrey, 93

House VI (Eisenman project), 9, 10f

How We Think (Dewey), 226–227

Hugo, Victor, 176

Human, 10–11, 13, 28

Humanities
 architecture, urban planning, and, 233–234
 on big problems, collaborative research for, 5–9
 crisis of, 203, 281n22
 as design oriented, 4–5
 digital, 4, 7, 278n7

diversity of, urban humanities and, 262
 generative, 278n7
 graduate education in, reforming, 5, 267n7
 isolation of, 5–6, 8
 multidisciplinary fields in, 4, 7–8
 porous pedagogies and, 202–204
 spatial turn in, 41–46, 270n17
 transnational perspectives of, 12–13
 in urban humanities, 3–6, 9, 12–13, 40, 233–234

Humboldt, Wilhelm von, 194

HyperCities (Presner, Shepard, and Kawano), 277n36

HyperCities digital mapping project, 22, 277n36

Hyperobjects, 4, 6

Iconoclasistas, 105, 105f

If-then logic, 162–163

Ignorant Schoolmaster, The (Rancière), 225–226

Image of the City (Lynch), 65, 89

Imagination, 165–166

Immigration
 in Los Angeles, studying, 67
 Los Angeles immigrant labor, 207–208, 208f, 209f, 210, 211f, 212
 to Mexico City, 248
 to Southern California, Mexican, 101–102, 101f
 transborder immigrant tool, 101, 101f

Inclusivity, pedagogical, 222–223

Industrial Revolution, 117

Infinite City (Solnit), 98–99, 99f

Informal city, 219

Informal urbanism, 60–61

Insertion, 157, 278n4

inSite/Casa Gallina, 239

Installations, 131

Intellectual lineage, urban humanities, 37–38

Intentional communities, 160

Interventionist mapping, 101–102, 101f, 103f

Intimacies, 12, 50–51, 263

Intimacies of Four Continents, The (Lowe), 50–51

Intimate publics, 96, 138–139

Inversions, pedagogical, 225–228

Ivory tower
 Freire on, 198–199
 pedagogy in, 196, 198–199
 workers in, 207–208, 208f, 209f, 210, 212

Izenour, Steven, 38–39

Iztapalapa borough, Mexico City, 33–34

Venturi, Robert, 38–39, 229
Vertov, Dziga, 118–121, 119f
Vietnam. *See* Ho Chi Minh City, Vietnam
Ville Contemporaine (Le Corbusier), 16
Visualization
  in critical cartography, 97–99, 99f, 100
  in spatial ethnography, 88–89, 96
Vitruvius, 40, 54

Walking (practice), 86
Web-enabled platforms, 131–132
Westwood, Los Angeles, 202, 238
White, Hayden, 158, 173–177
Whiteness, pedagogy of, 281n28
Whitewashed Adobe (Deverell), 66
Whyte, William H., 25, 88–89, 91f, 92–93
Wilhelm (fictional character), 194–195
Wilhelm Meister (Goethe), 194–196
Wood, Denis, 97, 109
Woodlands (McHarg project), 162f
Work, ethnographies of, 88
Workers
  in Gomez artworks, 210, 211f, 212, 213f
  in Los Angeles, immigrant, 207–208, 208f, 209f,
    210, 211f, 212
  porous pedagogies and, 207–208, 208f, 209f,
    210, 212
World cities
  core-periphery outlook on, 53
  interconnections of, 50
  narrative of, criticized, 53–54
  "World City Hypothesis, The" (Friedmann), 49,
    272n49
Wrestler *(luchador)*, 35, 35f, 171, 279n26
Wyman, Lance, 180

Xenogenesis trilogy (Butler, O.), 164
Xinhua Road, Shanghai
  history of, 185–186
  video project on, 183f, 184–185, 185f, 186, 187f,
    188
X-Men, 164

Yamashita, Karen Tei, 170–171, 279n26
YAMP (Yale AIDS Memorial Project), 132–133,
  134f
YaNeSen (Yanaka, Nezu, Sendagi), Tokyo. *See*
  Tokyo, Japan
Young-Law, C., 281n28
Yoyogi Park, Tokyo, 59, 146

Zeitschichten (time-layers), 106
Zhao Chen, 185
Zubiaurre, Maite, 207

Urban and Industrial Environments

Series editor: Robert Gottlieb, Henry R. Luce Professor of Urban and Environmental Policy, Occidental College